"Dr. Worthington has been a stalwart model of leadership for decades. I know you will be excited to read his memoir. He is a particular inspiration for young readers and will continue to make great contributions to our community as he is a great example of tenacious steadfastness. His dedication to this forward movement is evident in his work."

~ Taaj Jaharah M.A., M.S., R.M.T., A.T.C., L.A.T.
Movement Coaching; Serving the Professional Athletic and
Performance Communities

I0539230

"A true underdog story, with an unexpected twist regarding what truly matters in life."

~Remi Adeleke
Author of the aclaimed memoir, *Transformed*.
He was born in western Africa. Following his father's death, his mother, brother, and he relocated permanently to the Bronx in New York City. After years of making regrettable decisions, Remi joined the Navy in 2002 and later became a Navy SEAL.

"Thank you, coach, for the basketball training and advice you gave me during our one-on-one sessions and the support you've shown me throughout my basketball journey into the NBA. I look forward to reading your memoir, *In My Brother's Shadow*."

~Cameron Whitmore
An American professional basketball player for the Houston Rockets of the National Basketball Association (NBA)

"This impressive debut, *In My Brother's Shadow*, weaves a vivid and tragic story about a poor decision having life-altering consequences; Dr. Worthington's real-life *examples* provide tremendous life *lessons* in human nature and the importance of character, courage, and commitment in your daily lives to achieving goals."

~Roy Jones Jr.
Hall of Fame Professional Boxer, multiple world championships in four weight classes, including titles at middleweight, super middleweight, light heavyweight, and heavyweight

"I recommend diving into Dr. Rob Worthington's memoir *In My Brother's Shadow*! As we all make mistakes growing up, not everyone can overcome them. Dr. Worthington takes us on a real-life journey from adolescence to adulthood as he teaches us how to achieve any goal you set out to achieve!!"

~Brian Rowsom

A 1987 second-round NBA draft pick out of UNC-Wilmington, who played three seasons with the Indiana Pacers and Charlotte Hornets before continuing his career internationally with teams in Israel, Japan, and England. After retiring, he coached in the Ontario Pro Basketball Association and the American Basketball Association and was named ABA Coach of the Year in 2005. He is a 2009 Greater Wilmington Sports Hall of Fame inductee.

"*In My Brother's Shadow* is the book you would expect from Dr. Robert Worthington: Bold and exciting. Robert's book captures the idea that you can live any area of your life based on courage, love, and kindness instead of fear."

~ Clifford D. Garvey Jr
M.Ed., Prison Ministry Chaplain

"Regarding basketball, especially in the DMV, Dr. Robert Worthington is one of the GOATs for championing youth basketball. The youth basketball pipeline he has built throughout Columbia, Md., and Howard County continues to showcase talented student-athletes in the classroom and on the court."

~ Kelsey Nicole Nelson
A multi award-winning journalist and radio personality who has covered some of the top sporting events on local, state and national level.

IN MY BROTHER'S
SHADOW

A Gripping Story of a Bond between
Two Brothers, Invigorated by a Passion
for Basketball, Wedged Apart by Tragedy

DR. ROBERT WORTHINGTON

Foreword by NBA Hall of Fame Member,
Nate "Tiny" Archibald

For more information, visit https://inmybrothersshadow.com/

Hoop Voyage Publishing

ISBN: 979-8-218-96782-6 (hardcover)
ISBN: 979-8-218-46880-4 (paperback)
ISBN: 979-8-218-49660-9 (eBook)

Library of Congress Control Number: 2024917569

Cover Design by Markee Books
Interior Design by Amit Dey

TABLE OF CONTENTS

Foreword: NBA Hall of Fame Member Nate "Tiny" Archibald vii

Preface. xi

Acknowledgements xiii

Introduction xv

First Quarter:

1. The Effects of Sibling Rivalry 3

2. The Journey Begins: Finding a Home in Griffin Park 13

3. Welcome to the Family – Embracing New Connections 27

Second Quarter:

4. Basketball – The Drawing Board of Our Dreams 45

5. From Thriving to Surviving: High School, College, and Beyond . . . 69

6. Depths of Despair – The Unimaginable Happens 107

Third Quarter:

7. Bouncing Back: Resilience in the Face of Setbacks 135

8. Becoming a Coach 157

9. The Heart of a Champion: Reflections on the 2000 BCC
   Men's Basketball Team 183

Fourth Quarter:

10. A Journey of Personal Growth. 207

11. No More Excuses: Taking Responsibility for Our Choices . . . 233

12. The Invisible Victims: Exploring the Impact of Incarceration
     on Families 267

Overtime:

Glossary of Basketball Terms, Phrases, and Slang 295

Homage from Kith and Kin, Coaches, and Players 321

Music Playlist 359

FOREWORD

By Nate "Tiny" Archibald

There are times in your life when you will come across someone who gives you advice, makes you feel better about life, and sets you on the right path. You might wonder if that person is a friend, mentor, or both. Rob is a great teacher, coach, and a great person. It's that simple. He has a way of helping kids individually and collectively, not only to become better basketball players but better human beings. I've known him since 2005 when we were both hired as coaches for the Brevard Blue Ducks in United States Basketball League (USBL). The USBL was known as a developmental league for players with aspirations of playing professionally; many of the league's players would play in the NBA and professionally in Europe and other countries. The late-spring to early-summer professional basketball league would eventually close its doors for good, due mainly to the emergence of rival leagues, namely the NBA's D-League (recently changed its name to the G-League). The USBL has never officially announced that it folded, but league operations have been suspended since 2008.

Rob and I continued to work together conducting basketball clinics and camps, and it was there we formed a bond because of our shared passion for the game and our love for the kids we were training and coaching. It was never about the money for us, hearing young players say, "Coach, you helped me. I'll never forget what you guys taught me." Our bond was forged through connecting with the kids and teaching them the fundamentals of the game, and we had a great time doing it—we both wanted to do something to make the experience successful for the kids, and I have to admit, I learned from the kids as I learned from Rob.

Many of the kids we worked with did not have what I would call a fundamentally sound base, so that's what we worked on—structure first. Rob and I taught these kids to go out there and work on their skills and team play. It was as if he and I could read each other's minds when interacting with kids. We shared a mutual understanding about teaching the kids about keeping their egos in check, that nobody is more significant than anybody else.

Rob has a knack for putting kids in positions where they are just basketball players. What I mean by that is he teaches his students how to handle the ball from various angles; he instructs his students on all the aspects of the game because he knows that a student who learns the different types of ball handling, game skills, and mental toughness, poses a triple threat. Learning different angles of attack will make that kid a better basketball player, not just because he can jump or run. The player learns how to do all those things, and it helps his game—the combination of intimately knowing the game, no matter what position or skill, helps that kid on the court. Rob has a knack for bringing all that out in the kids he coaches.

The thing about Rob is that he will never give up on the kids he coaches, and that's what the game of basketball, and life, is all about. It doesn't matter if you get your butts whooped all over the court with a bad loss or not. You never give up.

When Rob and I were conducting clinics, we witnessed evidence every day that our efforts had a significant impact on the kids because they were there before we were; that's how much they wanted to play. When that happens, you think, *hey, those kids might not be the greatest basketball players, but they love the game*. It was satisfying that our students were starving for the information we gave them and implemented the tips we were giving them. The basic instruction and boosting each kid's self-confidence were unique about Rob's connection, and everybody loved that connection.

The thing that makes Rob extraordinary is that even though he had a considerable talent for playing basketball, he opted to go into the military to serve and protect his country. His unwavering confidence allows him to make decisions that benefit others, not only himself. He's had it since I've known him, and no one will ever take that confidence from him—he won't let them! He's not only got the courage; he's got the knowledge and experience to back it up. He hasn't always been allowed to demonstrate it because of how the world's system is set up, to exclude some (and I hope most of you reading this will know what I mean) from specific opportunities, the same opportunities that abound for others. But this one thing I know: Rob makes the most of every opportunity he gets. I deeply respect him for how he creates his chances by identifying limitations and pursuing different approaches without fear of failure. I have enjoyed a long-time coaching and personal relationship with him, and I've witnessed his passion for the game of basketball over the years. This book will be empowering for Rob's ongoing quest to use his life experiences to be a positive influence on the life of others.

~Nate "Tiny" Archibald

PREFACE

In My Brother's Shadow tells the story of the bond between two brothers, invigorated by a passion for basketball, wedged apart by a tragedy with life-altering consequences. All the typical challenges of childhood existed —who would get the new pair of shoes, the new bike for Christmas, or the "hand-me-down" clothes from your older sibling— along with the guilty feeling that comes over you when you develop a closer relationship with one sibling over another. The story tells of the incredible loneliness when our family was separated during our early childhood years, my mother and siblings moving to Florida, leaving me behind, to be raised by my maternal grandmother.

Finally, after nearly ten years, I was reunited with my two brothers, William and Derrick, my sister, Sharon, my mother, and stepfather, permanently in Orlando, Florida.

The decade-long separation had an impact on our relationship. Reuniting was difficult, becoming a series of daily contests between William and me; regular competitions to see who could run the fastest, jump the highest, climb the tallest trees, or spell the most words correctly. Usually, William won these contests. And it soon became apparent, our daily battles were not much competition, as William's talents seemed limitless to me, and each contest had a familiar outcome – he won. He was the fastest runner, the brightest student in school, the most talented artist, with the ability to draw almost any image from just a brief look. But there was one competition that stood out more than all the others, basketball.

Basketball at the park, or streetball, was played on an outdoor half-court made of asphalt with faded white court markings. The games were played with no referees, and all calls of fouls, traveling, or "carrying" would cause long delays as the two teams argued about whether or not it was a 'good call' or 'bad call.' Our passion became defining our identities in the park in the neighborhood. The park is where many of the neighborhood kids would earn their nicknames. I loved playing basketball on the blacktop asphalt courts at the park. In the evening, after school, or early mornings on a Saturday, 4-on-4 streetball games were the place to earn your reputation as a "baller." I was gaining a helpful "rep," and therefore I would usually get "picked" on a team unless the "big boys" were playing. But a familiar theme was beginning to emerge: "Weo" (the nickname given to my brother William) was the brother they "picked" first. When we attended tryouts for our first organized basketball team, Weo "made the cut," selected for the team. I was "cut," meaning I didn't get chosen for the team. The walk back home alone—well not completely alone because the other boys who were "cut" from the squad walked along with me—there were few words spoken. Weo stayed behind at the gym with his new teammates. Something had transformed the two of us into strangers, without a connection, heading in different directions, destined to make a fateful decision that would drastically alter our lives forever.

ACKNOWLEDGMENTS

I want to express my deepest gratitude to my family for their unwavering support throughout this journey: my spouse, who endured late nights and countless revisions with a smile, and my children, who inspired me with their boundless humor, imagination, and cheering.

Thanks to my editorial and production team, Lakaiya Purnell, Power Ratings, LLC, and Michelle Hill, Winning Proof, for their endless enthusiasm and tireless effort in making this book a reality. They are not just great professionals but are true friends.

This book would not be the same without the exceptional cover design by Markee Books Design (create@markeebookcovers. com) and the captivating illustrations by Jason (Jason The Artist @ Jasonartofficial on Instagram) McLaughlin; their creativity brought my story to life. I am deeply grateful to Amit Dey for his exceptional design work on the book interior and E-book formatting, as well as the accompanying website for this book.

Finally, thank you to the readers who embarked on this adventure with me for giving my life journey home in your imagination.

INTRODUCTION

The journey of writing this memoir has allowed me to reconnect not only with family members but schoolmates, lost friends, and former basketball teammates from around the world. I've discovered that my life may have had a more significant impact on other people than I've ever known. Rekindling these relationships brought back genuine excitement about sharing our memories. The process has taken some unexpected twists. I had hoped to ask questions of friends' memories to jolt my memories, but I ended up with as many questions posed to me as I had to ask others. People wanted to read more of the book; wanted to know what made me want to tell my story. Lamont Robinson, a former basketball teammate and friend of twenty-plus years said, "Man, this is great. I've always wanted to know what made you so determined and so driven, what it was that made you. I always wondered to myself, *Man, why does this guy work so hard? He's already the best player. Why is this guy working so hard?*" I responded to Lamont by asking him, "Why do you think?" — a rhetorical question I hope to answer along with many others throughout this book.

In sharing my memories about influencers in my life and how they shaped my life, I want people to know that a modest beginning is just the start of your journey. Through perseverance, dedication, and hard work, you can change your path. You deal with tragedy by engulfing yourself in a mission to overcome whatever obstacles are in the way of your success— all the while embracing the game you love like never before. Your determination, drive, and character change your situation, regardless of where you start. It's up to you ultimately. Other things will happen in your life that will create barriers to stop you from achieving the goals you set for yourself. And it's going to be up to you as to whether to overcome or to succumb to them. So, I want it to be about determination above all else, to serve as a motivational model to people. I want people to say, with a thumbs up, "Hey, you know what? You can still do it. It's hard, but you can do this." And that's what I hope comes from this book. There's no excuse. If you want to do something, you will do it. Believe in yourself; that self-belief will breed confidence and fuel your determination. Determination is not a skill you can learn in a workshop or classroom; it's a character trait cultivated over time. I believe that. And I do see so many excuses.

During a recent conversation with an educator, I was trying to be honest with him by saying that many of our kids, in particular, African American kids, are unfairly having the expectation bar lowered by teachers and administrators. "Do you know his father is in prison?" the educator asked, seeming to want to lower the bar for a young boy who wasn't following the rules. "Yes, I'm aware his father is incarcerated," I responded.

"Well, yeah, he may not have had breakfast this morning!"

"I don't understand why you're making these assumptions and excuses for his behavior," I said irritated. "He's not the first kid to deal with a parent being sent to prison. I've known more than a few kids who had to overcome similar situations. They didn't want a biased advantage, just the same opportunities as everyone else. Don't make things unequal for them by saying you go to the back of the bus, or you can't drink from this water fountain, or you can't walk on this sidewalk. Just be fair." During an evaluation for a promotion, don't limit my assessment to five if the max is ten. Don't say, "Well, you know what, we're going to make your max five," and then present it to me as if you're helping me. You're not helping me. I feel hindered. You're lowering expectations for me, and you're telling me you don't believe I can do any better. That's a problem. I want the same opportunities as everyone else, nothing more and nothing less. If given an equal chance, my actions will determine whether or not my life goes in the right direction.

And for much of my life, being a basketball player gave me that direction. I found that playing competitive basketball taught me more lessons than just how to plant my foot and push off in the other direction to spin into a layup and respond to life's challenges.

It may be a little naïve to think that we can all live our lives throughout the world in the same manner as we play on the basketball court. But you're judging a player on how well he passes on the basketball court. You're considering a player by how well he shoots. How well he plays defense. You're not judging him by whether he has dreadlocks or blonde hair. Whether he has blue eyes, brown eyes, or wears his pants too big. You're considering whether he can play.

The world would be a much better place if we were all judged fairly. I hope this book will allow people to see some parallels and life lessons basketball has taught me.

One of my coaches' consistent points was that there was no substitute for hard work. "The will to succeed is important, but more important is the will to prepare." If you want to excel at something, hard work is the only way. When I want to perfect my jump shot or make more free throws, the only way I can do it is through practice. I spent hours shooting jumpers alone at the outdoor asphalt courts in our neighborhood. My coach once told us it's essential to practice the right way. "Practices have to be harder than the games," he would say. In those practices, we relied on each other to help make the other a better player; iron sharpens iron.

A basketball court is an excellent metaphor for life. For example, the back-and-forth of a game is like what transpires in a person's life. Another example is the trust built between teammates on the court. When you pass the ball to another player, you're not saying, "I'm passing it to the Black guy or White guy," you're saying, "I'm passing it to the guy who can shoot." We're judged on what we do, not who we are or what we look like, and I think that's my basketball experience, over the past four decades. And I wish that would be the lens through which we look at the rest of the world, and the world could behave that way. Unfortunately, it doesn't. But it's the vision I want readers to have when reading the pages of this book, so that maybe it will inspire a tendency in others to look at the world through a little bit more of a positive lens.

There is a focus on basketball, but I hope the general life lessons learned from my early childhood to adulthood will also have an impact. Basketball has been an integral part of my life; it is difficult to separate my story without a game of hoops being included throughout the journey. It has shaped so many traits I credit for any success I've achieved in life, traits such as determination, dedication, loyalty, and commitment.

FIRST QUARTER

1

THE EFFECTS OF SIBLING RIVALRY

Sibling rivalry stories are told as far back as the famous biblical brothers Cain and Abel when the saying a 'blessing and a curse' was early uttered. Many firstborn children feel burdened by having to share their parents' attention with a younger brother or sister. However, the younger sibling can often feel as if he's in the 'shadow' of the elder sibling, struggling to prove himself. This is how it was for me and my older brother, William. This sibling rivalry drove many episodes for us from early childhood through adolescence into adulthood.

William and I were born eleven months apart at a military hospital on Fort Stewart Army Base, in the small southern town of Hinesville, Georgia. Fort Stewart, originally known as Camp Stewart, experienced a surge in its military population during the 1960s and '70s. The base, that initially had less than 5,000 soldiers, saw its numbers swell to more than 30,000 soldiers. This growth was primarily due to the reassignment of personnel in preparation for the United States' potential response to the Cuban Missile Crisis and its increasing involvement in the Vietnam War. The succeeding years would welcome the birth of my younger siblings, Derrick, and Sharon, at the same military hospital.

Our parents were married in Hinesville. My mother, Dorothy May Gaulden, was a nineteen-year-old baby-faced teenager from nearby Augusta, Georgia. My father, William Edward Worthington Sr., was a tall, slim, squared-jawline army drill sergeant from Harlan, Kentucky. Growing up as military brats, my siblings and I learned early in life the need to work together and to overcome adversity. And like most siblings, we felt a need to compete against one another at every opportunity. One of our earliest competitions happened in our backyard, with Derrick and me as primers and William as the judge in a spelling bee contest; I don't recall who won those contests, but William was usually the judge. He was an honor roll student, and if we needed any help with homework, we would go to him regardless of the subject. William would start the spelling bee by asking, "Can you spell…"

As the contest progressed, the words would get more complicated and more challenging. On more than a few occasions William would join in the competition. With William, it was no contest at all because he could correctly spell every word. He was always the smartest student in school, and in any contests involving sports, he was more physically gifted, making all our competitions decidedly one-sided. William was persuasive and creative, and he was brilliant at sketching with pencil strokes or other freehand drawings. I was an enthusiastic, skinny, wild-eyed kid with a six-inch reddish-brown afro, fond of making conversation with others. I was never much of an artist. I was so bad at drawing that it was a struggle for me to draw stick figures. But, if I wanted a new drawing, all I needed to do was ask William to sketch it for me. My favorite sketch that he would draw was a race car. Starting with a blank piece of paper, he would make a few lines, then a few circles, a few more lines, rotating the sheet to change the angle, and as if by magic, a new sketch of the Japanese anime Speed Racer race car would appear. The Mach 5 race car was based on the American Chevrolet Corvette, and William's sketch looked identical to the one on television. I was in awe of his talents, often asking, "Can you draw me another one, please?"

No one would ever mistake me for having a natural talent for drawing, but I was a natural talker. As a kid, I was told on more than a few occasions, "You're a chatterbox," and it was often said of me, "He's a very sociable little guy, isn't he?" Family movie nights would be more of the same; usually, my brothers were annoyed with me for talking too much during movies and episodes of the 70's sitcom, *Good Times*. A night at the drive-in theaters would also garner more than a few "shut up right now" looks from my mother. Kung Fu movies were our favorite. Most of the kids in the neighborhood loved to watch Chinese martial arts films, particularly films starring Bruce Lee. The 'Dragon' may have been the founder of the martial art style Jeet Kune Do, but he was also indirectly responsible for the destruction of many wooden broom handles in our house and others in the neighborhood. Thanks largely to Bruce Lee's box-office hit movie *Enter the Dragon*, his fighting sticks were nearly as popular at our neighborhood park as were slingshots.

Every kid in Griffin Park had to have a pair of 'fighting sticks' like the ones Bruce Lee used in his movies. The actual name of the weapon was Nunchaku, an Okinawan martial arts weapon made of two pieces of wood of similar length and a rope or chain about half that length connecting the wood. William, of course, would take the lead in making a pair of nunchakus for himself, me, and Derrick, our little brother. The latter was growing physically taller and visibly *bigger*/broader than us by the hour it seemed. We had our tasks; the first goal was to find two black hardwood rods of equal lengths. We encountered our first problem with our plan: neither of us knew the actual dimensions of the two rods. But we did have an old wooden

12-inch ruler. So, without much more debate about the idea, we recognized a wooden ruler fit perfectly in the back pocket of our jean shorts and would not be too noticeable under our shirts. We used old broom handles as the material with a hole nailed into each end and tied them together with an old bicycle metal chain. We spent hours practicing combinations of offensive and defensive moves, blocking, and strikes in our backyard. William was our instructor and teacher, but with no formal training in using the weapon, we could not avoid accidents. Unlike in the movies, there were no stuntmen to step in to safely perform a to avoid getting injured when landing during martial arts fight scenes. The results were predictable: many bumps and bruises from accidental strikes to anyone standing too close, or worse, self-inflicted injuries to your knees, hands, or head.

Martial arts movies would remain a sibling favorite for years to come. Bruce Lee's *Enter the Dragon* would undoubtedly be the first choice, but other Kung Fu movies impacted us as well. Movies like *Chinese Connection*, *Game of Death*, *Five Fingers of Death*, and *The 36th Chamber of Shaolin* were a close second to *Enter Dragon*. And all of these movies were regularly discussed in the neighborhood. If you're a fan of hip-hop and rap music, you may recognize the name '36th Chamber' from the pioneering group The Wu-Tang Clan. The group acknowledged the *36th Chamber of Shaolin* movie had a significant influence on them and was the motivation for the name of their debut album.

Regardless of how popular or how much influence Kung Fu movies had, they didn't keep our attention very long. Growing up in the '70s, we played stickball in the neighborhood streets and minor league baseball at Grand Avenue Elementary School baseball fields. We mowed lawns or washed cars on the weekends to earn money to see afternoon shows. And our favorite holiday of the year, other than Christmas, of course, was Halloween. I don't remember why, but costumes and candy may have had something to do with it. Kids from the neighboring communities would join together, running from house to house. This was one of the few times we could run, unsupervised for the most part, all over the neighborhood knocking on strangers' doors in the hope of getting a handful of free candy dropped in our trick-or-treat bags. Every kid would approach each house, yelling at the top of their lungs 'trick-or-treat' repeatedly until someone opened the door and began handing out as many SweeTARTS, Bottle Caps, Laffy Taffy, Charms Blow Pops, and Lik-A-Stix as possible. We always started the night walking through our neighborhood, Griffin Park. Still, the search for more candy and a chance to see more homes decorated with fake spider webs, plastic skeletons, jack-o-lanterns, and witches would always lead us to other communities.

Not every house required us to wait for an answer at the door; an open invitation was understood with a simple placement of a large container full of candy on the front porch. The night would usually end with a smaller group of us walking home, with the frightening thought of having our bags of candy grabbed and stripped away by older kids before we reached the safety of our home. Once inside our home, we would spread candy all over the dining room table or bedroom floor in preparation for candy swapping. Having four siblings of similar ages provided more opportunities for swapping for our favorite candy. This act also gave us a chance to eat as much candy as we could stomach before Mom would yell at us, "Do not eat all of that candy."

William, for some reason, always seemed to get the best of the candy swaps, convincing Derrick or me to swap one of his favorite pieces of candy for a handful of circus peanuts, which looked and felt like marshmallows; neither of us liked them. But William was the oldest, tallest, most confident one among us, so if he said it, then it was a good deal. Who was I to second-guess him? We all sought his approval, and William, known now by his nickname, 'Weo,' could usually talk us into doing anything. When our parents were away, he would be the enforcer of the household rules. "No name-calling, no running in the house, no television watching until all homework is done, no closing your bedroom door, no bad words (cursing)," William would say. And of course, "Be home before the streetlights come on!" If any of those rules were broken, he would 'tell mama'! William felt a sense of protection over us and some measure of authority over us younger siblings. He would always remind us, "Don't argue with me. I'm the boss when Mama isn't home, and what I say goes."

When Mama was preparing lunch one summer morning, she sent me to get a loaf of bread from the neighborhood corner store, Honest John Grocery, stocked with an abundance of inexpensive and high-calorie, unhealthy food items. The small, prefabricated panel mint green building sold everything from alcohol, cigarettes, and highly processed meats to home cleaning supplies. Low-income minority communities have a higher rate of obesity, partly due to less access to full-service commercial establishments and more access to small corner stores than affluent neighborhoods. Most people thought it was convenient to have a store so close. Still, they probably never considered the prices that Honest John's was charging for the hotdogs, snacks, and other packaged goods they sold, which were usually at a higher rate than more established discount food stores.

One day William handed me some money and asked if I would go to Honest John's and hurry back. I speedily jumped on my blue Schwinn bike with drop handlebars, racing-style saddle seat, dual-position caliper brake levers (a new Christmas gift) and headed out to the store. After purchasing the food, I was on my way back home when I saw my brother walking towards me. As he got closer, I began to slow my bike down by applying the rear brake and then the front brake. William began to speak softly, "Tan (a nickname my family, long-time friends, coaches, and some teachers would call me), Mama said for you to give me the change left over from buying the bread so that I can return it to Mama." Without hesitation, I said, 'okay,' and gave him all the change. I hurried off, pedaling fast enough to get through the crosswalk and avoid the oncoming cars. I arrived back home to find my mama in the kitchen. I handed her the loaf of bread, and immediately turned my attention to the back door, hoping to catch a glance at who was already outside at the blacktop courts. My momentary distraction was quickly brought back to the present when Mama asked, "Where's the change?" I replied, "I gave it to William, as you said." The stern look on her face as she spoke with a firm voice, "First of all, check your tone. I never said that." "But Mama, William told me you said to give him the change." William walked in before Mama chastised me with another 'I'm not one of your little friends' talks. "William Edward, did you tell Tan to give you my change?" In a calm and composed manner, he replied, "No, all I said to Tan was to ask him if he got the bread, that's about it." And of course, there was no debate about who to believe; one of the benefits of being the oldest. Not only was he the gauge for every important milestone, but what William said was believed. The oldest child had a different set of rules in the family; he got a little more leeway. That was just the dynamics in our home, it was one of the perks of being the firstborn. Parents usually trusted the firstborn to be in charge or to be the one who enforced the rules and would always tell the truth.

William was the pacesetter for the siblings who followed. He set a high standard, and I felt a desire to compete to earn equal recognition or achieve a similar level of success. And sports became a part of those dynamics. The 'park' in the Griffin Park housing complex had several asphalt basketball courts, but we usually only played on the court nearest our apartment, and a sports field where we played football and baseball. One of the neighborhood's most boastful and fleet-footed kids, Melvin, usually challenged anyone looking to play on a team to a foot race to prove how fast a runner they were. "Okay, let's race," Melvin would say. "See if you got wheels."

With a doubtful look, he would ask, "Do you even know how to play football'? Sandlot football, also known as street football or backyard football, was a variant of American football, with the ball being the only equipment needed. It featured full tackling and was popular in the playground. Playing sandlot football was one of the few times the younger kids interacted with the older kids and the big boys. I remember one game in particular when I scored my first touchdown. I took a handoff from our team's quarterback. I ran for a long touchdown, avoiding several tackles, including William's clumsy tackle attempt. This memory is significant because it was the first time that I felt athletic.

And it was the first time I had achieved any success in a competition against my big brother. I also remember the short-lived feeling as William would quickly come back and score another touchdown. His team won the game, but it was the first time I felt that I could have beaten him in a competition. We also played minor league baseball at the elementary school baseball fields and pee-wee football at the local YMCA. Derrick was an outfielder, playing right field due to his strong throwing arm. I played the infield third base because of my lateral quickness and ability to field ground balls. I wanted to be a pitcher and had a good fastball but little control to throw strikes. My baseball coach would always tell me, "You're not a pitcher; you're a hitter."

This competition didn't end with sports, it carried over to our household chores. The household chores can be described as a list of daily jobs assigned to each of us to keep our household running smoothly and efficiently. The chores list would always be posted on the front of the "fridge" (refrigerator) with a small imaginative magnetic decoration or two. The list was designed to make sure all of us shared the responsibilities of cleaning the house. The chores included cleaning your room, vacuuming or sweeping, taking out the trash, wiping down the kitchen cabinets, and everyone's least favorite thing to do, washing the dishes.

No one ever wanted to "do" the dishes. And we didn't have a dishwasher. We had to wash dishes by hand in the sink. We had a double sink, and we would use liquid dish detergent on one side and clean running water on the other. One day, William and I got into a heated argument about the chores assignment. I had looked at the chore list earlier, and it was not my day for doing dishes, but mysteriously the next time I looked at it, my name appeared as the dishwasher. Yeah, I was upset about this puzzling change to the chore list; no one confessed to switching the order of the list.

In those primary school years, many unexplained things happened where William seemed entitled to power. I wonder if it was due to the Adlerian theory, where firstborn children tend to be authoritarian, or perhaps it was due to parental favoritism. What was true was that Williams always seemed to get his way; everything seemed to go in his favor.

2

THE JOURNEY BEGINS: FINDING A HOME IN GRIFFIN PARK

Griffin Park, a federal housing project in west-central Orlando, Florida, near the historical Parramore neighborhood, would soon be my new home. Segregationist policies allowed the urban community to be encircled by two significant highways for decades, leaving its residents no choice but to breathe toxic fumes and endure the ever-roaring sounds of passing cars and trucks on all sides. The housing project, designed in the German-style "Zeilenbau" open blocks row with slab blocks, was named in memory of "Uncle Charlie Griffin," a 102-year-old formerly enslaved person who had lived nearby. In this historically black community, designated as a historic district in July 1996, pollution was a way of life for the low-income residents, who also had to deal with a high crime rate, the kind Americans tend to ignore. Segregation persisted, entrenched through housing and zoning policies and through the construction of urban expressways that turned existing racial borders into concrete barriers.

This impediment was not an unintended consequence; this was the entire point. As highway lobbyist Alfred Johnson later told an interviewer, some city officials in the mid-1950s were blunt about the goals of highway planning: Urban interstates would give them a good opportunity to get rid of the local "Niggertown." Founded in the early 1880s, Parramore was once a bustling middle-class community of black-owned homes, schools, businesses, churches, and hotels. It thrived well into the mid-20th century — even as black people were violently blocked from political power in Orlando and elsewhere in the country. Following Reconstruction, railroad systems were built around black neighborhoods across the country as a means of segregation. The railroad tracks divided Orlando into a black westside, including Parramore, and a predominantly white eastern corridor. In 1938, the city demolished housing in Jonestown, the first black neighborhood in Orlando, and two years later, most of the residents were relocated to the new Griffin Park "GP" projects. When Interstate 4 (I-4), the largest highway infrastructure project in Florida history, was constructed almost two decades later, it followed the route of the railroad tracks and further severed the Parramore community from the rest of the city.

This exposed the community's black residents to even higher levels of pollution. Today, I-4, State Road 408 (East-West Expressway), and various ramps form the loop that encapsulates Griffin Park within an "oval of pollution," as related by Robert Cassanello, a history professor at the University of Central Florida. I was just aware of the historical facts about the Griffin Park housing projects after nearly ten years of living there alone with my maternal grandparents, Claudia Mae (Kennedy) Gaulden and Clarence Gaulden. I enjoyed living with my grandparents, initially for just extended visits, then more permanently, lasting until I entered the fourth grade of elementary school. I don't know exactly how I came to live with them during these years, but I adored my grandmother and always loved talking to her. It soon became apparent that I was her favorite grandchild, not that she neglected other grandchildren, but she did show favoritism towards me; we had a stronger personal connection. I spoke to my younger brother, Derrick, about those years I stayed in Georgia while my mother and siblings moved to Florida with my stepfather. Derrick recalled, "Grandmama would get sick whenever we talked about you coming home with us." She had grown so attached to having me live there that she didn't want me to leave. Every summer, I would go to Florida to spend the summer school break. When I would come back to Georgia, there were times when we talked about me living in Florida permanently, but the thought of me leaving was very difficult for my grandmom. Recently, Derrick recalled what it was like in those years when I went back and forth between Florida and Georgia. "I wondered," Derrick said, "when I used to ask my mom when you used to come all the time why you just can't come back with us because every time my mom would get ready to take you and bring you back with us grandma would have a 'fit' like she was gonna have a heart attack or something — and I said, Mama, just leave him with Grandmama." Though I saw my mom and siblings quite regularly, I still longed for them when we were apart.

As a preteen or "tween," in 1973, I finally moved permanently to Orlando, Florida, to live with my mother, siblings, and stepfather, Adolphus "Buddy" Jones. Buddy was an army veteran and, like my father, one of approximately 300,000 African American soldiers who served in the Vietnam War. Although he never completed the legal adoption of my siblings and me, his long-term relationship with my mother allowed for a closer relationship. He became my first sports hero, as a six-foot three-inch athletically built 230-plus pounds former semi-pro football player and professional slow pitch softball player in the 1970s and early '80s. I became the waterboy for his football team and the batboy for his softball teams; therefore, we spent much time on the road together, developing an even closer relationship than he would have with my brothers. The summer of

1973 was sunshine-filled afternoons, as the large and increasingly visible black middle class made their way on I-95 South driving the 260-mile distance from Hinesville, GA to Orlando, FL. The drive was just over four hours from start to finish. Although I would regularly visit my mother and siblings, I spent my preschool and early childhood years living in Hinesville, Georgia (home to Fort Stewart, the largest Army installation east of the Mississippi River stretching more than 280,000 acres), raised by my maternal grandparents who became my source of oral histories and narratives of oppression of black people in the larger American society. This practice of kinship care, relative caregiving, or grand-families dates to pre-colonial Africa, and it's the backbone of our strength and resilience in the black community. I always knew who my mother was, and I saw her and my siblings quite regularly, but I enjoyed being raised by my grandparents. My grandmother made every decision regarding my second and third grade school education, vacations, church attendance, friend groups, and discipline.

There was a feeling of safeness to my grandparents' routine, and I blossomed under their watchful eyes. I have vivid memories of attending Sunday morning church services with my grandparents, the "hooping" or "whooping" tone of the pastor preaching the sermon of the day, the rhythmic and spiritual music of the choir with dominant vocals, expressions of faith, hopes and dreams. One of my most graphic memories is of my grandmother, Claudia, catching the Holy Ghost, shouting, and screaming, falling to her knees in prayer, worship, and praise for salvation, even at times losing consciousness or passing out for a short period. Some say that the first time they felt the Holy Spirit, it felt like intense peace and love, or a sense of inner knowing. But through the eyes of a young child, seeing your grandmother catching the Holy Ghost may seem dangerous, confusing, and frightening. Nevertheless, the adults in the church didn't seem too concerned; some of the women used handheld paper fans with a picture of 'Jesus' on it to fan my grandmother in an unbothered effort to keep her cool while continuing to sing along with the choir.

Growing up with my grandparents provided me with a stable and safe environment, along with a deep sense of cultural identity. However, like many grandchildren, my desire for independence grew as I approached my teenage years. Around the age of ten, I felt a strong pull to spend more time with my siblings. This longing led me to gradually drift away from my grandparents and extended family. Eventually, I expressed my feelings to my grandmother, asking if I could move to Orlando, Florida to attend school with my brothers. Finally, after years of summer visits, Orlando became my permanent home.

We resided in the predominantly black neighborhood of Parramore, Griffin Park federal housing project, one of Orlando's poorest communities, trapped by I-4 and State Road 408 (SR 408) and the suffocating air pollution from a few hundred thousand daily vehicle traffic. The nearby residents in the Griffin Park neck of the woods are low-income, making the housing complex district among the lowest-income neighborhoods in America. According to Neighborhood Scout, an electronically connected database of US neighborhood analytics assembled in the early 2000s, organized research shows the Griffin Park neighborhood has an income lower than 99.0 percent of all US neighborhoods.

In addition, 24.5 percent of children in Griffin Park district are below the federal poverty line and have a higher childhood poverty rate than 74 percent of U.S. neighborhoods. Over time, these environmental conditions would be suspected of causing chronic health problems in young children and leaving older residents suffering from health conditions like cancer, asthma, and other respiratory problems. But in the summer of 1973, my thoughts were focused on the fun time I would have with my siblings. We parked the car near the sidewalk, characterized by small cracks, pop-outs, and other surface deterioration that ran the length of the road in front of our apartment building, and began to unload my bags to bring into the two-floor building. The apartment at 812 Dunbar Court was painted a neutral beige, with brown-colored front doors and a single diecast, matte black aluminum light fixture about one-to-two inches to the right of the door. The front of the building had a single window and a double window on the first and second levels, each with the same brown-colored paint as the front door. We lived in this apartment unit for the next four years, 1973-1977. The small, low-income apartments had block walls and tile floors. Once you entered the front door, on the first floor was the living room with a couch, love seat, coffee table end, table, and an excellent twenty-five-inch color television. As you continued walking through the living room area, directly ahead were colorful beaded curtains hung in the doorway, dividing the living room from the kitchen area. The kitchen had a small dinner table, upper and lower-level cabins, a gas stove, and a single-door refrigerator. The second floor of the apartment included three bedrooms: one for my mother and stepfather, another for my sister, Sharon, and the third shared by my brothers and me.

Additionally, on the second floor was a hallway linen closet, which served as a place to store extra linens, toiletries, cleaning supplies, and more. The family bathroom had a single sink, toilet, and tub/shower. The apartment unit's backdoor was in the rear of the kitchen area; immediately outside the door was a small concrete block porch that you'd step down to, entering our backyard, a small, narrow rectangle space of about 120 square feet. The backyard was plotted more for quickly moving through rather than a space to gather or play. A short walk from our backyard was the neighborhood park, which consisted of several stones mixed with tar (asphalt) and concrete basketball courts with steel poles supporting aluminum backboards and baskets. An athletic field positioned between the basketball courts and fence line, less than 70 feet from Interstate 4 and State Road 408, with more dirt and red clay than grass, provided a place for us to play sandlot (backyard), tackle football, and baseball. All these games were competitive and followed the basic rules of football and baseball. During the summer months, the Orlando Housing Authority office, located in a building at the far end of the athletic field, had additional summer staff to supervise games and activities for the neighborhood kids, including arts and crafts and popular board games like Monopoly (all about buying, selling, and trading properties to win), Operation (save the patient, Cavity Sam, avoid the buzzer), Checkers, and Connect Four (the vertical checkers game).

We also played large group games like Red Rover, Freeze Tag, and Red Light/Green Light. Red Rover was the most popular of the three and involved two teams on opposite sides, spread out but holding hands, usually a distance at the end of each basketball court, to allow a running start between the two lines. One team says, "Red Rover, Red Rover, let 'Jellybean' come over." Then, that particular kid, Jellybean, sprints full speed towards the opposite team, trying to break through a gap between two people holding hands. If the player breaks through, he gets to pick a player and return to his original line with them. If he fails to break through, he must join the line of the team he couldn't break through. The other team now calls for someone to run right over, and this process would continue until one team has captured all the players. There were always one or two people injured playing the game, and occasional punches were thrown when some players got mad, but overall, we had fun playing the game. Years later, the Red Rover game would be banned as a school-sanctioned activity in most schools in the United States due to numerous children being injured.

The Griffin Park (Orlando Housing Authority) office also provided free box lunches for kids in housing complexes, including a cold sandwich, fruit, and a snack like a bag of chips or cookies. I don't recall how healthy or nutritious these meals were; the likelihood is that they were not full of essential nutrients. Each weekday during the summer months, around noontime, a sixteen-foot, white, refrigerated cold storage box truck would drive up in front of the office building, which was like a fire bell going off for all the kids at the park. The office staff assigned to lunch duty would walk up the ramp to enter the truck's trailer to unload the boxes of pre-packed lunches. A group of kids would always surround the car, not because they were excited about the box lunches, but because the food arrived packed in what we called 'hot ice,' which was actually dry ice (frozen carbon dioxide). Every kid in Griffin Park knew that you had to carefully handle hot ice if using your bare hands, because the surface temperature could reach minus 109 degrees Fahrenheit, potentially causing severe freeze-burn injuries. Nevertheless, we were all fascinated by the idea of touching such a hazardous substance; the danger was exciting. But nothing was more thrilling than playing sports.

We played Little League baseball at Grand Avenue Park; my brother Derrick, Melvin, and I played for the George Stuart team, while Wayne, Tim, Walter, L.C., Bruce, Vince, and George played for different groups in the same league. Many of the same guys also played in flag and tackle football leagues. However, our most memorable and competitive games were sandlot tackle football, played at the Griffin Park recreation field. The flag and tackle football leagues were supervised and coached by adults, who also scheduled practice, organized the games, and, on many occasions, provided transportation to and from practice and games. But we played ten hours of sandlot tackle football and pickup basketball games for every hour of organized baseball or football. In these games, we scheduled ourselves against other nearby neighborhood kids from Grand Avenue, Parramore, and our biggest neighborhood rivals, Carter Street. Neighborhood pickup games were organized in one of two ways. The first method was just showing up to a park with a reputation for 'good ball' play. The second was by inviting kids from a specific neighborhood to play at our park or their park at an agreed-upon time. Usually, game invites got passed along by word of mouth. Neighborhood pickup game rules were mostly the same everywhere: bring a ball, games would be shirts versus skins, no zone defense, and individual players called their fouls. And there was rarely anything that caused more bickering and arguments in pickup basketball games than calling a foul. A player who believed he had been fouled would call out, "Foul!" The play would stop, and the basketball would be awarded to the fouled player's team. If you did not call the rules honestly, you would be labeled a cheater. Although it generally wasn't as simple as that; a guy would argue that he didn't foul you, or if you got fouled, you should've called it immediately, or 'we can shoot for it.' These were the rules that settled all on-court disputes.

Another rule that caused a lot of disagreement was a player calling 'and-1,' which means the player is calling a foul, and the basket counts if the ball goes in. If the shot misses, the player gets the foul call. Most players argued that this interpretation of the rule would allow a player to have his cake and eat it, too! We eventually settled on a strict 'no and-1' rule. If a player calls and-1, regardless of whether the shot goes in or not, the player must take the ball back to the top and doesn't get the points. Visiting players unfamiliar with our 'home court' rule would frequently get pissed-off angry when they learned of the rule. Still, eventually, they would accept it and ultimately admitted that it largely eliminated the reoccurring problem of players calling fouls every time an intense game was close to game point.

While we enjoyed playing various sports, riding our bikes throughout the neighborhood, and other outside activities, pickup basketball quickly became our favorite pastime. Pickup basketball or streetball first became popular on the streets or playgrounds of the major cities across the United States – hence its name, streetball. Every city where streetball is played has unique rules, styles, and heritage. The most famous location associated with streetball is Rucker Park in Harlem, New York, widely recognized as "the mecca of basketball." In 1950, a New York City Department of Parks and Recreation employee, Holcombe Rucker, organized the first 'Rucker Tournament,' a summer basketball event intended to help keep disadvantaged neighborhood kids off the streets and to get more than a few of them into college basketball programs. The Rucker Tournament became renowned for its exotic style of play, boisterous and unruly crowds, its role as a grooming ground for future basketball greats, and as a showcase for numerous National Basketball Association (NBA) stars. Notable players who played at Rucker Park include NBA greats Kareem Abdul-Jabbar (Lew Alcindor), Wilt "The Big Dipper" Chamberlain, Julius "Dr. J" Erving, Nate "Tiny" Archibald, Earl "The Pearl" Monroe. More recent NBA stars like Shaquille O'Neal, Kobe Bryant, LeBron James, and Kevin Durant also played at Rucker Park. Other Rucker Park greats who never played in the NBA include Joe "The Destroyer" Hammond, Earl "The Goat" Manigault, and Rick "Pee Wee" Kirkland, who become immortalized in the repeated streetball stories in every hood in the United States.

One of those hoods was Griffin Park, where the basketball courts provided local kids their concrete jungle, opportunities for 'you had to see it to believe it' moments, and the chance to enhance their own legends. In the mid-1970s, a unique one-on-one battle on the courts of Griffin Park sparked passion, excitement, and never-ending debates about the outcome. Over the years, the accounts about the one-on-one battle between two of Griffin Park's most talented players, Arthur 'Marvin' Jackson (6'2") and Oscar "OD" Daniel (6'1") varied with each retelling of their encounter, elevating each player to mythical status within the Griffin Park housing projects. Marvin was a fundamentally sound player. He used a power dribble to set up his opponents for a perfectly executed drop-step, a basic low-post but effective move. On the block, he would usually explode off two feet to the rim for an automatic basket. 'OD' was an explosive athlete, with a smooth, left-handed, free-flowing jump shot, who rarely missed a shot, regardless of the difficulty. OD was such a deadly perimeter shooter that the legendary "Chocolate Thunder," Darryl Dawkins, would routinely stop by the Griffin Park courts and challenge anyone who could beat OD in a one-on-one game. The person who beat OD would win a hundred dollars. No one ever collected the money, as OD regularly won games by scores of 30 to 2 or 30 to 0, while each basket counted as two points. Dawkins, a six-foot ten-inch center as a high school senior, averaged 32 points and 21 rebounds a game, leading his high school team, Maynard Evans High School, to the state championship. Although colleges heavily recruited him, Dawkins decided to enter the NBA draft directly out of high school, becoming the first player to do so. I would attend the same high school nearly a decade later.

The retelling of these types of stories became folklore in Griffin Park. Marvin and OD's one-on-one contests stood above all others in the mythology of GP streetball. The battle took place on a hot summer morning, with the sky blazing blue and the sun celebrating yellow, accessible, and bright. The usual "thwack…thwack… thwack" of a basketball bouncing off the hot asphalt courts in Griffin Park combined with the loud shouting, cussing, and chaotic debates of the crowd, created a symphony of sounds like music blasting at its highest volume on the courts. The anticipation and anxious suspense over… 'Ball'! Standing at the top of the key were two of Griffin Park's best basketball players, Marvin and OD. With the offensive player saying a single word, "check," the battle would begin.

The outcome of the encounter repeatedly changed with each retelling of the story. Some versions recall OD consistently making jump-shots from 'downtown,' as long-distance shot after shot, 'swish…swish…swish' through the hoop. "Nothin' but net!" yelled a spectator standing on the sideline. Another person insisted Marvin struggled to contend with OD's hot shooting and fell behind 20-2 at one point in the game. However, other people recalled a much closer game, with OD making long-distance shots to take an early lead before the tide turned. Marvin responded by checking the ball and 'bellying up' to OD at the inbound point. The defensive adjustment allowed Marvin to get the ball on offense. He immediately started using his size, strength, and butt to back OD down in the low post while protecting the ball with his body to score basket after basket, with both right- and left-hand layups and mid-range jumpers. He was "on fire." As the game went back and forth, the action became more and more physical. Each player shoved, pushed, and threw the occasional elbow on defense to ensure the other would earn every point. The contest became so rough that the players nearly got into a fistfight. Finally, the game came to an anticlimactic ending, with no consensus on a winner.

Both players would become high school basketball stars at their respective schools, Marvin at Boone High School, and OD at Jones High School. Marvin's team won the High School State Basketball Championship in 1977. Both players would be selected to the area all-star teams and the All-Central Florida Basketball Team. The All-Central Florida team was comprised of fifteen of the best high school basketball players throughout metropolitan Orlando, including Orange, Osceola, Seminole, Lake, Brevard, and Volusia counties. Being recognized as one of the best players in the area by the opposing team coaches became a fantasy for me and many of my peers. Although still in grammar school, elementary and junior high, we understood basketball was thoroughly established in our neighborhood's cultural fabric and was seen as a sought-after path to success at the high school, college, and professional levels — the hoop dream of every young basketball player in the hood. The mythical stories of older players celebrated the thrill of earning a nickname based on their style of play or attitude and chasing 'the hoop dream.' At Griffin Park, the basketball courts featured hoops mounted on nonadjustable straight steel poles without pole padding. Each hoop had a white, fan-shaped aluminum backboard with a twenty-four-inch horizontally and eighteen-inch vertically orange shooting square, known as the 'sweet spot,' and chain nets attached. Some players utilized the sweet spot for bank shots, but nothing compared to the satisfying sound of the chain net's metallic swish from a made shot.

The court was outlined with a faded, solid, white-painted line illustrating the sideline, baseline, and halfcourt (division line). I am not sure if any of these measurements adhered to regulations for high school, college, or professional basketball distances, but to all the kids who played on the court, it mirrored the 94-by-50-foot National Basketball Association (NBA) hardwood courts. The foul (free throw) line, fifteen feet distance from the front of the hoop, was also painted with a white semi-circle and a straight line marking the shooting area. The teams comprised four players each; one team was skins (players removed their shirts), the other was (shirts), and players kept their shirts on. Both teams were required to play man-to-man defense; every player had to 'guard' their man, and no zone defense was allowed.

A player, usually the player who picked the team or the best shooter, had to 'shoot for the ball,' i.e., shoot from the top of the key, to determine which team gets the ball first. If the player made the shot, his team got the ball, if he missed the shot, the other team got the ball to start the game. Game play begins with the offensive team's player 'checking the ball,' tossing the ball to his defender to ensure both teams are ready to play; the defensive player checks to see that his team is prepared; then passes the ball back to the offensive player to begin play. Another unwritten rule required that the ball be 'checked' after each made baskets, the ball goes out of bounds (out), a foul is called, etc. Because pickup games don't have referees, players call their fouls (defender's illegal contact with the offensive players), calling out "Foul!"; generally, the play would stop. The player who was fouled would take the ball outbounds. These calls were also the root of many of the arguments on the court, as some players had an unspoken rule of 'no blood, no foul,' especially as a team was getting close to the game point. After each made basket, the offensive team would take the ball out of bounds, 'make it, take it.' The game is won when a team has scored thirty points (each basket is worth two points) and has a winning margin of two baskets. We would play those four-on-four pickup games for hours. These contests would be intense, with their own rules and rituals but the most important was being 'picked' for one of the four spots on a team. Being the first pick was important; the moment hastily established the hierarchy of ability while offering regular ballers the chance to exchange casual nods of greeting and acknowledgment.

Another ritual was the anointed best players, on-court alpha, who would customarily give his approval of the game ball, inspecting it the way your grandmother handles produce at the market— carefully checking feel and pressure on. No one ever had a pressure gauge to accurately check the ball pressure. But someone would hold the ball up to face level, extend their arms out, and let it drop. If the ball bounced above the player's waistline or slightly higher, it's good. If the ball bounced up to the player's chest or higher, it was over-inflated, and if the ball bounced below the player's waistline, it means the ball was 'too flat' and under-inflated. Starting the game would be delayed until a ball was found that wasn't 'too flat' or 'that shit got too much air in it.' Once found and agreed as acceptable, 'Yeah, that one's good.' Once the games began, the style of play would usually consist of players passing the ball less, showing their ball-handling skills by over-dribbling, lots of isolation, and guys taking tough shots in a vain effort to repeat a 'move' they had seen their favorite NBA player do. We would play basketball at various parks for hours, sometimes losing track of time, at least until near darkness. When I was growing up, every kid on my block knew the rule that in the summertime, all of us kids had to be home before the streetlights came on. If you didn't make it in time, you'd be sorry.

3
WELCOME TO THE FAMILY – EMBRACING NEW CONNECTIONS

I n the summer of 1974, I awoke early to gather my bags. Still half-asleep but energized by the day's excitement, my mental fog from sleepiness quickly dissipated. I tip-toed around the bedroom to avoid waking my two brothers sleeping on the floor to be the first one in the bathroom. Even though I had traveled to Orlando, Florida many times, it was only for summer visits and vacations. This time, it was to move permanently to live with my mother and siblings. After the chaotic process of the three of us brushing our teeth, washing our faces, and getting dressed in one bathroom, my brothers and I eagerly loaded all my belongings into my stepfather's 1972 light-blue Oldsmobile Cutlass Supreme. With its roomy interior and stylish body, ensuring we left enough room for all three of us plus my sister, Sharon, to sit in the backseat, with our parents in the front seats. Buddy liked to hit the road early in the morning, just after the sun came up, to 'get ahead of the traffic' and allow for more stops and sightseeing opportunities. Inside the house, my brothers and I could barely contain our excitement for the upcoming road trip as we sat at the dining-room table and quickly gobbled down a bowl of Honeycomb cereal and debated loudly about the iconic commercial with the 'Honeycomb Hideout' clubhouse and its catchy theme song 'Honeycomb's big, yeah, yeah, yeah! It's not small, no, no, no…. Honeycomb's got … A Big, Big, Bite."

After eating, my siblings and I would all wait outside by the car, anticipating hearing the words, "It's time to get on the road." The nearly three-hundred-mile drive from Hinesville, Georgia to Orlando, Florida was long drawn out, with plenty of annoyances along the way, including being crowded into the backseat with my siblings, William, Derrick, and Sharon, and repeatedly being told "No" by my mother when I would ask for my favorite soft-serve ice cream, Dairy Queen. We would belatedly be allowed to buy one souvenir priced under five dollars at a gas station or truck stop, only to find a better one later at the official Florida Welcome Center just after we crossed the Florida-Georgia state line, where we always stopped for free orange juice. But the most frustrating thing was our continuous pleas to Mama and attempts to overcome her skepticism that we needed a restroom break at nearly every rest stop on the interstate.

As a family, we made the Florida-to-Georgia road trip so often over the years that we created games like spotting moving cars or trucks with license plates from specific states or excitedly interacting with semi-trucks, or 'eighteen-wheelers,' by pumping our arms out of the car windows in the hope of getting the truck drivers to sound their air horns. The gesture shows mutual respect between truck drivers and other drivers on the road. We kept a keen watch through the rear window to see if any vehicles were speeding up behind us; then we would immediately start screaming for Buddy to move over from the left lane, the "passing lane," into the slow traffic, proper lane. Other highway etiquette included blinking the car's headlights at oncoming traffic to warn of cops or speed traps ahead. If a semi-truck attempted to merge in front of you, a quick blink of your headlights let them know they had room. Continuously blinking your backlights (hazards) signaled your thanks if a truck allowed you to merge in front of them. And NEVER use your bright lights to communicate.

We finally arrived in Orlando after roughly five hours, an extra hour due to sightseeing stops at historical landmarks or driving on a heavily traveled freeway along the Atlantic coastal plains. This route included crossing the historic I-95 St. Mary's River Bridge, an alluring and majestic blue-colored truss swing bridge (constructed in 1927) connecting Georgia and Florida as it crossed the St. Mary's River.

Though it was a recurring trip over the summers for about ten years, the approximately 263-mile road trip to Orlando felt uniquely different this time. This trip was not a summer visit but a permanent relocation, resulting in me experiencing mixed feelings of anxiety, joy, and a sense of peacefulness; I was finally home. As our vehicle stopped in front of the Griffin Park housing complex at Dunbar Court, we parked on the paved roadway. The complex provided no assigned parking spots for its residences. As my siblings and I began to get out of the car, I gathered my personal belongings, and more than usual, my brothers William and Derrick helped me carry all my stuff. As we began to walk towards our apartment, talking and laughing, I felt a weird feeling growing inside me, like seeing your best friend you've been missing for a couple of years or finding a lost shirt you've been looking for the past six months that was your favorite.

When I entered the front door, I felt like shouting at the top of my lungs, "Oh, Lucy, I'm home!!!" — a line from the TV show *I Love Lucy*, but I resisted my thoughts of being witty; I did not want to expose myself to the relentless teasing I was sure to get from William for the rest of the night. After getting all our things out of the car, we suddenly had a burst of energy and excitement and William, Derrick, and I raced towards the stairwell. Everything was a competition, running full speed up the stairs in a sprint to our bedroom. The three of us shared one bedroom with twin-sized beds, two side-by-side and wall-to-wall for Derrick and me. And a third twin bed in the front of the room closest to the entrance for William. The bedroom wasn't huge but was roomy enough for a four-drawer chocolate-colored, four-foot dresser with a curved kick plate and round wooden knobs, and two drawers each for Derrick and me that sat in between the head of our beds. A second four-drawer dresser in our closet belonged to William; it was missing the lower drawer, so we used the space as a step-up to reach the closet's top shelf, which was more than eighty inches from the floor.

The bedroom also had a single window, which allowed us to have a view of the roadway used for parking in front of our apartment and a direct view of the heavily overgrown grass and weeds of the rickety, weather-beaten abandoned building that sat across from our apartment unfinished for all the years we lived there. The finishing touches that transformed our bedroom into a sanctuary were the floor fan and a small TV atop the dresser between our beds. We didn't have air conditioning in our apartment; in fact, less than half of all homes in the United States had AC installed by the end of 1975. But we had what we thought was the next best thing to keep our room cool, a box "floor" fan. It was a light, green-colored TG&Y Champion box fan. Its blades were enclosed in a shallow square box, with grilles on the front and back to allow air to pass through.

The box fan was typically set on the floor near the head of William's bed. On more than a few occasions, we placed it in the bedroom window to pull air from outside and efficiently cool all sections of our room. My brothers and I became rather creative in how we used our box fan, including taking our flat sheets off the beds and laying them over top of the box fan to make a "fort." We never had duct tape to seal the ends of the sheets, so we used schoolbooks, chairs, shoes, or anything lying around heavy enough to hold the sheets in place. Finally, we would pull the open end of the sheet over the box fan and turn the power switch to its highest speed. The air would flow inside and fill the sheets, then we would carefully crawl into the fan fort through the opening. We'd usually have pillows, snacks, and maybe a flashlight for storytelling. The fan was noisy, but we enjoyed every moment in the fan fort, even falling asleep inside. The constant, cool, and powerful wind blowing our sheets into the air was a great way to stay cool, with the only drawback being the few occasions we would wake up the next morning, having lost our voices. Even after we knew the constant air blowing on us would cause this to happen, we repeatedly built our fan fort anyway. It was like having nightly sleepovers and it became a terrific bonding exercise for my brothers and me.

Before You Fall Asleep

Bedtime was an essential custom in our home, as it is for many families when the twilight hour falls, children yawn, and bedtime routines engage all our attention. We had to be in bed between 8:00 and 9:00 p.m., but we rarely fell asleep right away. My mother always told us that having a consistent bedtime routine would result in a more restful night's sleep, improved cognitive functions, better decision-making, and increased ability to absorb more knowledge in school and retain it longer. But most important to her was the belief that a consistent bedtime routine improved our sleep quality, provided a sense of security, and fostered a positive relationship between my siblings and me. Only years later did I learn why 'bedtime' was so significant to her.

Reflecting on a haunting memory from her early childhood, as she grew up in the 1950s in Blackshear, Georgia, a southern city known as home to a temporary prisoner-of-war camp for thousands of Union soldiers during the American Civil War. Blackshear was a Sundown town. Sundown towns are all-white communities that intentionally exclude African Americans or other minorities from residing within their boundaries by forced expulsion, violent threats, or economic coercion. Numerous Sundown towns and counties appeared in Georgia during the late 1950s and early 1960s. My mother shared with me an eerie account from her childhood. She recalled being awakened in the 'wee hours of the morning' by the frightened, quivering, and trembling sound of her mother's voice, urging her to get out of bed and grab her blanket quickly. The family's life was in danger. As the family huddled together at the front of the entrance of their home, standing outside in the front yard of their home was the white landlord who had rented them the house. Several other white men joined him with fire torches and threatened to burn down the house and everyone inside if the family did not leave at this very moment! Fearing for their lives, the family left the only home they had known on foot with only the items they could carry, walking more than thirty miles to her grandparents' house in Baxley, Georgia. Mom remembered being so frightened and exhausted by the ordeal she had to be carried on the backs of her father and her older brother for the majority of the distance until they reached their destination. The family would spend the next year sleeping together in one room under the watchful eyes of her father, mother, and grandparents. This bedtime routine fostered a sense of security and intimacy for the entire family.

Like many families in the United States, our bedtime routine consisted of taking a bath or shower, brushing our teeth, and a bedtime story (we told ourselves) or a short talk with mom before saying good night. And the final step every night before we got into bed was to recite the Lord's Prayer: *"Our Father, Who art in heaven, hallowed be Thy name; Thy kingdom come; Thy will be done on earth as it is in heaven. Give us this day our daily bread and forgive us our trespasses as we forgive those who trespass against us, and lead us not into temptation, but deliver us from evil"... now and forever. Amen!"* My mother always reminded us that praying together helped us stay grounded and feel connected with God and gave us a feeling of protection that God is always watching over us. However, our sibling rivalry shenanigans resulted in round-the-clock conflict, and this necessitated a continuous reminder from Mom that 'God is watching' —three words we repeatedly heard in her efforts to resolve our never-ending sibling competitions. Most sibling relationships have some degree of jealousy or competition. The arguments and bickering back and forth over such inconsequential things as who gets to open the front door, who gets to check the mailbox, and who sits in the front passenger seat in the car seem everlasting. When an expected car trip was approaching, everyone would yell 'SHOTGUN,' meaning you get to sit in the passenger seat instead of the back seat. And a foot race to the car to claim the front seat would erupt, triggering an argument about who first reached the passenger door handles. The losers of the foot race, usually Derrick or me, would be teased and told, 'Boy, you are so slow,' a judgment that often went too far. Mom would eventually have to intervene and remind us, 'God is watching,' omniscient words meaning God knows everything there is to know in the universe. That usually stopped the bickering, at least for a short time. On numerous occasions, our sibling rivalry would erupt over meager quarrels over who was asked to do something first. These disputes would escalate to the point where Mom would have to assume her regular role of mediator. Mom recalled one such argument: "I asked all three of you to do something for me, and neither of you wanted to do it, but within minutes, you all are in a knock-down drag-out squabble over who was going to do what no one wanted to do in the first place. All of y'all go sit down somewhere and be quiet."

Nevertheless, nothing led to more arguments than who would be the first in the bathroom. We only had one small bathroom, with a tub-shower combo, a single sink with a porcelain coating over a cast iron base, and an off-white color 'Standard Carlyle' toilet, shared between all six of us. This circumstance heightened the importance of being the first to reach the 'washroom,' resulting in quite a few arguments in the early years. Sometimes, we tried to work out our differences before bedtime, agreeing on the order in which each of us would go in the bathroom, only to have another sibling, usually William, ignore the previous agreement. Derrick, the youngest and tallest of us, would also "butt in" line, but not due to any sense of entitlement. It was more as a mischievous act or his disregard for following rules. Years later, when reminiscing about our childhood, Derrick would describe himself as being 'bad as hell,' always getting into confrontations, breaking house rules by going into the refrigerator, the closet, and wearing other's clothes without their permission. His memory was accurate; it was frustrating, invasive, and disrespectful for a sibling to take your clothes without asking and, to add salt into the wound, to wear your clothes around you. We even tried to resolve this issue by designating certain clothes we could all share and others that were completely off-limits. That wasn't a solution that actually worked, as for some reason, the 'off-limit' clothes always seem to be the most desired ones. Derrick thought this was hilarious. But this joke was short-lived, as he soon outgrew all my clothes, growing taller and heavier than nearly all of the kids our age in the neighborhood. In the coming years, we would eventually settle into our roles at home and enjoy our time together far more than not being together, even if it was not always in harmony.

The Perfect Weekly Tradition – Family Movie Night

Having a TV in our bedroom, even a tiny nineteen-inch RCA portable television (TV) with access to about twelve channels, offered us convenience and fun, as we were able to watch some of our favorite shows and movies without leaving our bed. But it didn't come without rules; our behavior could result in the TV's removal quickly. But like all things between my brothers and me, what shows to watch on the TV became a regular source of disagreement between the three of us, especially during the Saturday morning cartoon lineup. We would bicker over watching shows like *Scooby-Doo*, *The Jetsons*, or *Hong Kong Phooey*. The disputes would usually be resolved by turning the channel to ABC to watch the DC Comics superhero show *Super Friends* or we would watch *Speed Racer*, a Japanese manga about automobile racing, and my personal favorite. The main character's car, the 'Mach Five,' is a white-colored Formula One open-wheel two-seater racing car. It had a red 'M' on its hood and a yellow number 5 encircled in red on its doors with a set of 'special devices' used under any circumstance. I was astonished by the dazzling features and adeptness of the Mach Five. I was so fascinated by the Mach Five that I talked about the round-the-clock racing car so often that William decided to draw me a picture of it and tape it to the wall near my bed. He was an impressive freehand artist and could draw something from just a short observation. William's drawing was indistinguishable from the images we watched on TV in the afternoons. I was amazed by his drawing abilities, a talent not genetically passed down to anyone else in our home. This was just the beginning of the many times William's talent and abilities would leave me awestruck.

Due to our early bedtime routine, there were only a few television shows we regularly watched. During the school week, normally we watched programs with black characters, like *Good Times*, *Different Strokes*, *The Jeffersons*, and, because it was Buddy's favorite show, *Sanford and Son*. On the weekend, we watched cartoons and shows like *The Flip Wilson Show* (a one-hour comedy variety show and one of the longest-running syndicated programs in American television history) and *Soul Train* (a musical program featuring in-studio dancers and singers showcasing the latest music and dance moves). We loved to watch the *Soul Train* commercials with pro-black advertising for products targeting black people's natural features, such as skincare and hair, for example, Afro Sheen, Ultra Sheen, and Taking Care of Business (TCB Naturals hair care line). And, of course, the show's end always had the host, Don Cornelius (with his perfect shape Afro hairstyle), stating in parting, "We wish you love, peace ... and *soul!*"

The most memorable multi-episode television program we watched together as a family in the living room on the twenty-seven-inch floor model TV was Alex Haley's *Roots*. The groundbreaking

1977 television miniseries presented viewers with an unflinching encounter with the brutality and rupture of American slavery and the horrors African Americans endured at the hands of white slaveholders. The eight-segment miniseries aired on ABC and was watched by nearly half of the United States, an estimated 140 million viewers captivated by the brutality of slavery and its effects on generations of African Americans in America. We were transfixed by the prime-time phenomenon, spellbound by its cruelty and inhumanity, but also fascinated by its characters like Kunta Kinte, Kizzy, Fiddler, and Kizzy's son, Chicken George. We talked about the groundbreaking series before we went to bed at night, at school during the day, and after we came home in the afternoon. The 1977 miniseries *Roots* had a massive effect on how we watched television within our household and had a significant impact on American culture, including inspiring a nationwide interest in genealogy research, particularly among African Americans. In addition, the miniseries was considered a step forward in America's confrontation with its racial history and, at the time, was the most viewed program in American television history, with an estimated eighty million viewers. Although watching our favorite TV shows provided a barrel of laughs and good times, it paled compared to family movie night outings to the drive-in-theater (an outdoor cinema).

On weekends, we frequently made the short two-mile drive to the 'Orlando Drive-In' off South Orange Blossom Trail. The outdoor drive-in featured categorized parking for approximately 300 cars, offering every guest a perfect view of the forty-two-foot-long and sixty-foot-high screen, along with individual speakers that hung off the car window. Movies were shown every night starting at 7:00 p.m., with two movie shows on the weekends. Many of the shows we wanted to watch were Kung Fu movies, especially those with actor and martial artist Bruce Lee. We became familiar with him by watching him on several episodes of the *Batman* TV series as Kato, sidekick to the Green Hornet. Still, of his Asian-style martial arts,

Kato became our favorite. Lee was also the founder of Jeet Kune Do and is considered by many to be the most influential martial artist of all time. His movies, *The Chinese Connection, Fist of Fury*, and *Enter the Dragon* helped ignite a Kung Fu craze in the 1970s, with his idolization magnified by his sudden and mysterious death at the age of 32 in 1973, at the height of his popularity. Even though we felt thrilled by the excitement of martial arts and Bruce Lee, there was a much greater connection to the 1970s blaxploitation films. These "black movies" were designed to captivate inner-city Black American viewers and provide black actors and actresses leading roles that directly confronted racial issues. Including movies such as *Coffee* and *Foxy Brown* (action/crime), starring Pam Grier, the first black female action hero and 1970s pop culture icon. She became the object of affection for virtually every pre-teen and teen boy in every black community in America.

Even famous American movie critic Roger Ebert, a middle-aged white man, duly acknowledged her extraordinary beauty, stating that she was an actress with a "beautiful face and astonishing form" and that she possessed a kind of "physical life" missing from many other attractive actresses. Although we certainly felt a deep understanding and emotional connection to these black movies, more than a few of them created a sense of discomfort and conflicting attitudes from all of us. "Blaxploitation" was both demeaning and empowering. It was empowering because, for the first time, we got to see people who looked like us on the big screen —these black characters were the stars of the show, not domestic servants or criminals. But at the same time, these movies could be demeaning with little depth to the characters and displaying behavior that was full of cliché and racist memes intertwined throughout the plot narrative. Some other blaxploitation movies we watched at the drive-in theater included *Blacula*, a vampire horror film that left me afraid to be alone in a room for weeks, *Uptown Saturday Night*, the action/comedy/crime trilogy, *Let's Do It Again* and *A Piece of the Action* featuring the duet of Sidney Poitier and Bill Cosby. Also, we watched the musical drama *Sparkle*, inspired by the legendary Motown 'girl group' The Supremes. Without question, my two favorite movies ever seen at the drive-in movies were the coming-of-age comedy-drama movies, *Cooley High*, a film that followed the narrative of high school best friends with a joy-turned-tragic storyline, heightened and reinforced by the soulful sound of Motown music throughout, and the movie, *Cornbread, Earl and Me*, which elicited deep emotion from me and enhanced my passion for basketball more than any movie ever before. The plot centers around a high school basketball player nicknamed "Cornbread," the pride of his urban neighborhood, destined for basketball stardom at the college and professional levels.

After an afternoon of playing pickup basketball, Cornbread and two local kids are the last in the neighborhood store when heavy rainfall begins to come down just before they head home. To settle a playful argument between the two kids about how fast Cornbread could run home in the heavy rainfall, Cornbread begins running off as the kids count out loud. At that moment, a white police officer steps out into the street and mistakes Cornbread for a suspect he had been chasing on foot, pulls his gun and fires a fatal shot that hits Cornbread in the back, killing him. The police department begins a coverup to protect the officers (there was a second Black police officer involved who did not fire his gun). Members of the oppressed African American community do what they can to find justice for Cornbread and his family. To this day, when I hear the theme song for this movie, it's still very emotional. The song lyrics, "In the heat of the night hear the bump of the ball on the floor of the court on the sides of the hall he's cornbread…cornbread…ah he's cornbread… he's the man with the plan he's got a basketball in his hands…. he's cornbread."

Primary School Years and Enjoyable Pastimes

My primary and secondary school years began in Florida during a time of increased movement towards integrating schools. This movement occurred as numerous other major events were happening around the United States, such as the Kent State massacre and Jackson State University shootings during student protests, the Watergate scandal involving President Nixon, the last crewed mission to the moon by Apollo 17 (for more than fifty years), the ending of the Vietnam War, the founding of two of the most successful companies in US history, Microsoft and Apple Inc., and the ongoing struggle of states to integrate public schools by allowing black and white kids to attend the same schools together. Florida's public-school integration did not happen until nearly twenty years after the Supreme Court outlawed racial segregation in public schools. The ruling, ending the five-year case of *Oliver Brown v. Board of Education of Topeka, Kansas*, was unanimous. However, not all states accepted the Supreme Court's decision. In the state of Florida, widespread racial segregation continued in public schools until the near end of the decade, when federal and state officials approved the desegregation plan.

However, giving equal access was not fully recognized. This atmosphere of fear and uncertainty greeted most black students as we trembled, broke out in cold sweats, and experienced a rapid heartbeat when walking up the steps to a new school. The first school I attended in Florida was Delaney Elementary School, a neighborhood mainstay for decades, and most children walked or biked to school. There was no air-conditioning and no covered area for parent pickup. The red brick building had white-block letters spelling "Delaney School" above the main entrance and two dozen rectangular windows with white casing framing around the windows. The main entrance had twelve concrete steps and a sweeping, white-colored staircase with black wrought iron rails, leading up to a door that was just a few steps from the principal's office. We didn't attend the school very long, as it closed a few weeks after the school year began for unknown reasons, resulting in all the kids being assigned to different schools. The summer before attending my second elementary school in Florida, I played on my first organized sports team, a boys' flag football team. Many other kids from Griffin Park also participated. After the first half of the summer, a planned trip for all the teams in Central Florida —nearly thirty teams and hundreds of kids— was scheduled for a weekend at "Camp Wewa" or "Land of Many Waters." This was an appropriate name as three lakes surrounded the camp location.

One of the longstanding traditions for all campers who attended "Camp Wewa" in Apopka, Florida was to sit around a campfire with all the other attendees and listen to the folklore stories told by camp counselors. One such folklore, "Orange Blossom Trail," is a story recounting how the spirit of a Native American warrior haunted the trail. The warrior's ghost was rumored to wander the trail, with visitors reporting cold spots, and orbs with a blue glow seen at night. The frightful tale was horrifying for a group of young kids and the situation would get worse as we set out on a group ghost hunt, with the group warning all of us to be on the lookout for something shaped like a ball with a hazy blue glow. The frightful haunt didn't last very long as someone in the front group screamed, yelling the words "RUN!" At that very moment, I thought I saw a blue light as we ran away from the area as fast as we could. The entire experience left me shaken and fearful about sleeping alone for weeks.

The summer months passed quickly, and it was time to attend my first full year of school in Florida at Grand Avenue School, a two-story Mediterranean Revival structure constructed in 1926. Its physical characteristics were of the Mediterranean Revival style, including its stucco walls, pitched tile-clad gable roof, multi-paned windows, decorative gable vents, medallions, and the projecting parapet entry with columns and an arched doorway. I would attend this school for three years, from fourth through sixth grade. These three years were milestones for me, my brothers, and many other neighborhood kids. We all began showing growth in various ways, including socially, academically, and physically. Derrick's growth spurts continued, I became more comfortable in my surroundings, and William became increasingly independent and showed signs of puberty.

In addition, we became more involved in sports, showing vast improvement in coordinated movements by playing basketball and baseball or participating in martial arts classes. In sixth grade, my final year of elementary school, I played on my first organized sports team, a little league baseball team named 'George Stuart,' sponsored by the company George Stuart Inc. (the largest office-supply company in Florida at the time) and the founder of little league baseball in Orlando, George Stuart Sr. Two of my teammates were my brother, Derrick, and Melvin Laws, another Griffin Park kid with whom we spent most of our childhood in competition. Several kids from Griffin Park played on various teams in both the major and minor leagues, including Tim, Vince, Bruce, Walter, George, 'Pee Wee,' Eddie, and Tony, to name a few. The baseball league teams played games at the Grand Avenue athletic complex, with multiple baseball fields and lights for night games.

The first time we put on our George Stuart uniforms consisting of jerseys, pants, socks, shoes, and a red baseball cap with a white check mark, it was the most awe-inspiring feeling I'd ever had. The league was divided into two separate divisions: the Major League, for ages 9-12, for more skillful, knowledgeable, and experienced players, and the Minor League, for ages 5-12, for less experienced players seeking to improve their skills in order to get selected for the Major League. Grand Avenue Little League Baseball was also very popular with kids from other neighborhoods in Orlando and the neighboring communities. We enjoyed the excitement of playing games in a competitive environment, and little league baseball was our introduction to organized sports and its benefits of strengthening the participants' self-esteem and confidence.

SECOND QUARTER

4

BASKETBALL–THE DRAWING BOARD OF OUR DREAMS

L eaving elementary school behind and transitioning to junior high school was a mixed bag of emotions, swings from exciting to scary, stressful, or even overwhelming with more homework, more subjects to study. This new stage of my life brought many changes, including cliques, crushes, more classes and new teachers, physical and emotional changes, and basketball tryouts!

William was entering his second year (eighth grade) of Junior High School and his second school (Cherokee and Howard) in as many years. He attended Cherokee Junior High School in seventh grade, where he attended his first tryout for the school's boys' basketball team. He was one of twelve players selected and would become one of the team's top players. I vividly remember the long walks from Griffin Park to Cherokee Gymnasium to attend William's basketball practices. A group of us would walk the nearly two-mile distance along Orlando's historical Cherokee Trail with its historic homes, many of which dated back to the 1870s. Finally, reaching the peaceful aura of Lake Cherokee was an indication that we were close to reaching the school. The sight of the white signs with red borders warning of danger, "BEWARE OF ALLIGATORS" and "DO NOT FEED THE WILDLIFE," served as visual reminders that a laid-back atmosphere could abruptly be interrupted by an alligator or snake sighting. Cherokee Junior High School, built in the 1920s, was hidden on a side street but very distinguishable with its arched entrance and terracotta embellishments. The local newspaper, Orlando Sentinel, once characterized the school's Mediterranean Revival construction as a blend of Moorish and Spanish architecture, with colorful, decorative terracotta features and one of Central Florida's architectural treasures.

The gym where the team practiced wasn't as decorative or colorful as the outer structure of the school, but I was still impressed because it was the first indoor facility I had ever been in with Maplewood floors. I remember watching the team practice intently, vividly recalling the sound of sneakers squeaking and skidding on the hardwood floor and the loud sound of the coach blowing his whistle. All the players would come to an immediate stop, as the coach warned all the players to stay focused on the team's goal and pick your effort and intensity. However, the one thing that made an impression on me the most was watching William shoot the basketball and listening to his coach enthusiastically praise him for his 'perfect shooting form and technique.' William was tremendously consistent in his shooting. I had never seriously considered the mechanics of shooting a basketball, including sight, balance, hand position, elbow-in, alignment, rhythmical shooting motion, and follow-through…also known as 'flipping your wrist.'

Playing pickup basketball or 'ball' at the playground, players were judged by their ability to make shots. If you made shots, other players would pass you the ball and expect you to make the next shot, and if you made multiple shots consistently throughout a game, you earned the reputation of being a shooter. However, I came to better understand shooting mechanics from attending

William's basketball practices. Follow-through and flipping your wrist when taking a jump shot helps provide the all-important spin and control on the ball, increasing the likelihood of a successful shot attempt. I was so fascinated by the praise and adoration William received from coaches and players alike about his shooting motion that I obsessively questioned him about the 'flip-wrist' technique he used with his jump shot. He would get irritated and usually tell me to practice more: "Tan, stop asking me the same question; go work on your game," he would say. But my questions persisted, even during frequent one-on-one basketball games, most of which were not competitive as he would usually win quite easily.

William, using my name to emphasize his point of me practicing more to improve my game, just fueled the fire burning inside me to improve as a basketball player. "Tan," a nickname given to me by my Aunt Eloise, my mother's youngest sister, when I was seven years old, was used by all my family members, friends, and some schoolteachers, a reflection of affection from my family and a signal of familiarity and bond from friends. We would play basketball every day, and each loss tormented me, and I increasingly irritated William with more questions about his shooting form and my insistence to continue playing one-on-on" basketball games. I would say "let's play again," even though the games would usually result in another defeat for me. On some occasions, William must have noticed the sad look on my face because after his usual "good game, boy," he didn't walk away to play with the 'big boys'; instead, he sat next to me on the wooden stump on the side of the basketball court and shared a few encouraging words with me. With a slight smile on his face, he looked at me and said, "Tan, man, just keep working on your game. You have to learn how to accept a loss. Being a good loser and a gracious winner are both skills; you have to be able to handle both." Or he would say, "Tan, man, I can't let you win; for it to be real, you must earn it."

He also explained to me how flicking your wrist when taking a jump shot stabilizes the flight of the basketball and increases the chance of making a basket. This technique creates a backspin on the ball, which improves your shooting accuracy and distance. William didn't just work on his shooting form on the basketball court. During walks home from school, he would pretend he was shooting a shot in a game, quickly going into his shooting motion, elbow tucked, fingers spread on the basketball, raising great with his jump shot and releasing the ball at the top of his jump, elbow above his earlobe, flip-wrist and follow through until the ball swishes through the net. He would repeat this imaginary game in his head over and over again on his walk home from school. In addition, all of his pretend jump shots were performed with a quick release, eliminating any wasted movement in his shot delivery (to avoid getting his shot blocked). William continued to improve his basketball skills, achieving high success on the court, and excelling in the classroom. Unfortunately, he only attended Cherokee for one year, as the school closed its doors to junior high school students due to a controversy about the original purchases of the property where the school was constructed.

During the summer between my first year of junior high school, seventh grade, and William's second year, eighth grade, we played lots of basketball at the Griffin Park asphalt basketball court and other neighborhood parks around the city. Playing pickup basketball at Griffin Park courts, like many across the country, would have dozens of players gather daily, for hours of fierce and intense competition. The loser had to leave the court. These cutthroat games were very effective, although not necessarily the best approach, in helping me to improve as a basketball player. Pickup games allowed us to develop our skills in a more game-like setting, without referees and scoreboards, and get exposure to different playing styles and strategies. The high intensity, competitive nature, and customary 'trash talking' motivated you to play better or intimidated you into playing worse. Also, the combination of all these challenges allowed us to develop mental toughness early on, which is the ability to stay resilient and confident when faced with challenges or pressure.

Pickup ball is the most organic form of basketball, where you carve out your name and legacy at the neighborhood park, which could lead to bigger, more organized things, or not, and just playing for the love of the game.

Additionally, playing in organized leagues or team practices can provide more structured coaching, team-oriented development, and exposure to advanced tactical concepts. So, while pickup games are valuable, they are most effective when combined with other forms of training and competition. However, many players in NBA history, some of the best players in NBA history, honed their skills through street/pickup ball; players like Wilt Chamberlain, Connie "The Hawk" Hawkins, Kareem Abdul-Jabbar, Julius "Dr. J" Erving, Earl "The Pearl" Monroe and Nate "Tiny" Archibald. Many other players played at the famed Rucker Park and reached legendary status but never played in the NBA, including Joe "The Destroyer" Hammond, Richard "Pee Wee" Kirkland, and Earl "The Goat" Manigault, to name just a few; there were many more! Many of these players have shared their memories about playing pickup or streetball and saying it is where you learn grit, competitiveness, physical toughness, mental toughness, creativity, fun, your identity on the court, basketball IQ, and how you're going to respond to trash talk and intimidation. Whether playing in your neighborhood, in an organized rec league, or for major high school, college, or professional basketball teams, hooping is hooping!

The unwritten rules of pickup basketball—like no clock, no foul shots, no fouling out, no timeouts, no five-second calls, no shot clock, and players calling their fouls—may vary by region but are more or less universal. They have been established over time and respected over generations as the most efficient and fair way to compete in good competitive pickup basketball games. One of the 'big boys' (recent graduates from high school), 'Pee Wee' Medlock, from Griffin Park, once told me, "You can watch how someone plays pickup ball and learn everything you need to know about that person." For many of us in the Black community, basketball, an overwhelmingly Black sport at all levels, personified our vision board, dreams, and goals for the changes we'd like to see. In these early years, and maybe even true today, basketball embodies dreams of success and possible escape from the ghetto and poverty. Still, in many communities, pickup games are played for the sheer opportunity to challenge oneself. Additionally, some players may have a strong passion for the game and approach every opportunity to play as a chance to improve and enjoy the sport.

The competitive nature of basketball and the desire to win brought out our competitiveness, and we sought out that competition as often as possible. It was simple: nothing compared to neighborhood bragging rights. Traveling around to different areas in the city we would play pickup basketball games for hours, since if you won, you stayed on the court. Soon, word of mouth preceded a 'baller' on the court. Earning a reputation of being good or great at basketball would earn you considerable respect and recognition at basketball parks in surrounding neighborhoods and throughout the entire city. And every weekend, you would be presented with the opportunity to raise your renown by taking to the court and destroying your neighborhood competitors.

Junior High School Aha Moments

Though Howard Junior High School was my brother William's second junior high school in two years, his reputation as an outstanding basketball player preceded him, and the boys' basketball coach, Coach Allen, wasted little time in letting William know that he was looking forward to seeing him in attendance at 'Rangers' basketball tryouts. Coach Allen's teams were known for their attacking, fast-paced style of offense, and his teams always seemed to put up impressive assist-to-turnover ratios and offensive efficiency numbers. The team would suit up an impressive lineup of players, including two post players over six feet tall in center 6'3" Willie C and 6'2" forward Lee White. Both had long arms, often described as 'lanky,' and were athletic. The team's point guard and floor general was a small, muscular guard nicknamed 'Little Man,' who possessed incredible quickness and speed.

The fifth starter of the group was my brother William, known more by his nickname, 'Weo,' a sharpshooting wing player with a tremendous shooting touch and skillful offensive abilities. I was also familiar with several of the team's top reserve players, Lenny "Tank" Grace, and two seventh graders, 'Pee Wee' Jackson and Tim Swanigan, who lived in Griffin Park and were frequent competitors in our regular neighborhood pickup basketball games. I knew the team's core players exceptionally well and thought it would be a tough challenge for any team to beat them. Because this was the first year William and I would be attending junior high school simultaneously, the opportunity to become teammates was intriguing, but unfortunately, it would not happen.

Before entering my first year of junior high school, seventh grade, we moved from the Griffin Park housing project into a neighborhood whose school district, as designated by Orange County Public Schools (OCPS), was outside of the attendance zone for Howard Junior High School, where my brother had attended the previous, and was assigned to attend for the upcoming, school year. I wasn't available during this time because I no longer lived in the Howard school zone and interdistrict enrollments, possibly attending schools outside your assigned school district. I was assigned to Memorial Junior High School, home of the Soldiers, renowned for its outstanding football teams. After my initial disappointment, I refocused my attention and excitement on participating in my first junior high school basketball tryout for my new school as a seventh grader. However, I was familiar with the topic format of a basketball tryout, including the basic skills of dribbling, shooting, passing, and layup lines from youth basketball tryouts that typically last one or two hours. Junior high school tryouts were more extended, usually two to three hours, and had the added challenges of drills, sprints, and competitive scrimmages to assess teamwork and basketball IQ. Although the tryout was much more competitive and the players bigger and more athletic, the environment was similar to what I had experienced in youth basketball tryouts, but without the encouraging words from my watching from the sideline.

Memorial Junior High School, located just five miles southwest of Howard, had a history of being a high school, a junior high, and a city hall. The home of the 'Soldiers' had a reputation as a 'sports school,' mainly because of its celebrated and dominant football program, which had won multiple county championships and sent numerous former players onto NCAA Division I Football Bowl Subdivision (FBS), National Football League NFL and professional teams. Buddy, my stepfather, a former high school, college, and semi-professional football player, was enthusiastic about me attending a traditional 'powerhouse' sports school. "Honestly, Tan, just hang in there," Buddy said. "Trust me, I know the feeling because I went through the same thing in school. At the time in your life when you are developing your independence, you are forced to spend entire days in an environment that rewards rule-following."

Buddy and I had built a strong bond over the years, mainly through sports, from attending pay-per-view professional boxing and Florida Championship Wrestling events to the many weekends traveling on the road to his semi-pro football and softball games. He was a big advocate for all of us to participate in sports. A bonus to attending Memorial was that one of the best basketball players in Griffin Park, Greg Register, was also attending the school and a returning player on the school's basketball team. Greg was older than me and in the same grade as my brother. He was also taller than most of the kids in the neighborhood, and he had long arms, which made it easier for him to shoot over opponents and grab nearly every rebound that bounced off the rim. It's advantageous to get your hands/arms as close to the basket as possible for the highest percentage shot and to shoot over others, or as a defender, to reach high to block another's shot; thus, Greg was exceptional at using his length. Greg reassured me about tryouts for the team and told me what to expect and what I should do to make the 'cut.' He said, "Tan, you got to play aggressive, solid defense on every play." He explained to me that the head boys' basketball coach, Coach Myers, was only going to keep two seventh graders on the team. "So, man," Greg said, "You got to be running the floor aggressively, and when you do get the ball, are you taking good shots?" Greg was the star player on the "Soldiers" team and possessed a combination of exceptional athleticism, size, and basketball IQ. Learning from him and my brother gave me a great advantage over the other seventh graders and an outstanding chance to be one of the two who would make the 'cut' for a roster spot on the team.

After several days of tryouts, the day came for Coach Myers to announce the final roster spots for the team. I was confident that I would make the final cut —I followed all of the advice Greg and my brother had given me, and I made the few shots I got to take. And when any of the coaches spoke to me or the team, I listened attentively with my ears and my eyes. The last day of tryouts was on Monday; now it was time to find out who 'got cut.' We had twenty-six kids trying out, and the final roster consisted of only twelve players. The team's starting lineup was going to be unchanged, with all five starters returning, including Greg, DC, Mac, Marvin 'Man' Williams, and Streeter. The two top reserve players were back and wouldn't be replaced. Therefore, only a few new players would be added to the team, and I was confident I would be one of them; I had practiced so hard for this moment. As the coach blew his whistle and called everyone into a semi-circle gathering, I stood next to Greg. Looking confidently at Coach Myers, I patiently listened to his message to all of the guys who attended the basketball tryouts, making it through the first two team cuts to arrive at this point, the final team cut. Cutting a player is never easy; the emotions will run high for the coach, parents, and athlete. Unlike high school, junior high school teams do not have varsity and junior varsity teams, with a total of 20-24 roster spots; there's only one team with 10-to-12 roster spots, divided up between returning players, which usually determine how many roster spots are genuinely available and the best eighth and ninth graders trying out for the team.

In many instances, coaches would also elect to keep the two best seventh graders, as those players could play with the team for three years. I was confident I would be among the two seventh graders selected for the final team roster. Coach Myer's first announcement was shocking. I don't recall what he said at the beginning or end of this statement, but I vividly remember what he said in between, "This year's team will not include any seventh graders." I was stunned by his announcement, standing on the court with slumped shoulders and a flat gaze; I don't remember whether the coach explained his decision. I was shocked; even as other team members patted me on the back and shared encouraging words about the following year, I still tried to comprehend and deal with the disappointment of being cut from the team. I don't know if my conflicting emotions included anger toward the coach, but I wanted to talk to him about why I was cut.

Coach Myers was open to speaking with me and provided feedback for the decision he made on not having any seventh graders on the roster. He explained that he didn't believe I or any of the other seventh graders performed well enough to be selected over the other players. However, he added, "You were the best seventh graders we had in the tryouts." He understood my disappointment but said, "It's important to remember that this setback doesn't define your abilities or potential." I listened to him and used the experience as motivation to set new practice goals and work even harder to improve my basketball skills. I was receptive to Coach Myer's constructive feedback; it included areas he suggested I needed to improve. But as a twelve-year-old who had played basketball since I was eight, I felt the game had been taken from me. I even felt embarrassed by the decision; other players from my neighborhood were selected for their school teams, and like me, they were seventh graders. I took a few days to allow myself to feel the disappointment; it's a normal reaction, but afterward, after some reflection and talking to my brother and to some of the players who made the team, I embraced being cut as an opportunity to grow and improve as a player. The following Monday in school, I went to Coach Myers's office before class to discuss the feedback he gave me, in particular for areas of improvement. I told him I would use this time to demonstrate my commitment to developing my skills and basketball IQ to make the team next year. He smiled, his face conveying confidence and sophistication with his well-groomed full beard and mustache, and said, "Robert, I can't wait to see the results."

In the meantime, I looked for other ways to stay involved with basketball, such as joining a competitive youth basketball team at the Young Men's Christian Association (YMCA) of Central Florida. The YMCA league allowed me to play on a team, emphasizing skill development, teamwork, good sportsmanship, and character development. Additionally, the team's coach named me team captain, a new leadership role that required me to set the standard for my teammates, holding my teammates and myself accountable for our behavior on and off the court. The team captain role was the first time I was in a leadership position responsible for more than just my performance, and I embraced the responsibility wholeheartedly. Finally, I work hard to develop my skills on the court and understand what it is to be a leader with integrity and purpose. The most important thing was that I always got encouraged. I stayed positive, focused on improvement, and open to new opportunities, primarily next season's basketball tryouts.

Although I didn't make the cut to be part of the Soldiers' basketball team in my first year of junior high school, I was determined that this would not be my last encounter with Coach Myers. I never attended another Memorial basketball team practice that year. Still, I was fortunate enough to attend several of my brother William's practice sessions and scrimmage games as they prepared for the season. Shortly into the 1978-79 basketball season, two of the best teams in Orange Country were scheduled to play one another in a highly anticipated matchup between two undefeated teams, Howard Junior High School (4-0) versus Memorial Junior High School (4-0). The game was being hosted at the home gymnasium of Howard with its out-of-the-ordinary structure style, including red color rails lining the top of the gym ceiling, its walnut hardwood bleachers, large scoreboard directly behind the baskets, and bright red colored doors conveying the impression that you were entering a Roman arena.

This was the first time I was attending a game where my school, Memorial, was competing against my brother's school, Howard. The atmosphere was electric, and the bleachers were overcrowded. The roar of the crowd was deafening when the teams entered the gym to the funk-disco beat of the R&B number one hit song "Le Freak" by the band Chic. As the teams ran around the perimeter of the court, the teams split off, each taking opposite end halfcourts to begin their warmup routine. When the game finally tipped off, it was fast-paced action, with high-flying layups, long, high-arching jump shots, and intense competition. The game's thrilling momentum swings—one team going on a scoring run and the other responding with a scoring outburst of its own—created an electrifying atmosphere. Fans were kept on the edge of their seats with roaring approval or disapproval at the back-and-forth action. Howard had the more athletic players, showing top-tier athleticism at both the offensive and defensive ends of the court. Going into the fourth quarter of the game, the home team had a lead, and my brother Weo was having an outstanding game, hitting some clutch, long-range jump shots, and by the end of the third quarter, had already scored in double-figures, leading all game scorers. Reflecting on the game they played against one another, Greg recalled Weo and other Howard players' trash-talking him before the start of the fourth quarter, "We got y'all," "I told y'all this was gonna be easy,"…"Ref can't help y'all, game over."

But the game changed dramatically in the final quarter; led by an exceptional individual performance by Greg, the Soldiers team seamlessly moved the ball, executing well-designed plays, outmaneuvering the Howard team and its talent, but outplaying them in pivotal moments of the final minutes to win the game. The home crowd wasn't happy about the game's outcome, yelling at the referees and accusing them of cheating. Attending this game was the moment I realized how important basketball was to me; I wanted to be on that court so badly that it hurt. I wanted to play in a 'real' basketball game and not wait until next year's basketball tryouts. The opportunity presented itself with an invitation to play in several recreational basketball leagues at the local YMCA and Boys & Girls Clubs of America. However, the talent level of the players was inferior, competing in games with officials enforcing all the rules and spectators cheering and booing provided an opportunity for me and other players to develop fundamental basketball skills and learn important life skills such as how to participate as part of a team and communicate with coaches, officials, and teammates. Both of these leagues helped to better prepare me for my basketball tryouts as my stamina increased with conditioning from running a mile or court sprints with William and repeatedly going through basketball drills.

The summer before the next basketball season, my eighth grade in junior high school, we moved from the Griffin Park housing projects to the urban housing community of the Carver Shores neighborhood, named after the prominent African American scientist and inventor George Washington Carver. Our new home would be much larger, with four bedrooms, a living area, a family room, and an add-on room for additional space. The major improvements in size and quality of our new living conditions should have been joyous. Still, the excitement was half-hearted as the location of the new residence was outside of my previous school district, requiring both Derrick and me to transfer to a new junior high school. William did not have to change schools because he was entering his final year of junior high school. Therefore, William would continue to be a rising basketball star and an honor roll student at Howard Junior High School. Derrick and I would have to attend Robinswood Junior High School in Pine Hills, an Orlando subdivision, for the upcoming school year.

The disappointment of leaving Memorial was magnified when I was also cut from Robinswood basketball tryouts, leaving me no option but to play another season at the Boys & Girls Club. Fortunately, I had one of the better basketball prospects in Orange County to practice with and continue to play one-on-one basketball games against almost daily. I continued to lose those games. But my confidence was growing due to all of the practice games (and losses) playing against my older/taller/better sibling. Because William was such a talented basketball player, I wanted to challenge myself against him as often as I could. It was like having my basketball audition against an older and better opponent regularly, forcing me to develop my skills further.

During the last weeks of the summer, I noticed a school assignment in the mail. I was astonished to see in bold letters that **Memorial Junior High School** was my assigned school for the 1980-81 school year! Due to a clerical error at the Orange County School Board, I was erroneously reassigned to Memorial Junior High School for my ninth-grade year. I was looking forward to returning to my old school, eagerly anticipating basketball tryouts, and displaying my newfound confidence and vastly improved basketball skills to Coach Myers. At the same time, William had entered his first year of high school at Wymore Tech High School in Eatonville, a suburb of Orlando, and the oldest black-incorporated municipality (1887) in the United States by African American freedmen (formerly enslaved people). The school also had a rich history of basketball success, giving it its identity. The school's basketball program made numerous (qualifying for six final four appearances) trips to the Florida High School Activities Association (FHSAA) state boys' basketball championships, including two state championships and four state runners-up finishes. The school has had only three coaches, as each of the previous two coaches remained there for extended periods, achieving two dozen twenty-plus win seasons and only one losing season in over four decades. William would transition nicely to his new school, making the honor roll each quarter of the school year, excelling on the 'Bobcats' basketball team, earning a spot on the roster, and being one of its best offensive players. The Bobcats "We Run and Gun" (WRAG) offense was perfect for William's game; it had lots of pressure, transition, and perimeter shooting.

WRAG was geared towards the guard's dribble penetrating, attacking, and kicking out for the baseline deep corner shot, William's preferred spot on court to shoot the ball. The team's three best players, 6'6" Hollis Mack, 6'4" Kenny McCain, and 6'2" William Worthington were all ideally suited to play in Coach Calvin Lang's fan-friendly, high-scoring run and gun offense. The team continued its traditional on-court success, making the 1981 FHSAA basketball playoffs, winning Class AA district and regional playoff games versus Groveland and the heavily favored Lakeland Sante Fe Hawks, each of which were one-point victories. In the regional playoff game, the Bobcats were led by McCain and Worthington, scoring fifteen points apiece, and Center Mack contributed eleven points and key rebounds to secure the victory.

The win sent the team into the Class AA Section 5 Championship game versus Flagler Palm Coast Bulldogs, with the winning team advancing to the state finals. The Bobcats led the Bulldogs by two points going into the fourth quarter. A cold shooting spell by the Bobcats—missing six consecutive shots and turning the ball over several times—allowed the Bulldogs to expand their lead. The Wymore Tech team could not recover from this deficit, losing the game 71-67 and ending their season one game short of the state championships. Exacerbating the disappointing feelings, William had his worst game of the season, scoring a season-low one point in the heartbreaking loss. Simultaneously, I was making my first appearance as the starting shooting guard in a junior high school basketball game for the Memorial Soldiers. The team's roster was comprised mostly of ninth graders who were multi-sports athletes, creating a mentally tough team that played the game with an advanced level of competition experience, leadership, and teamwork. Despite the availability of a lot more talented and experienced players, two seventh graders were 'cut,' continuing a tradition the majority of coaches replicated each year.

Coach Stanley was now the head boys' basketball coach, replacing Coach Myers, who was still a teacher at the school. I was somewhat disappointed that I wasn't going to have an opportunity to display the improvements in my skill level to Coach Myers; I had played the scenario out in my mind repeatedly, showcasing my ability to dribble, pass, and shoot the basketball, being the hardest working player in the gym. I was committed to being the first player in line for drills and ensured that I touched every line running 'suicide' conditioning drills. I was single-minded in my effort to separate myself by displaying improved basketball skills, being the most vocal and enthusiastic player in the gym and hustling on every play! This approach didn't lead to having many friends on the team.

However, one teammate in particular, Steve Griffin, and I developed a good friendship after an initial rough start, largely due to the fact we were both ultimate competitors. Steve was one of the best basketball players on the team and the best football player in the entire school. The five players who made up the starting lineup for the 1980-81 Soldiers included Steve, Al, Mark, Allen, and me; all five of us were multi-sports athletes. Our starting lineup was not composed of the usual point guard, shooting guard, small forward, power forward, and center positions. We started each game with a three-guard lineup, and Coach Stanley would make adjustments based on the flow of the game action. Although our team had more than our share of outstanding athletes, the team's performance was consistently inconsistent. The coach's staff encouraged us to continue to work hard in practice, explaining that it was a long season and everyone experienced ups and downs throughout the season.

As the team captain, I spoke with Coach Stanley about the frustration spreading throughout the team, dealing with inconsistency in our play. I was not immune from the inconsistent play of my own. In one game, I would score double-figure points and lead our team in scoring and to victory. The next game, I would score six points on 3-for-12 shooting, and even though I tried to make up for my less-than-stellar offensive output at the defensive end of the court, we routinely lost the games where I didn't perform well offensively. The poor performance led to more than a few long talks with Coach Stanley in his classroom, during which he attempted to walk me through both the team's and my struggles. He explained to me, "You have to embrace the bad shooting performances for what they are, and if you shoot 6-of-7 or 1-of-5, you shouldn't get too excited or dejected over either."

The goal was to remain even-tempered and confident and use this mental approach to my advantage. He and I would always agree that any concern about my performance should remain secondary to the focus on doing everything I can to help the team win. And I always put winning as my priority, whether I was shooting well or not. Although many of my teammates didn't think so, accusing me of being selfish and stuck, only concerned with scoring my points, the jealousy was a major factor in why we finished the season in the middle of the pack of teams and made an early exit from playoffs. The final loss of the season came at the hands of an opponent whom we had defeated twice during the regular season, Westridge Junior High School.

The last time I would take the court with my teammates was for an exhibition game versus the school's teachers. The game was entertaining and a way to bring everyone together for a fun game. My favorite part of the game was going up against some of my teachers, hearing them talk good-natured trash talk to me and some of my teammates, and being able to talk trash back to them a little bit. I hit several long-range jump shots in the game, and one teacher, who was not participating in the game, Mr. Anthony, came up to me after the game to tell me that I was "a baller and the best player on the team," and that he enjoyed watching us play. The friendly competition was exciting with the final score of 56-48, the teachers losing by only eight points.

We had a final event, the end-of-the-year sports awards ceremony, in which all of the sports teams over the past school year were given awards to the best athletes in their specific sport. The awards included best hustle player, best defensive player, most improved player, and most valuable player (MVP). The MVP award, or Most Valuable Player award, is an honor given to the player who is considered to be the best performer and most valuable to his specific team. He is deemed to have had the most outstanding season on the team. During the days leading up to the award ceremony, members of the team and other students openly debated about who would receive what awards. But there was one particular conversation that stood out for me.

During one of our lunch periods, I was walking alone towards the school cafeteria when I noticed a group of my teammates having a heated debate standing near an outdoor bench in front of the cafeteria. As I discreetly approached, I could overhear one of the players, our point-guard, speaking very loudly and clearly, "Man, if Tan wins the MVP, I'm going to be sick." I was shocked, so much so that I didn't hear the remainder of the conversation as I turned around and walked in the opposite direction. I wasn't sure where I was headed, but I ended up in a familiar place: Coach Stanley's classroom. I told him about the loud conversation I had overheard and how the words coming from my teammates' mouths were shocking; not only were these my teammates, but some of these guys were also supposed to be my friends. This 'aha moment' of jealousy or resentment was distressing, so I asked Coach if he was planning to give me the MVP award…and if he was, I did not want it! Coach listened to me patiently, allowing me to vent my frustration and emotions about what I had overheard. Afterward, he told me that he didn't feel obligated to give the MVP award to anyone who did not earn it. He then asked me if I believed that I was deserving of the award. I responded by saying, "It doesn't matter; I don't want it because my teammate does not think I deserve it." He then explained to me what his criteria was for the MVP award; the player who received the award not only had to possess exceptional talent, but exhibit leadership, and impact the team's overall success…and he believed I was deserving of the award!

On the day of the awards banquet, coaches, players, family, and friends gathered in the school auditorium to honor the best moments and athletes of the season. When the basketball awards were announced, "the 1980-81 boys' basketball Most Valuable Player (MVP), Robert Worthington"…I don't remember the reaction of my teammates or if any of the other spectators applauded or not. But I do recall the look of approval on Coach Stanley's face. As I walked up on stage, extending my hand for a respectful handshake, Coach quietly mouthed the words, "You deserved this." As I accepted the award, I said, "Thank you" to my coach. I felt gracious, humble, and grateful; the honor validated my efforts to improve as a basketball player. I acknowledged my teammates with a nod of my head as I walked back to take my seat…after the award ceremony was over, most of my teammates congratulated me on winning the award. As I headed home, I reflected on the evening and the proceeding days when I overheard comments that I was selfish because I scored more points than some other players…they never mentioned the fact that the coach was calling the plays for me to score.

Finally, I thought that this would likely not be the last time I would experience some resentment from teammates, but under no circumstances would I ever back down from my efforts to play at the highest level my skills would allow so that I could better fit in or be more "accepted" by the teammates. Doing so would be far too high a price for "belonging." Besides, what kinds of teammates or friends would ever want you to deliberately hold yourself back from reaching your potential so they can feel better about themselves? When I got home that evening, William was sitting at the dining room table eating a bowl of cereal. When he saw the trophy in my hands, he shouted, "Tan, what award did you win!?" Before I could respond, he grabbed the trophy. He read the inscription, "Tan, man, I knew you were going to win MVP…. man, bruh, I'm so proud of you. I knew you gonna win it, MVP. "Wrapping his arms around my head and pulling me closer to him, he handed me back the trophy, he said "We got to play one-on-one tomorrow."…which was always the ultimate challenge for me!

My journey in junior high was coming to an end, and it was now time to move on to new challenges in high school. Although Coach Myers was not my coach during my ninth-grade year at Memorial, he was still a teacher at the school, and we spoke frequently about the improvement he noticed in my game and the potential he thought I had to becoming a high school basketball star. Sitting in the school parking lot after school one afternoon, in his 1970 red convertible Oldsmobile Cutlass (he loved that car), he shared with me that he had recently accepted the junior varsity boys' basketball coaching job for the Boone High School Braves, a program led by legendary varsity basketball coach Wayne Rickman (winning state basketball championships in 1977 and 1983). He told me that he wanted me to come to the school to play for him. I was elated; I had wanted to play basketball for Coach Myers for years, and now he was offering me an opportunity that, two years earlier, he didn't think I deserved. I told him I wasn't sure how I could attend the high school, considering I didn't live in the school district, nor did I have transportation to get to and from school. He reassured me that he would take care of all my transportation needs, picking me up every morning before school and dropping me off after school and basketball practice in the evening. I told him I would have to speak with my mother about it, but I would consider the offer.

The next morning, in my first class of the day, US Government, I spoke with my favorite teacher, Mrs. Little, about the offer that Coach Myers had presented to me. I was a little surprised by the quick change of her facial expression, from her usually soft and gentle smile, full of kindness and empathy, to a half-smile with a look of 'the hell you are'. We discussed the matter until class started and continued the conversation after class was dismissed. As I was just about to walk through the classroom door, Mrs. Little stopped me, "Robert, let me speak to you for a minute." "Yes, ma'am," as I made a quick U-turn back into the classroom, stopping in front of her desk. "Robert, what happens if you can't play basketball…will the coach still give you a ride? What happens if you are not as good as he thinks you are? What happens if he gets fired from his job as coach? Who will give you ride to-and-from school? Robert, you do not need to go to a school where you have to rely on someone else's generosity to get to and from that school. And his act of goodness is based on how well you play basketball for his team." "Yes, ma'am," I replied. I decided not to attend Boone but instead went to my assigned school, Maynard Evans High School.

Caught In My Girlfriend's Bedroom Closet

Summer break for middle school kids who live in Orlando, Florida is usually filled with perfect weather, an abundance of parks, and permanent vacation vibes from the constant flow of visitors worldwide. And that world-famous mouse down Interstate 4 (one of the busiest roads in the Sunshine State) at the world-famous magic kingdom, Walt Disney World. Summer break 1981 in Orlando was highly distinct; most people remember two unforgettable happenings: the massive Winter Park sinkhole and the Rolling Stones concert. The sinkhole swallowed up a private home, a luxury (Porsche) car dealership, various businesses, and a community swimming pool, totaling more than four million dollars in damages.

The overwhelming excitement and anticipation of Mick Jagger and the Rolling Stones, performing with opening act Van Halen for two nights at the Tangerine Bowl in a concert known as "Rock Super Bowl XII" concert was exhilarating. More than sixty thousand tickets were sold in ten hours. The two concerts grossed nearly two million dollars but weren't without some controversy. According to a New York Times article, legendary lead vocalist Mick Jagger said, "The front rows in Orlando were filled with twelve- and thirteen-year-old girls, some of whom were making the unseemliness suggestions." Maybe Mick should blame the behavior of the teenage girls on the lyrics of the Stones' hit song "Under My Thumb." Nevertheless, I fail to recall much about either of these two milestones. But the summer of 1981 is plastered into my memory for another highly anticipated experience…a planned summer visit to see my girlfriend at her house without parental supervision! No, I was not *only* thinking about sex.

However, my thoughts would repeatedly return to sex as a teenage boy. Still, this preoccupation would be occasionally interrupted with thoughts of basketball, great conversations, and debates, grades in school, and other teenage stuff. But my relationship with my girlfriend Alicia was special. I genuinely enjoyed talking to her. We were both athletes at our junior high school and often spoke to one another during school and afterward. But dating happened by accident, I think! The school day had been long, including two hours of after-school sports practice. Alicia and I found ourselves alone without our normal group of friends, allowing us to talk alone for an extended period without others' interference. We eventually decided to walk home together, a distance of about four miles and more than sixty minutes. The walk seemed to last hours; our conversations were interesting and familiar. I was amazed at how easily we went from one topic to another. About midway through our walk, we were surprised by Alicia's boyfriend at the time. He rode up from behind us on his mini bicycle, an old-school crate bike with an ape handlebar and bucket saddle seat. He never said a word, he just slowly rode his bike between us until he was out of sight. I don't recall if Alicia and I ever talked about what occurred. We paused, became silent for a few seconds, and continued our walk and conversation as if nothing had happened.

Nevertheless, shortly after the surprise 'ride-by' incident, Alicia and I ran into each other at school. She told me that she and her boyfriend had a break-up. She didn't seem too upset about it. This is how we accidentally began dating. She spellbound me; I'd never had such an intense crush on someone before. We would talk all day and night, and I often fell asleep on the phone talking to her. But the school year was over, and I wouldn't see her every day. Two long weeks had passed since summer break began. Although we spent hours on the phone talking, we agreed that I would visit her on a weekday afternoon when her parents would be at work. I had never been to her house before, and we had never had a one-on-one conversation behind closed doors, much less a closed bedroom door!

Finally, the big day arrived! I hurriedly got prepared; I had a long shower, dressed in a clean white t-shirt, sports shorts, high-top Converse, and crew socks. Lastly, I sprayed some Afro Sheen on my hair and picked it out. I was ready, out the door for my long walk to Alicia's house. After enduring the more than ninety-degree Florida heat, crossing numerous highways, and darting in front of speeding vehicles, I arrived at Alicia's house. Standing in front with emotions stirring, I nervously rang the doorbell. Alicia answered the door wearing a yellow-colored one-piece pull-up, strapless top, and shorts…I was spellbound! I wasn't sure if she noticed, but I could barely look into her eyes or at her beautiful smile and dimples. I couldn't stop staring at her bra-less top, revealing her perfectly shaped breasts and erect nipples. I don't remember even walking into the house, but we eventually ended up in her bedroom, sitting on the edge of her bed. We talked and laughed loudly until suddenly she stopped talking, looking as if she heard some strange noise; she nervously whispered my name and said, "Tan, I think my dad is home!" A feeling of extreme nervousness and fear came over me as we both quickly jumped off the bed. Standing at the foot of the bed, Alicia grabbed my arm and pushed me toward her bedroom closet.

Initially, I was hesitant to go into the closet. Well, until I heard the deep baritone sound of her father's voice, thenI quickly went into the closet! Alicia opened her bedroom door, and her father walked into the bedroom; he asked what she was doing. I don't recall her answer, as I was too busy praying to God to save me! I promised God that if you allow me to live through this 'mistake,' I would never…ever go into Alicia's bedroom again! After what seemed like hours, her father left her bedroom and headed back to work. Alicia returned to the room to let me know the coast was clear, and I came out of the closet. I made a quick beeline for the living room. I tried to play it cool, but I was scared to death. It was the most frightening moment I had ever experienced; I had taken a significant gamble that nearly resulted in severely negative consequences!

5
FROM THRIVING TO SURVIVING: HIGH SCHOOL, COLLEGE & BEYOND

Attending high school in the 1980s occurred simultaneously during the early stages of the digital revolution, the rise of personal computers, and the birth of the internet. It was an exciting time, but I felt apprehensive and nervous about the unknown and the formidable transition from junior high to high school. Several school officials believed the processes to be the most significant and complex transition an adolescent would experience to this point in their lives. August 25, 1981 was my first day of high school at Maynard Evans High School; first-year students typically had to attend orientation sessions, receive their class schedules (although you could also pick up your schedule from the school office before school year), and become familiar with the layout of the school. This included knowing hallways 100, 200, and 400, where my locker was located and the most crowded area in the entire school. The 400 hallway was also where most hall monitors were: an adult paraprofessional staff member, an upper-level student volunteer, or one of the school's coaches. I also received the 'first day of high school warning' from my brother William, "Tan, don't block the hallways with your friends and don't walk into the school like you own the building. You are just going to irritate the upper-level students." I don't know if I had the same advice for Derrick, who always walked slowly but was unlikely to be bullied by anyone! Because it was the first day of school, my mother ensured we had all the essential supplies such as notebooks, pens, pencils, lunch money, gym bag, and any required paperwork or forms the school may have requested. I wasn't too uncomfortable walking through the hallways of the school; I knew many of the kids were from my neighborhood or had attended Robinswood Junior High School, which I attended during my eighth-grade school year.

The school was huge, and the layout was unfamiliar. I spent fifteen minutes walking around the hallways looking for my first-period French class. But by the end of the first week, I had fully adjusted, and it became routine. But my excitement about the school had not subsided, and I was looking forward to the start of basketball season. The school is located in the heart of West Orlando. It is the home of the Trojans, where local basketball phenom Darry Dawkins became the first high school basketball player to go directly from high school to the National Basketball Association (NBA). (Philadelphia 76ers selected him in the 1975 NBA Draft, first round, with the fifth overall pick.) His legend loomed large over the school and the boys' basketball program! It's a little embarrassing to admit this truth, but, basketball, not academics, was why I was excited about attending Maynard Evans High School. Spending my adolescence years in Carver Shores, a southwest neighborhood that offers residents an urban feel and opportunity for affordable home ownership, wearing the green and white uniform of the Trojans was considered quite the honor. And kids in this neck of the woods dreamed of wearing those colors, even with my short flirtation with the thought of attending Boone High School.

The Trojans had built an impressive reputation on the basketball court over the previous decade, from 1971 to 1981. They were led by six-foot-ten-inch-tall Dawkins, who averaged thirty-two points and twenty-one rebounds per game over his high school career, culminating in a pivotal win and the 1975 Class 5A Boys Basketball State Championship. This success continued with a long list of great players who followed. Opposing teams were more than a little apprehensive about facing off against the Trojans basketball teams, especially in their home gym, where the opposing schools found it so difficult to win games, other coaches began referring to the gym as 'the Snake Pit.' The Trojans were so dominant at their home gym that opponents would resort to just playing 'stall ball,' holding the ball for as long as possible without taking a shot—an advantage they were afforded due to no shot clock at the time, and a strategy that would be successfully deployed years later.

A few Trojan basketball traditions that didn't strike fear in opponents and were more than mortifying for the Trojan players were, in the words of my good friend Moses Gordon, "Coach gave us John Stockton shorts, let me rephrase that, Booty shorts, way up the leg shorts." We had the shortest uniform shorts in high school basketball history, well at least during those times. Adding insult to injury, paired with our uniform were green canvas Chuck Taylor All Stars – Converse shoes, even with the availability of Air Jordan 1, Nike Air Pegasus, Saucony Jazz, Adidas ZX, and other high-top designed leather basketball shoes. I never asked any of our coaches what values or culture we were upholding by wearing "daisy duke" basketball shorts and canvas Chuck Taylors. The last season an NBA player wore a pair of canvas Converse All-Stars was in 1979. But if the 'tradition' was intended to create a sense of unity for us as players and how we bonded as a team, it worked. We were all equally embarrassed. Still, we displayed great confidence in being a part of the team, and we trusted one another!

William was not as fortunate in his junior year as he was in his sophomore year, at least not on the basketball court. He found scoring more challenging and had more than a few 'differences' with the team's coach regarding his rotation patterns. In the classroom, he regularly made the Principal's Honor Roll each quarter he attended Wymore Tech. William was an outstanding student who maintained academic recognition with distinction in all of his classes, usually with above 3.6 GPA, without exception each year in school. Academic success didn't come as easily to me. I was not an honor roll student, but I was hardworking, submitted most of my assignments on time, and actively participated in all my classes to get better grades. Academically, William and I were at opposite ends.

My 2.3 GPA was slightly below average, and although it was a passing C-grade average, it was not considered a strong academic record if you're planning to seek acceptance into college. The transition to high school presented other challenges. For most students, walking through the hallways was a daily ritual (stopping by your locker, seeing who was in school and who was absent, catching up with friends who don't live in your neighborhood, and making it to class on time, etc.). The lunch period was more about our social life or lack thereof than whether we ate a healthy meal. We mostly sat at the same table at lunch every day, with usually the same group of friends. The normal essential topics of conversation in the lives of teenage boys are sports, girls, more sports, more girls, and a lot more about girls, specifically if anyone had a girlfriend or rumors of what girls the guys may like.

Undeterred by the end of the school day, most of these conversations continued after school, usually over the home telephone (we didn't have cell phones or the internet) or by writing notes someone passed along to you in class; generally receiving an end-of-class note was a suggestion that a particular girl was revealing a romantic interest in you. The next day at school, one of your friends, who was friends with one of her friends, would ask if your 'crush' (the girl you were attracted to) had a boyfriend. You would spend all day nervously awaiting an answer and holding your breath that you would not see her in the hallway at her locker before you knew the answer to your question. This approach to dating continued for most high school boys, in particular for a sophomore. In high school, the progression up the social ladder of popularity had to begin all over again. Being a member of the basketball team played a significant role in enhancing my popularity in high school in several ways.

Foremost, as an athlete, I received far greater attention and recognition for the achievements of being a part of the Trojans basketball team, something that elevated my social status. Additionally, sports provided a sense of community and belonging, as teammates bond together, and fans rally around the team. Maynard Evans High School was similar to most high schools, they didn't give as much attention to academic extracurricular success as to athletic success. School administrators promote the school's athletic programs in ways other extracurriculars do not. Athletes can wear their team's uniform tops to school, and pep rallies are held during the school day to encourage team spirit and support team members. Parades and other social events are held to celebrate the team and individual players' success. Sports banquets are held, and the entire student body is invited to attend to present awards and school letters.

Finally, athletes use special facilities, like team locker rooms, weight rooms, basketball courts or sports fields, swimming pools, etc. Beyond a shadow of a doubt, being a member of the school's basketball team aided in my climb up the social ladder. But even with being popular, I wasn't exempt from the emotional ups and downs of a high school crush. The first time I saw Rebecca, she appeared nearly flawless in her beauty, with a smile that conveyed happiness and good humor. I was so captivated by her beauty that whenever she was nearby, she thoroughly held my attention. I could not stop staring at her, something I tried hard to conceal. If she ever noticed me staring at her, she 'played it off' well, never letting on that she knew how fascinated I was with her. I don't know if 'love at first sight' is a real thing or not. Still, the phenomenon of having intense feelings for someone the second you see them perfectly describes how

I felt when I saw Rebecca. Although I would speak to her from time to time in school, we had no classes together as she was a year ahead of me. It was months into the school year before we had ever had a one-on-one conversation. I returned from our casual conversation feeling as if I had been friend-zoned!

However, the following week, everything would change; our high school basketball season was starting with a home game against a conference rival, Oak Ridge High School Pioneers. As members of the junior varsity team, we took the court before the varsity teams. Nevertheless, as our team ran out of the locker room and came into view of spectators, the noise was electrifying. High school basketball is one of the most entertaining sporting events you can attend at the high school level. From the proximity of the spectators in the wooden bleachers to the court at the Evans High gym, known as 'The Snake Pit,' to the accelerated pace of the entire event, from team warm-ups to gameplay, to the raucous cheers of the energized crowd, the atmosphere of a high school basketball game is thrilling. The home opener against the Pioneers was a nail-biting close game, with both teams battling fiercely for every basket as the lead exchanged several times.

The home crowd was on their feet, cheering and shouting encouragement to our team and their favorite players. During a critical phase of the game, with less than two minutes remaining in the fourth quarter, our starting point guard, JoJo Harris, dribbled through a defensive trap in front of the visiting team's bench near the half-court line. As he continued to speed-dribble up the side-line, he used a crossed over dribble to change directions. He headed towards the top of the key, and as two defenders closed in on him, he quickly stopped his dribble. He made a perfect bounce of the ball to me on the right corner of the court. As I received the pass, I squared my body towards the basket and shot a high, arching jump-shot, 'swish, nothing but net' as the shot goes in! It was a beautiful offensive play. It was set up by a fantastic pass from our point guard, which led to us finally taking the lead. The crowd went wild with excitement as the scoreboard showed the home team with the lead. The game was still neck and neck, as we traded baskets back and forth with the point spread never growing beyond two points. The clock was ticking down, and the tension was palpable. We had the ball, and we tried to run down the clock. We'd pass the ball around the court, trying to find an opening; suddenly, I made a back-cut towards the basket and received a back-door pass from our starting forward, Moses Gordan, leading to a right-handed underhand layup or "finger roll." This play put us up by four points with three seconds left on the game clock! The crowd erupted in jubilation and triumph.

We had won our opening home game! I had the best game of all junior varsity players, leading the team in scoring, including the two crucial late baskets. As we left the court, I heard more than a few "you the man" comments directed towards me. I am grateful for the fans' appreciation of the team's performance, and winning always makes the post-game interactions better. However, what happened after my teammate and I emerged from the locker room was completely unexpected. We walked up the bleachers to scattered applause to take our seats behind the team bench and watch the varsity game. I noticed that Rebecca was in attendance with her sister and some other female friends sitting in the next section over from the team. As I walked past the girls to take my seat, Rebecca reached out and touched my leg with a shy, playful, and flirtatious touch, a sign that maybe I wasn't permanently stuck in the friend zone or at least she noticed me! The next day in school, we talked about the game and the cute moment we shared with her touching my leg. Before heading off to class, she gave me her phone number and a friendly hug. Our phone calls became a daily routine, and they were always flirty, playful, and full of compliments.

However, other than maybe a handful of times of walking to class together, and one funny encounter we shared with another female friend, one where they made lighthearted fun of me in gym class by putting eyeliner on me as a joke…but regrettably a more romantic relationship never developed. During the high school years, plenty of other social occasions arose, none more sought-after than pre-midnight informal gatherings in (occasionally unfamiliar) local neighborhoods known as 'house parties.' These teen house parties provided an opportunity to hang out with friends and meet new ones from surrounding areas. They were generally hosted at different private houses throughout Orlando. But for the three years I attended high school, the most popular and unforgettable house parties were typically held in Carver Shore's predominantly Black neighborhood (the community where I lived), at the house of one of my best friends, JoJo Harris.

For the majority of the parties hosted at the Harris house, the man at the controls of turntables or CDs playing the songs to keep everyone dancing with his high-energy, humor-infused style of disk jockey was the legendary DJ, Dr. Ant. Because the location was just a few blocks away, William and I would regularly walk together to the house parties. However, this routine didn't last beyond the first year, mostly because we attended different high schools and hung out with a different circle of friends. William and I rarely arrived and departed together from one of the weekend house parties. Because most house parties happened on a Friday night, the same night most high school basketball is played, I routinely attended with one or more of my teammates during basketball season. In the first year of playing basketball for the Trojans, our junior varsity (JV) won the country basketball championship, losing only two games the entire season.

In the championship game, we played against a familiar opponent, and the only team that defeated us during the season, Bishop Moore Catholic High School. We were determined not to lose to them again; my teammates Moses Gordon and John Hadley were too big and athletic for the other team's post players. And I had quite a good shooting night. The sportswriter of the local newspaper, The Orlando Sentinel, wrote a column the following day where he described the performance as "Robert Worthington, a 5'10" sharpshooter, contributed some consistently accurate long-range shooting throughout the game for the Trojans." After winning the JV Championship as tenth graders, the three of us, John, Moses, and myself, all believed ourselves to be "called- up" from the JV to the Varsity team for the remainder of the season. But unexpectedly, the varsity team lost in the early district playoffs, ending their season shortly after the junior varsity team's season ended with a championship. I was shocked to learn of the varsity game results and disappointed that I wouldn't get an opportunity to play on the varsity team. Coach King and I had a lengthy conversation about how I was feeling. He assured me that he thought I was good enough to be on the varsity team but also felt I could use "a little more seasoning." I agreed with his assessment; I'd only played one junior high school basketball season. Therefore, my lack of experience playing organized games was a weakness, and I looked forward to resolving this by playing as much basketball as possible during the summer months.

The summer between my tenth-grade and eleventh-grade year in high school presented me with endless opportunities to improve my basketball skills, including playing one-on-one games against my brother, pickup games throughout Orlando, playing in the summer basketball league at the Dr. James R. Smith Center, and hours of ball handling and shooting drills in our driveway at home where we had a garage-mounted basketball hoop. During the first few weeks of summer break, Greg Register and I planned to meet up at Barker Park, a popular outdoor park located on the north shore of Clear Lake. The park was favored for its view of the cypress-lined lake, boat launchings, Barker Park Bridge, multiple pavilions for picnics, and the availability of a lovely outdoor asphalt basketball court, where the basketball bounces fast and high on its surface. Greg was a long-time friend and former high school basketball star at Orlando Jones High School, a school formerly known as the 'Orlando Colored

Academy' and one of the first public high schools to allow Black students to attend. Jones was also one of our biggest rivalries dating back to the late 1960s.

When Evans High School matched up against Jones High School, basketball games were played, the gymnasium or football stadium was jam-packed with spectators, and the atmosphere was electrifying. As Greg and I met up on the bridge, we leaned over the rails and talked briefly. He informed me that Jones High School alums hosted a summer gathering at the park. I told him I was okay with going since I had attended junior high school with many of the students at Jones, and therefore would not feel out of place. As we walked off the bridge toward the basketball court, we noticed Coach Belvedere, the Jones varsity boys' basketball coach, walking toward us. He gestured to Greg to come over to him, leaned over, and whispered something in Greg's ear. As the coach slowly walked away, still looking at me and smiling, I refocused my attention on Greg, who was laughing as he walked back toward me.

I was puzzled. Did Coach Belvedere not want me to attend the event? Did he ask Greg to tell me to leave? "Greg, is something wrong? What did Coach Belvedere talk to you about?" I asked. Greg continued to smile and replied, "No, he was asking me if you were a shooting guard from Evans High School and if you were looking to transfer to Jones High School for the upcoming school year." As Greg and I continued to talk, Coach Belvedere walked over to us and said in a beguiling manner, "They don't have anything like this over at Evans now, do they? This is a family atmosphere with barbecue and playing ball. You come over here to Jones, this is what it's gonna be like. You know what I'm talking about?" I smiled at the coach's words and walked to the basketball court. Greg and I laughed about the encounter later that day, but he was right about one thing: No other schools hosted an alum gathering like the Jones High School Tigers alums!

The following day, Sunday morning, I shared the story with my brothers. Derrick looked at me and said, "Tan, boy, you better stay your ass at Evans" then he walked off disinterested. He was never big into sports. On the other hand, William strongly believed that I may be considering changing schools, though I had yet to think it through. Still, my older brother felt I should remain in the familiar surroundings of Evans High School. He thought I had established myself on the school's JV team and that I was best positioned to be selected to the varsity team, given my early success and feedback from the team's coaches.

1-on-1 Rematch Against My Brother

Growing up in Griffin Park, I really wanted to beat my older brother, William, in a one-on-one basketball game. It irritated me that I could never beat him. It also motivated me to get better every day. William once reminded me that losing a one-on-one basketball game gracefully is a skill, just as is winning graciously. Still, I'm sure that advice was a little easier to give since he usually won all the games. But I never lost self-confidence and was determined to improve, starting with my outside shooting game. I spent hours developing my jump shot and improving my ball-handling skills. I would even shoot outside shots when the park lights were off, so I would listen for the sound of the ball moving through the nets to determine if the shot went in, 'all net.'

As the weeks passed and hours of practice added up, I saw a noticeable improvement in my athleticism, stamina, speed, and agility. My jumper improved significantly in fundamental form and in consistency of hitting long-distance shots. So, when our usual back-and-forth about basketball turned into yet another one-on-one challenge, I walked on the court this time believing that I was a much better player than at any other time over the years' past when evaluating my game against my big brother. We would typically shoot for the ball to determine who started the game on offense, but William was confident that didn't matter, so he self-assuredly said, "You can have the ball." I was okay with his overconfidence; he had earned it. I dribbled the ball to the top of the key, passed the ball to Weo, and said "check" to begin the game. The winner of our one-on-one matchup would be the first player to score eleven baskets, earning one point for each basket., and after each basket was made, the ball had to be taken behind the key.

The game was back-and-forth, much more so than usual, until I made consecutive basketball after consecutive misses by William. I was leading ten to nine and taking the ball to the top of the key for a chance to score the winning basket. I slowly dribbled to my right, then quickly speed dribbled forward, crossover dribbled back to my free-throw line elbow and shot a mid-range jump shot that I had shot over and over again during my practice shooting sessions. 'Swish,' nothing but net as the shot went through the basket. I looked at William, unsure how he felt about losing to me for the first time, but his face was emotionless as he said, "Good game, Tan. Man, your set-shot has gotten so good." We would play two more games, each winning one. We never talked about the game's outcome other than his reference to my 'set shot' being better. However, years later, he wrote me a letter and shared his true feelings about the one-on-one basketball I had won.

"I remember when we played one-on-one ball, the losses you took, and the look on your face. Yet I also remember my love and pride every time you picked that basketball back up and said, 'Check.' Tan, boy, I loved you then, and I love you now, and I almost cried when you finally won a one-on-one game against me. Man, you played, boy! And I felt light-headed, as if I was the one who won that game! But let me tell you a little secret, little brother: I tried to win that game and wanted to win badly. But there was a part of me that kept 'rooting' you on, and years later, I realized what that part of me was, bro...My heart holds each

of my family members inside of me…Man, this has me in tears right now, bro, and boy, I'm so glad you can't see me now cause I know both of us would break down."

I didn't need to celebrate my first win in a game against William; in fact, I felt embarrassed that I had won the game. He's the big brother, he's supposed to win. During the one-on-one matchup, William didn't seem himself. I wondered, was he not motivated, as his physical performance was a noticeable decline? We had so many high-spirited battles over the years. William was always motivated and energetic from the first game to the last. But this game was different; he appeared lazy and unmotivated, unable to perform at his typical high-skill level. I was bewildered and somewhat rattled by his performance. What was happening? Was he allowing me to win? A few weeks later, the questions would be answered.

Early on a school night, we all piled into the car and made a hasty trip to the hospital emergency room. William had complained about feeling dizzy and nauseous after sitting in a cold bathtub of ice-cold water; Mom said nervously, "We're going to the ER." We rushed to Orlando Regional Medical Center (ORMC), a hospital with a reputation as one of the most advanced medical care centers with the best outstanding rehabilitative and emergency care in Central Florida. After hours of waiting, a doctor finally walked into the ER and asked, "Is Mrs. Worthington in here?" As he walked over to my mother, his facial expression indicated the news he was about to deliver wasn't good. As he began to speak, I stared directly at his mouth as he explained to my mother that William had contracted a bacterial infection known as spinal meningitis, which caused the swelling of the protective membranes, blanketing the brain and spinal cord.

The diagnosis sounded frightening, but I don't believe my mother or any of us realized how awful the condition indeed was. The doctor warned us sternly that the infection can spread rapidly through the body. Before being hospitalized, William had complained of not feeling well, with symptoms ranging from a high fever and headache to joint pain and muscle spasms. He even got into a bathtub full of ice-cold water to break his fever. I had never heard of the disease, but we would soon learn that the condition could have profound consequences, which, if left untreated, could cause brain damage in a matter of hours, and even death within twenty-four hours. As a family, we were very fortunate that the illness was diagnosed early. Although William spent more than ten days in the hospital receiving intravenous and oral antibiotics, the doctors told us that he would make a full recovery. Spinal meningitis is life-changing, with the likelihood of wide and varying challenges, including the possibility of suffering from clumsiness or coordination issues, lack of concentration, loss of balance, vision problems, and a change to your personality or behavior.

During the next few weeks as William was recovering from meningitis, I visited him in the hospital several times. Once he was released and returned home, he still needed more time to fully recover. We had the chance to talk much more than we had in recent years. William and I always had a pretty good relationship, with occasional sibling fights and arguments that were usually resolved within a few days as if nothing had happened. But in the previous few years, between the ninth grade and eleventh-grade high school, we had seen less and less of one another as we attended different schools and hung out with different friends.

I no longer had any idea how to spend time with him. But his unfortunate illness had created an opportunity for us to reconnect, mostly because we were both home at the same time. We even pulled out the old family favorite board game, Monopoly, which we hadn't played in years! We reminisced about the hours William, Derrick, Sharon, and I used to play Monopoly in our pre-adolescent years, frequently arguing about who would get which one of the classic Monopoly game pieces, including the race car, thimble, shoe, dog, top hat, iron, and wheelbarrow. William always got to play with the race car piece. In the middle of our game, Sharon walked into the room and asked if she could join the game; before she sat down, Derrick walked in; everyone was home at the same time, a rarity in our lives. He noticed that we were playing Monopoly and started laughing before saying, "Man, we used to play this damn game so much back in the day." We all laughed, and William asked Derrick to come join in; after initially saying he had to go meet up with a friend, he quickly changed his mind and joined in the game. We had a great time playing the game, swapping old stories, and remembering all the silly things we used to do; it was so reminiscing of our preteen years, with lots of happy recollections and thinking back to stories from the past. I was the first mocked, for as we flashbacked down memory lane, William recalled the unfortunate accident from the time we were all in the living room playing a game of darts; we were using darts made of yellow plastic wings with metal steel tip points and a dartboard cabinet to protect the walls from damage.

The four of us, Sharon, Derrick, me, and William, took our turn throwing three darts at the board one at a time and trying to rack up points. At the end of each of us having a turn to throw the darts, we added the points earned, and the next player threw. William was the last to throw in the first rotation; he decided to make it more challenging by turning his back to the board and throwing the dart between his legs to the board. The idea was exciting; we all anticipated his hitting the dart board without scoring any points, so we laughed at him. Well, it was worse than I could have imagined; as William positioned himself to throw his dart, I sat in a recliner chair near the dartboard. I could see the dart coming directly at me as if it were moving in slow motion…it didn't just miss the dartboard, his first dart landed into my left shoulder, leaving a puncture wound that wasn't painful! After realizing that his dart didn't hit its intended target, he rushed to my aid along with Sharon and Derrick. "Okay, everyone, stay calm," William said and whispered to me not to say anything to "Mama."

I nodded my head that I wouldn't tell her. "We have to stop the bleeding," Derrick said as he and William applied gentle pressure to my arm. Sharon ran to the bathroom to grab a clean towel, which she wet with warm water to clean the wound after William had pulled the dart out of my arm. I don't recall if we ever finished playing the game or why I thought it was a good idea sit near the dart board. As William finished his story, my sister looked at me with a smile and asked, "y-you play darts?" …I responded with a quick "No." But I believe Derrick had the best 'remember when' moment when he retold the story of Sharon missing curfew time to be in the house; like many families in those days, curfew time was always the same time, "home before the streetlights come on." Since she was late, she was very fearful of being punished with a 'spanking,' being hit on buttocks with an open hand. Sharon was so afraid that as she approached the backdoor of our apartment, she paused; as the backdoor opened, our step-father Buddy stepped out, and a 'tough parent' voice told Sharon she was going to get a spanking, never mind the fact that Buddy has never, ever given any of us a spanking….it was not a serious threat, but to Sharon's ear, it was, and she took off running towards the road.

Derrick, William, and me all went running after her; Sharon had never run that fast before and ran nearly out the housing complex before we were able to catch up to her. We laughed, well, not all of us; Sharon didn't recall this particular memory fondly, still insisting that she was "running for my life," sparking another round of laughter from all of us! As the days and weeks of summer passed, William slowly regained his total health and returned to playing competitive games we both loved, like flag tag, pillow wrestling, and, of course, basketball, although not regular one-on-one basketball games yet, mostly just shooting competitions like around the world, where players take turns making shots around the court, usually starting with a layup and moving on to other spots. In the classic game, H-O-R-S-E, a player begins with a shot anywhere on the court; if he makes it, the next player will follow with the same shot; each missed shot will give a letter to the player until one player spells out H-O-R-S-E with missed shots. Finally, we began playing our traditional one-on-one basketball games on the home court in our driveway and returning to the asphalt courts of Carver Shores Park for pickup team games in the evening.

One afternoon, as we sat in the family room watching TV, our conversation turned to the pending end of summer and the new school year. During the discussion, he shared with me more unexpected news: he would be transferring to Evans High School for his senior year of high school. The shockingly surprising news left me somewhat stunned, but I quickly realized what this news meant; for as long as I could remember, I wanted to play on the same basketball team as my brother. At long last, we would have an opportunity to play together in his senior year of high school; my anticipation for the start of basketball tryouts was more emotional than normal…but something was wrong from day one in the gym.

Basketball Tryout with My Brother

Basketball tryout week at Evans High School always began with meeting new and returning players in the legendary 'Snake Pit' gym, where the coaches explained that we would be physically and mentally challenged like no other time in our lives. As the coaches spoke, I looked around at all of the players standing on the court with looks of nervousness or anxiety in their eyes; because the junior varsity and varsity tryouts were combined, there were nearly a hundred players in the gymnasium all at once, and more than half of them new players, including my brother.

William and I arrived at the gym separately. I hadn't seen him in school all day, so I wasn't sure how he was feeling about a new start with a new high school team, but I had no real concerns that he would handle this tryout as he had so many others: he would be a standout player and be one of the few new players to make the Trojans team roster! Day 1 of tryouts started with the rigorous two-mile endurance test, which all players needed to run in under fourteen minutes. This test was one of the primary evaluation criteria for newcomers looking to make an excellent first impression. My brother William and I didn't run together, but I watched for his positioning in the large group of athletes running around the track. William and I finished in the top half of runners, mainly because of our competitive nature, as neither of us relished long-distance running. But we understood the endurance run was more of a mental challenge than a physical one and that the coaching staff was using it to test the mental toughness of guys trying out for the team.

In addition, running is an essential part of basketball, as developing good stamina will allow players to remain energized throughout an entire game. But without failure each year, the endurance challenge had the effect of reducing the number of players returning for Day 2 of tryouts. The second day of tryouts, after the worst players have been weeded out on Day 1, is progressively more competitive than the first. Unlike the first day, there's no endurance test at the track; all of the evaluations for the next three days would be through fundamental skill drills and lots of running on the basketball court. The second day was also when the Trojan station drills were introduced. They included bench jumping, footwork drills, ball handling, passing drills, Mikan layup drills, jump rope/short hop, rebounding drills, and zig-zag defensive drills. You had to be prepared to sprint and run suicides in between the various parts of the tryout. Coaches want good athletes and players who are in shape. But the most important was your dedication and commitment; attitude is everything!

This was true even though some of the other drills like three-man full-court weave, full-court defensive slides and closeouts, and "suicides" are dynamic and emphasize aggressiveness, competitiveness, proper execution, pressure on the ball, traps, and overall conditioning. We also did fundamental skills drills, such as ball handling, dribbling, passing, shooting, and footwork, each at a separate station (basket), rotating every ten minutes on Day 4 tryouts. Finally, we did one-on-one challenges of junior varsity versus varsity and controlled scrimmages. Day 3 would be the day of the first cut, well, at least for the players who hadn't cut themselves earlier in the week. This was the first day I noticed something different about William's play. He didn't seem himself in either the individual or team drills. He was struggling to make shots, his shooting touch and form was off, he wasn't able to get past defenders, and he had significant problems making contested layups—all skills he had previously done effortlessly. He wasn't the player I had seen for so many years; something had changed! William and I never spoke about his lackluster performance during tryouts, and he never told me that he wasn't returning the next day; he just never showed up. I was disappointed and confused by the sudden change to the circumstances.

A week earlier, I was living a dream, finally getting the chance to play basketball with my brother; now, without much warning, he was not in the gym for the final days of tryouts. What was the cause of such an unexpected outcome? Had he not fully recovered from the complications associated with spinal meningitis, including problems with coordination, movement, and balance issues? Had the Trojan coaching staff informed him that he was being cut from the team due to his lackluster performance? Whatever the reason, the dream of playing with my brother ended during the first week of basketball tryouts. When my brother William didn't make the final cut for the Trojans basketball team, it was shocking to me… to that point, he was the best basketball player I had seen. And since our days of playing pickup basketball in the neighborhood and my first introduction to organized team basketball with the Lake Como basketball team (a local travel team) tryouts, he was always the standard by which I measured myself, both on the court and in the classroom.

The finality of the thought of playing him hit hard because this was his senior year; there would not be another year that we would both be in high school together. The feeling of having a dream that almost comes true is a combination of the dream's vividness and the possibility that it could happen...and then you awake and realize it was just a dream! A few weeks later, he would drop out of high school; a former high school basketball standout and academic high achiever who bordered on the intellectual ability to be 'gifted' had decided to drop out of high school in the middle of his senior year.

When William dropped out of high school, he never talked to any of us in our household; he just decided he no longer wanted to attend school. His decision was baffling for multiple reasons. First, he was a great student, regularly making the honor roll throughout his school years. Even if it feels boring or irrelevant, just staying in school almost guarantees you'll end up in a better place than if you dropped out. Unfortunately, according to a recent America's Promise Alliance report, those factors rank among the top reasons kids take themselves out of school. None of the primary reasons that correlated to high school dropouts applied to him, for example, poverty, lack of resources, high incidents of racial discrimination, and low expectations. When I asked him why he dropped out of school with about a half-year remaining before he would graduate, he replied, without making eye contact, "Tan, I just lost interest in school"; with that answer, he walked away.

He would eventually obtain his GED with scores among the highest in Florida. We never discussed it again. He began working a minimum wage job in the Florida Orange Groves as a fruit picker shortly afterward. He didn't move out of the house, but we saw him less and less frequently, as he would leave in the early morning hours before I left the house to catch the school bus. He usually worked twelve-hour shifts, and when he returned home, he went directly into his bedroom before reappearing briefly to go into the bathroom for a shower. He became almost hermitlike, never really coming out of his room when he was, and when he did come out of his room, he would go out the door within a few minutes. His desire to play basketball no longer existed; his attention to fashion details was not visible in how he dressed, and his bubbly personality and habit of playing jokes on family members no longer interested him. The effervescent brother I had known my entire life seemed to be experiencing a disconnect from his regular thoughts, emotions, and desires. At this point, I didn't know how to help him or if he knew how to help himself. The look on his face would be someone feeling unsure about their identity, having trouble making decisions, and maybe feeling overwhelmed by what was happening in his life. I didn't know what was causing this dramatic change in his personality. Was it fear of judgment, a feeling of low self-esteem, or trauma from the unexpected decision he'd made by dropping out of high school? I wish I'd asked him some of those questions. Regrettably, I did not. Years later, William would tell me that in those last few years, he felt like his life had no direction and that he had lost sight of the person he wanted to be.

1982-83 Trojans Basketball Season of Expectations

The 1982-83 Trojans basketball team had incredibly high expectations, and for good reason. The team was returning four senior starters, including the ranked small forward in Orange County, the versatile multi-sport star 6'5" Tony Fluker, the leading scorer from the previous season. Also returning was 6'4" senior Cleve Williams, a pure shooter wing player; 6'9" center Daryl Wesley, who possessed a seven-foot wingspan; and 5'10" point guard Joe Wright, who, despite his primary focus being that of a facilitator, was also a competent scorer. In addition, the team welcomed junior transfer Darryl Jackson, a standout from Eatonville Wymore Tech.

The coaching staff was also enthusiastic about the potential contributions of a trio of junior varsity standouts, including 6'4" Moses Gordon, 6'5" John Hadley, and me, at 6'1" moving up to the varsity team after winning the junior varsity Metro Conference championship, losing only two games all season. The team's high expectations weren't limited to internal expectations. They entered the season with a top five ranking, fifth in FHSAA Class AAAA Boys Basketball state polls. They were the preseason favorites to win a second consecutive Metro Conference Boys Basketball title. The sixteen-year head coach Richard "Dick" Hulette led the coaching staff, with the highly regarded veteran coach Bob Gordon on the bench as the top assistant, and first junior varsity coach and former Trojans player coach Calvin Lingelbach completing the staff. We were reminded consistently about the "Trojan way" of doing things, expectations that all players be accountable to the team themselves, respect the keystone principles and traditions of the program—abiding by team rules, being on time, always displaying respect and discipline—and accept that you will be given consequences for actions that go outbounds of those expectations. These principles were the foundation of our season. We had to be accountable on and off the court.

The team roster final spots were filled by an experienced and athletic group of players in reserve roles for the team, including 6'0" senior point guard Shannon James, 5'9" junior Leonard Allen, 6'6" junior power forward Tim Sherry, and 6'1" combo-guard Dwyane Foreman. We started the season with an impressive seven wins in our first eight games, entering the holiday tournament (November – January) season with 'swagger,' inner confidence, and belief that we were one of the state's best high school basketball teams. Entering the sixteen-team Burger King Whopper Shootout basketball tournament at Valencia College, we fully expected to be playing in the championship game at the end of the tournament. We lived up to those expectations, defeating two local powerhouses in the semi-finals, Orlando Boone with a record of 6-2, led by dual of 6'4" Andrew Hungerford and 6'3" Lenny Grace, and the Oak Ridge Pioneers in the championship game. During the Christmas break, we traveled with the entire team in a Royale Motorhome vehicle for the five-hour drive to Tallahassee where we competed in another sixteen-team tournament with several unfamiliar teams from around the state and outside the state.

We began play in the Governor's Cup Basketball Tournament, hosted at the Tallahassee convention center, with a match-up against James A. Shanks High School (Quincy, FL) and their all-state, All-American 6'0" point-guard Andrew Moten, who had received a full college scholarship to play for coach Norm Sloan at the University of Florida Gators. (Moten eventually became an All-SEC First Team selection and NBA draft pick for the New Jersey Nets.) In the first half of the game, Moten was hitting shots from everywhere on the court, and we had no answers to stop him from scoring. By the end of the first half, he'd scored twenty-one points, more than half of his team's total! Our coaches were not happy, in particular, head coach Richard "Dick" Hulette, who was known to lose his temper during games, times outs, halftime, or nearly any other situation where he didn't think we were performing up to our abilities.

No player was immune from his verbal castigating; he would approach you with both hands on his hips, his eyebrows lowered, lips tightened, and would embarrass you in front of fans, friends, and family alike. More than a few parents believed coach Hulette's behavior crossed the line into being abusive. However, as a player who was a part of two teams he coached for several years, I didn't believe his actions were abusive. Although I certainly didn't want to be the target of his verbal chastising. Sometimes, he didn't use profanity, preferring phasing like "Good golly" and "great day in the morning" to get his points across to players on the team, but we never felt like those were personal attacks. He demanded that everyone give their best efforts. But not even the varsity team's assistant coaches, Gordon and Lingelbach, were exempt from Coach Hulette's temper tantrums.

During the halftime coaches' discussion about defensive strategy to stop or at least slow down the scoring output of Moten, Coach Lingelbach (one of his duties included assessing the opposing team) shared his thoughts about Moten with Coach Hulette. He said, "Coach, that Moten kid has like twenty points at the half, and if we don't do something to slow him down, he's going to end up with forty points." Coach Hulette responded with an outburst, "Well, aren't you some type of mathematical genius? Twenty plus twenty would equal forty. We can figure that one out, Einstein." Coach Lingelbach walked away and later recalled that he hadn't uttered another word the entire game. We eventually made a run in the second half to keep the score close, but led by the spectacular play of Moten, we lost the game to Quincy Shanks. After an opening loss, we rebounded with three consecutive wins—two against local teams, Florida A&M University Developmental Research High School (FAMU) and the Tallahassee Maclay Marauders, as well as against Malone High School, featuring All-State and McDonald's All-American Honorable Mention, Blake Miles. These victories helped us capture the consolation bracket championship, ending the holiday tournament on a high note and entering the New Year with an overall 11-3 record.

Championship Tournament Upset

After the holiday tournament play was over, we went 7-1 in the two tournaments and had an overall record of 11-3. Our record made us feel like we were still in the driver's seat for another Metro Conference championship, District and Regional game. We were en route to making our first final four appearance in the state high school basketball championship tournament since the 1975 state championship win with the legendary Darryl "Chocolate Thunder" Dawkins. We were confident that we were still one of the best teams in the state, but we were not overconfident. Our coaches kept us aware that regardless of how teams performed during the regular season, postseason and tournament play is a new season.

We entered tournament play as regular season co-champions, with Oak Ridge (20-6, 9-3) an overall record of 22-6 and a Metro Conference record of 10-2. "I'd rather have a piece of the pie than none," said Evans coach Dick Hulette. "Last year we backed into it (Metro championship), but this year we wanted to win it outright." The Metro Conference consisted of the following teams: Orlando Boone High School, Orlando Colonial High School, Orlando Edgewater High School, Orlando Evans High School, Orlando Oak Ridge High School, Winter Garden West Orange High School, and Winter Park High School. Not unexpectedly, we entered the Metro Conference tournament as one of two teams, Oak Ridge being the other, favored to win the Metro Conference tournament championship. We had a tough matchup against the Pioneers, losing both our home and away games against them earlier in the season.

During our road game versus Oak Ridge High School, we were behind in a closely contested game, so our coaches decided to switch to our press defense. I was substituted into the game along with senior point guard Shannon James. The coach instructed us to apply pressure to the Pioneer's guards for the entire court length before and after the ball was inbounded. Our pressure defensive strategy emphasizes backcourt ball pressure and setting sideline traps to disrupt the opponent's offensive flow. It didn't take long for the defensive pressure to produce a turnover. Shannon, protecting the middle court area in help defense, cut into the passing lane on a cross-court pass, tipping the ball ahead as he sprinted towards the loose ball. I joined the chase, not sure if I would get the steal or receive a pass from Shannon, who finally recovered the ball just before I reached it, resulting in the two of us getting tangled up and nearly falling to court! Shannon regained his balance, separated from me, and made several quick dribbles left-to-right hand before laying the ball up with his right hand over the outstretched arm of a defender, getting fouled in the process.

The basket counted, plus a free throw. Following the made free throw, as we backpaddled to the other end of the court, ready to play defense, Shannon quickly turned towards me and asked, "Tan, what the hell were you doing? You almost made me miss the shot." I responded with a puzzled look on my face, "Trying to get the loose ball," We 'dapped' each other up and quickly turned our focus back to defense. Although the full-court press got us back into the game, we would lose to the Pioneers for the second time. Still, we were certain that a third meeting in the Metro Conference tournament would have a different result. First, we had to play against an Orlando Boone Braves team that we had already beaten three times this season, a feat even legendary North Carolina Tar Hills basketball coach Dean Smith, an astute coach, wrote, "It was extremely hard to beat a good team three times in a row." Coach Smith was referring to the common belief in college basketball that it's harder to beat a good team three times in a row. The high variability of outcomes in college basketball can make two-time winners seem less secure in the third game. I don't know if we felt less secure in the third; we were pretty confident that we would win the game…the other team just outplayed us!

But now, at the start of the conference tournament, we had to beat them for a fourth time. The Braves had been playing well as of late and we knew they were talented with outstanding players, including 6'4" Andrew Hungerford, 6'3" Lenny Grace, 6'2" Anthony Shorter, 5'11" Craig Mateer, and a player I had been competing against since elementary school, 5'8" Wayne "Pee Wee" Jackson. Nevertheless, we were the better team, with more talented players. As the old saying goes, 'It's hard to beat a team so many times.'

However, that generally applies to relatively evenly matched teams, which we didn't believe was the case with this matchup. Regardless of our belief and previous success, the Braves players would prove us wrong —we were not the better team! On March 2, 1983, in our fourth meeting of the season, we lost to Orlando Boone in the Metro Conference tournament after they had previously lost to us three times during the basketball season. The Braves' victory was fueled by the powerful pairing of Lenny "Tank" Grace (thirty points) and Andrew Hungerford (twenty points). This dynamic combined to score fifty points and controlled the game on both ends of the court. "We did one thing well, we showed up. It's straightforward, we just showed up," said Coach Dick Hulette to reporters after our upset loss. The expected state championship run for us had ended at the hands of a familiar foe who displayed unexpected greatness, the ability to just instinctively play the game, executing the right play at the right time and adapting to every game situation on the basketball court, with high-level basketball IQ. The upset lost to Boone was so surprising. Later that night, I received a phone call from Joe Harris, the starting point guard on our JV team. He was incredulous at the news that we had lost. "Tan, tell me, man, it's not true. Y'all lost to BOONE?"

"Yeah," I responded.

"Man, how, what happened?" he asked, unwilling to accept it.

"Joe, man, I don't know what happened; we just didn't play a good game." My words were unsure, as if searching my memory for some unknown answers. "They just beat us."

Joe let out a deep sigh, with the sound of disbelief still in his voice; he spoke softly, "Alright, man, I'm going to bed."

In a championship game earlier in the evening, Joe had led our junior varsity team to a victory in the JV Metro Conference championship game win over Oak Ridge, scoring a game-high twenty-two points, as the team completed the season with a 19-3 record. Therefore, his disappointment was for more reason than news of our shocking loss; Joe had fully expected to be 'called up' to the varsity team as we continued our run to Lakeland for the state tournament. Furthermore, we were not the only upset victims of the Orlando Boone Braves team; they not only won the Metro Conference championship, but they also continued to capture the 1983 FHSAA Class AAAA Boys High School State Basketball Championship—a blueprint for winning an unexpected championship.

Years later, Lenny Grace and I got together for breakfast to reminisce about those games all those years ago, especially about the Braves' upset of the Trojans in the 1983 Metro Conference tournament, which was still a source of aggravation for me. I reminded him that we had a 3-1 record against them that year and believed they'd robbed us of our state championship. Barely turning his attention from his breakfast plate, Lenny, with a look of indifference, responded with four simply words, "Tan, you need therapy," as we both laughed aloud at the suggestion.

Senior Year, New Season, New Coach, Same Goal

The first day of school as a twelfth grader. Senior year was supposedly a time to relax and prepare for the transition from underclassman to top dogs in the school. It was filled with counselor meetings, recruiting visits, and telephone calls from coaches, and the anticipation of what college or university life would be like after receiving a basketball scholarship. All of this would only be possible if I were truly ready to be a starting varsity basketball player, had improved enough to become a varsity star, and was mature enough to become a leader on the varsity basketball team—accomplishments I had never achieved before. But during the prior summer months, I played a great deal of basketball, from pickup games around the city to the summer basketball workouts we did at home gym, with returning and former Trojans participating in hours of full-court five-on-five basketball games.

During one of the summer team practice games/workouts/two-hour sessions, Coach Gordon was picking teams, and he selected me to play on a team where I would not be playing my natural position of guard. I responded with a visual reaction of displeasure by throwing my arms up in the air and mouthing the words "oh man." Coach reacted immediately, "Robert, get off the court and get out of the gym." I was shocked at hearing his words The gym went deathly silent as I walked off the court and out of the gym. I leaned against the pay phone at the front entrance of the gymnasium; I didn't know if I should leave or wait to speak with Coach Gordon after the workout. It seemed like an eternity, which in reality was more like two hours, before other players began exiting the gym and leaving. Some of them spoke to me, while others walked past me without uttering a word. Finally, Coach Gordon walked out of the gym and began walking towards the front where I was still leaning against the pay phone. As he approached closer to me, I adjusted my posture and stood upright, prepared to take whatever reprimand I had coming. But there was no lecture, no scolding, he just walked right past me silent.

I was in a panic. Did he cut me from the team? Was my senior year of varsity basketball over before it ever started? As I walked over to the bus stop, I was overwhelmed with unreasoning and overpowering fear that my high school basketball career had ended so abruptly. The bus ride home was long and filled with an extreme feeling of anxiety; I was stunned that the coach didn't speak to me after practice. I needed to speak to him. It was the weekend, and my thoughts were all over the place, but all I could think of was speaking to the coach as soon as possible. There was no way I would wait until Monday to speak with the coach. I finally calmed myself down enough to dial the coach's phone number; there was an answer after a few rings, «Hello." I knew the sound of the voice, so I just began talking, "Coach Gordon, I'm sorry about what happened this afternoon. I know my actions were disrespectful to you and the other players. I was just being selfish in wanting to play in my regular position." Coach listened quietly and waited a few seconds after I had stopped speaking before he responded. "Well, Robert, I appreciate you apologizing and accepting responsibility for your actions."

"Yes, sir," I responded.

Coach continued speaking, "But you don't understand what I was doing. I know what position you play. I put you in that position.

I wanted you to go in and play a forward position to show some of those other guys who were dogging it that we didn't need them. I wanted to use your versatility and understanding of what we're trying to do to send a message to the team."

He continued to explain that my physical reaction to his choice to play me out of position was a challenge to his authority, and he was shocked that I acted in such a manner. But then I was surprised by what he said next: "Robert, I want to apologize to you as well; I was so determined to teach those guys a lesson that I overreacted to your outburst." That wasn't something I expected or that he had to do, but it taught me a lesson about true leadership. You don't just hold everyone around you accountable to one standard without holding yourself accountable to the same standard. Own your mistake. Don't make excuses for yourself. And say you're sorry sincerely! By the end of our short phone conversation, I felt the weight of the world had been lifted off my chest. But I had another question to ask him. "Coach, am I back on the team?" I asked, uncertain what his response would be. "Robert, you were never off the team," he promptly responded with a chuckle!

Another team tryout signaled the beginning of the final opportunity. We would have to fulfill a goal and expectation, and we vowed to one another the first day we walked into the "Snake Pit" to win a state basketball championship. The disappointment of losing in the Metro Conference tournament last season still had not disappeared. Still, the lessons learned from that experience would help prepare this year's team to be more mentally prepared. The first-year students from the '83 team all returned for this final run, including me, 6'4" Moses Gordon, 6'5" John Hadley, 5'9" Leonard Allen, 6'0" Tim Sherry, 6'1" Dwyane Foreman, along with several additions from junior varsity conference champions, led by 5'9" JoJo Harris. We also got a major addition to the team in the Bishop Moore Catholic High School transfer, a highly touted front-line player, 6'7" Jimmy Kuhl. Another new change to the 1983-84

Trojans was the return of Evans High assistant coach Rudy Tapia as the team's new head coach following former coach Richard Hulette's step down after last season. Coach Tapia had spent the previous ten years building the Edgewater Eagles into a highly regarded program. Once again, the Metro Conference coaches picked Evans High School "unanimously" as the favorite to win both the Metro Conference and Class AAAA District 10 titles. The coaches picked Oak Ridge to finish in second, Winter Park the third choice, Boone, the defending Class AAAA state champs, was picked fourth, followed by West Orange, Edgewater, and Colonial. We started playing for the season with the Metro Conference Jamboree at Boone High School.

All seven teams played, and the pre-season ranking held with the two top teams playing like it, the jamboree. We got out of the gate on fire, winning our first seven games to start the season with a 7-0 record, including a win against one of our biggest rivals, Jones High School, by a score of 67-54. Kuhl had his best game of the season scoring twenty-five points and grabbing twelve rebounds. It was my first experience with the Evans-Jones hyper-enthusiastic and exceedingly large groups of spectators that attended the game. "When I came here to Evans, they told me this game was a big rivalry. There sure was a big crowd tonight," Kuhl said. I didn't have a great game, but I scored fifteen points, including thirteen points in the first half, which included a long-distance jumper at the first-quarter buzzer that put us ahead to stay, sending the large home crowd into a frenzy! The early season success allowed everyone to play without pressure and to have fun.

Tim Sherry, a senior power forward and a valuable substitute player for our starting post players, years later remembered some hilarious newspaper stories written during the season: «In a regular season game," Tim said, "which we won, you had a good game. The next day, the Orlando Sentinel did a game re-cap that read something like this: *KUHL LEADS EVANS TO VICTORY . . . Evans star Jimmy Kuhl scored eight points and grabbed six rebounds, leading the Trojans to a decisive victory. The junior had four points and a rebound in the decisive second quarter. Senior Robert Worthington chipped in twenty-two points in support of Kuhl's effort.* Tim recalled asking me if I had seen the newspaper story, and we joked that I needed to contribute less to get the headlines. Another funny story Tim remembered: "We had beaten Colonial High School basketball team the night before by about fifty points. You scored twenty-five points, while I hit two free throws in the last minute of the blowout. The next day, I (Tim) told a girl that you (Tan) and I combined scored twenty-seven points. And you said, with a sarcastic expression on your face, 'Yep, Tim hit the clutch free-throws.'"

But the hot start to the season would not last. We lost seven of our next nine games to fall to a record of 1-2 in conference play and 9-7 overall. The loss included a 50-48 overtime loss to Coach Tapia's former team, Edgewater Eagles. The game was sloppy, with pressure defense by both teams causing several crucial turnovers (we had eleven turnovers in the first half) as each team went on double-digit runs at different game periods. In the final minutes of the fourth quarter, the teams traded game-tiring field goals, including one by center John Hadley, to tie the game for the first time 44-44 with less than two minutes to play. One Eagles guard made a mid-range jump shot to put his team back up 46-44, setting up overtime, forcing a ten-foot jump shot by me with six seconds left, all even 46-46. But at the end of the overtime period, the Eagles got a buzzer-beating jumper to win the game. The losses continued to add up as we lost a road game at Orlando Jones, 49-41. We finally got back in the winning circle with a road win at Winter Haven High School, 82-51. Hadley and I led the way, scoring twenty-one points apiece.

The frustration of losing so many games after such a great start to the season was also causing tempers to flare up in our team practices. Our team practices were always very competitive, but there usually weren't many physical altercations. But on this particular day, that would change as Jimmie and I were going at each other pretty hard physically and exchanging words back and forth. I thought he was fouling me unnecessarily, and he told me, "Stop crying, Robert."

I replied, "Okay, do it again." Another teammate, Tim Sherry, later recalled the incident: "I remember you giving Jimmie Kuhl a 'duck lip' with an elbow to the mouth one day in practice. You had complained to me earlier, saying, 'If he elbows me again, I'm going to beat his ass,' and sure enough, he elbowed you again." Coach Calvin Lingelbach recalled the same incident with Kuhl, which he described this way: "A day before a big game, you got into an elbow-throwing contest with one of our bigs, and you hit him in the upper lip with your elbow, making him look like a fish. The next night, he had his best game; you had a strange way of preparing our team for a big game." I don't remember the details of the incident between me and Jimmie, but I remember calling him at home and apologizing over the telephone.

But things just kept getting worse. We had another home game to Orlando Colonial, a team picked to finish last in the conference and came into the game with a 7-14 record, winning the game 44-41. We would rebound against Lakeland High School, 75-40, followed by a loss in the next game to Metro Conference rival Oak Ridge, 64-55. Although I led the team in scoring in both games with nineteen points in each, with a 2-3 conference and 11-8 overall record, scoring points wasn't getting the desired results. "We're history in the Metro Conference," said Evans Coach Rudy Tapia.

Although we did not come back to win the Metro Conference title, we did qualify for the playoffs, winning a district home game before losing in the regional championship game. The basketball game was played in front of a large crowd; our big guys got in early foul trouble and poor shooting before fouling out of the game in the final minutes of the fourth quarter. The heartache of a season-ending loss can be overwhelming. We had not succeeded in achieving the lofty goals we had set for ourselves. But our coaches didn't allow us to hang our heads, encouraging us to remember the life lessons emphasized throughout the year and the core values of hard work, honesty, and teamwork. *"The true measure of a man is not how he behaves in moments of comfort and convenience but how he stands at times of controversy and challenges." -MLK.*

With the season over, the next phase of our journey was the post-season individual awards, team sports banquet, and the college recruiting process. Moses Gordon (13.1 ppg; 8.8 rpg) and I (15.5 ppg, 5.6 rpg) were selected for the 1984 All-Metro Conference and All-Orange County boys' basketball teams. In addition, another teammate, John Hadley, earned honorable mention honors. I was excited to share the news of my post-season awards with my brother.

Even though we had fallen short of winning the state championship, I, along with several of my teammates, was recognized as being among the best high school players in Central Florida, and those efforts earned me an offer of a full basketball scholarship to college. But it would be days before I could share the news with my brother or talk about those options offered to attend college. He was usually not at home for days at a time, and on those few occasions he was at home, he remained locked inside his bedroom nearly the entire time. William seemed to have lost his way, no longer interested in playing basketball or pursuing higher education after receiving his GED. Nearly 98 percent of colleges in the US accept GEDs as a legitimate high school diploma equivalent. As a GED holder, William could have applied to attend community college, technical schools, and universities to earn a college degree or pursue vocational training.

Our relationship, so intertwined just a few years ago, had become the complete opposite. The breakdown in our relationship, a bond our passion for basketball fueled, now appeared so far apart. Although we had continued to live in the same house over the years, we barely saw one another. He occasionally came to the park to play basketball but rarely stayed longer than a game or two. Even though it's not uncommon for relationships to change over time, there are many reasons why siblings may be acting differently. It was the lack of communication or outright avoidance that distressed me. We had always communicated openly and honestly with each other about how we were feeling, providing a perspective of understanding even if we disagreed. But this was different, a sort of 'sibling alienation,' or maybe he was going through something that was causing him to withdraw.

New Teams in College and Beyond

When I received the call over the PA system to come to the front office, I was sitting in Mr. Bailey's fifth period typing/keyboarding class. Valencia's College Head Men's Basketball Coach, Tom Garcia, was on campus to convince me to commit to playing for his college team next season. I had never met Coach Garcia, but he was pretty convincing. He referenced two familiar players, former Trojans Tony Fluker and Cleve Williams, who had signed basketball scholarships to play for Coach Garcia and his Matadors College men's basketball team. I had not planned to attend a community college or junior college (JUCO). Still, as a non-qualifier, I had to meet the initial NCAA DI/DII academic eligibility requirements after graduating high school. Valencia presented me with the opportunity to improve my grades and academic standings and further develop my physical strength and basketball skills in preparation for transferring to the next level.

An added benefit was that junior college programs also help athletes adjust to the highly competitive nature of college sports. Valencia College is a public college in Orlando, Florida. The college is part of the Florida College System, with an enrollment of 16,112 undergraduate students. The decision to attend Valencia also gave Moses Gordon and me another chance to be teammates again, as he also decided to attend the same college. Coach Garcia had given both of us a chance to play college basketball but warned us that college basketball would be much more physical than high school, and the academic demands would require discipline and diligence to successfully meet the requirements to remain eligible to play after the first-semester break. "You always have to sweat out the semester break and worry about who's coming back and who is not," Garcia said. He also expected Moses and I to play a significant role on the team as freshmen. On the first game of the year, we traveled to Jacksonville, Florida to play a road game against Florida State College at Jacksonville (FSCJ). Moses and I were in the starting lineup as freshmen for our first college game. We lost the game, although Moses and I didn't play too badly in our first college action. Moses recalled a game years later: "Tan and I went to Valencia College, and in our first game, Tan had an awesome game. Tan had thirty points, and I got four dunks." He then recalled something I do not remember, as the post-game interview. "We were interviewed after the game, and my brother stood with us. The three of us were interviewed, and it was the first time I heard Tan speak in a soft voice like Michael Jackson. I always joked with him about that, laughing at his soft tone of voice during an interview!" But the joy of our reteaming up in college would be short-lived. Although I had other double-digit scoring games, my play on the court was inconsistent. Players I had easily outplayed during pre-season scrimmages and practices were now getting more game minutes than I was, and deservedly, they were outplaying me. What created more anxiety for me was that my performance in the classroom was even poorer than my recent performance on the basketball court. In my first year of college, I was thrown into disarray by a tragic event with life-altering consequences. This event caused great uncertainty as to how the future would look, or if the future had to be someplace other than here! I don't know if this defining event was one of those times that you know you're looking back on one day and saying, "If it wasn't for that, some things probably would have played out differently for me."

Nevertheless, my college basketball career ended abruptly. I joined the Unites States Air Force not out of any deep sense of duty and commitment to serve my country but because I needed to find a different path. I continued to play basketball while traveling to countries worldwide, including Germany, Spain, the Netherlands, the United Kingdom, Panama, and Guam. In addition, I had the opportunity to compete with and against top competitors at military bases around the United States, as many members were former high school and college basketball players. I excelled playing basketball in the Air Force. During my assignment to Germany for the US Air Forces in Europe (USAFE), I led the league in scoring and was invited to be a member of the All-Air Force men's basketball team (twelve-man roster). Reflecting on the highs and lows of my journey of achieving some goals and failing to achieve others allows me to look back at both the moments of significant progress and the challenges I faced, using them as valuable learning experiences to understand personal growth and resilience throughout the process, allowing me to learn valuable lessons from both experiences in order to better approach future goals with a balanced perspective. Although I've had to overcome some serious challenges along my journey, the hardest thing I have ever experienced in my life occurred during my first year of college: my brother's murder conviction. I don't know if I will ever get over the feelings of sadness and guilt that overwhelmed me!

6
DEPTHS OF DESPAIR

My senior year of high school felt like it all happened in a blur. I wished it could've lasted longer! I'm preparing for college because it's the summer after high school graduation. It has been nearly two years since William walked off the basketball after the second-day tryouts of my junior year, ending my dreams of playing on the same team as my brother and his subsequently dropping out of school more than halfway through his senior year of high school. Although we lived in the same four-bedroom house since junior high school, we barely saw one another. William had grown increasingly distant, seemingly emotionally indifferent to every household member, including me. He would go into his bedroom, lock the door, and spend a long time alone for hours every day, only exiting briefly to go into the kitchen or bathroom. I wasn't sure what had caused this shift in behavior. Was it typical conduct for a teenager on their way to adulthood, or maybe depression or anxiety? Whatever the reasons, it was a major factor in the fractioning of our family connection. William spending more and more time in isolation became almost normal, or at least it became acceptable as the attempts to get him to join us in the family room for a movie, come into the living room to talk and laugh or play pickup basketball at the park had become a hopeless undertaking. He would leave the house in the early hours of the morning, day after day to catch the bus to his job—one that we pledged to ourselves we would never do—picking oranges. Because we had lived in Florida most of our lives, we were aware of how large of an industry Florida Orange Groves was in the state. But the only experience we had picking oranges was a summer day during the time when we lived in Griffin Park. My grandmother's brother, 'Uncle Willie,' convinced my mother to let him take the boys over to the orange groves and "show them how to work." It was the hardest day's work we had ever done, from the wee hours in the morning to just before dawn hours. Hand-picking crops of oranges required you to climb up the orange trees using a sixteen-foot ladder, with nylon sacks hanging across your back. Once you've harvested the oranges by hand and dropped them in your sacks, you would have to climb down the ladder and dump the oranges into a wooden crate or box.

At the end of the day, you would be paid a rate of 70-to-90 cents per ninety-pound box, less than minimum wage salary. It left a negative impression on William, Derrick, and me, and we vowed that we would never again work another minute in the Florida orange groves, under no circumstances. William was especially committed to never touching a wooden harvest storage bin again. Yet, all these years later, he would routinely walk several blocks from our house to get on the 'orange grove bus,' driven by a longtime neighborhood resident we all called Mr. Parramore. Why William decided on the cheap labor of a daily orange grove picker, a manual job he had previously shown nothing but disdain for, is still unclear. In addition to insufficient pay, citrus picking is also considered by many in the industry the most dangerous job in agriculture. The process of picking oranges has mostly stayed the same in the past thirty years. It is considered a dangerous job for several reasons, including citrus pickers often use ladders to reach oranges, which can lead to falls and serious injuries. The risk of injury is increased by unpredictable weather conditions that can make the ground slippery. Also, orange grove pickers must carry bags weighing over ninety pounds over their shoulders, risking muscle, tendon, and nerve injuries. In his 1996 book *Oranges*, writer John McPhee said of the orange grove pickers: "Their work is so hard that only people of considerable toughness of body and spirit last very long in the groves." And there's the prolonged exposure to the Florida heat; the average daily temperature range in the summer months is typically between 73-and-95 degrees Fahrenheit, making heat stress or heat stroke a real concern.

Yet, this former high school basketball star, an exceptional student who was incredibly skilled in the techniques of "realistic art" or sketch drawing, was resigned to working a low-skilled job for very little pay. On the few occasions we did see one another, we usually just exchanged a "Hey, what's up, man?" with the usual response, "Nothing much," followed by a quick exit from the room. We never spoke about his job, the fact that he no longer played basketball, or that he seemed no longer to care about his personal appearance, something he cared deeply about in previous years. His behavior drastically changed from that of the big brother, who had ultimate confidence, positive self-image, and self-esteem, whom I admired my entire life. Shortly before I began attending my first college class or basketball practice at Valencia College, I participated in one last high school athletic event, the Orange County one-on-one Boys Basketball Tournament hosted at the very same college where I would later be suiting up for my freshmen basketball season in the coming months. The one-on-one tournament included sixteen of the best high school basketball players in Central Florida, playing in a single elimination player-seeded bracket made up of four different rounds. All sixteen players played in the first round, with the winners moving on to the second round. William was excited about the tournament as he recounted a high-spirited debate with another passenger on the bus ride home about who would win the tournament. "Tan, boy, I'm betting on you to win it." I didn't take his words to mean he was "gambling" on me to win, but he had full confidence that I would win. It had been quite a while since we had an engaging back-and-forth about basketball, and the fact that it regarded playing one-on-one brought back so many memories of all those one-on-one games we had played against one another.

On the tournament day, I didn't see William before I left for the college campus, but he assured me he would attend before I played my first game against an unknown opponent. As I arrived at the West Campus Fitness Center parking lot, full of vehicles and spectators walking toward the gymnasium, I could feel the excitement growing inside me. I entered the gym and headed directly to the scorer's table to check in and learn who my first-round opponent would be. The gentlemen at the table asked if I had an Evans team uniform and a change of gym shoes; I replied yes to both questions as he checked several boxes of the paperwork. "Robert, you will be playing on court number one against Orlando Jones High School's Steve Griffin," he said. What a way to start the tournament playing against my former junior high school teammate and one of my best friends! I sat in a sideline chair across from court number one, unzipped my gym bag, and pulled out my game shoes while continuously glancing around the arena, looking for any sign of my brother; he never showed up. Two other high school classmates, Tim and Chip, yelled my name, "Tan, we in the house," announcing their arrival to support me, and this helped to distract me from my brother's absence. As the three of us chatted, I quickly looked at the score clock, less than thirty minutes remained before the whistle to start the first game. I needed to go warm up. I won the one-on-one matchup against my friend and former teammate, moving on to the tournament's second round. I got a second victory in the second round, moving into the tournament's semi-finals. The matchup in the semi-finals was against another familiar opponent, the starting forward for the Oak Ridge Pioneer, Bo, a 6'8" athletic player with a massive wingspan but not one of the more prolific scorers from the team. I was confident in scoring over a bigger player in several ways—shooting long-distance jumpers, contested mid-range shots, or driving past the bigger defender off the dribble once he attempted to close the distance and contest my outside shots. But the outside shots I had routinely made in the earlier games, I was missing. I even missed a driving layup during a critical phase of the game. I had miscalculated the impact Bo's size and length, 6'8" height with a 7'2" wingspan, would have on my ability to make shots accurately and consistently over the much taller player. Bo won the semi-final and one-on-one tournament championship in the next game. I was disappointed, but I truly believed I would win the tournament. I did learn a lesson about the impact a much taller player with an extra-long wingspan could have on my ability to make shots…something I needed to improve going into my college season!

It was a few days before I had an opportunity to speak to William about the outcome of the tournament. He was a little disappointed that I didn't win the championship. "Tan, man, what happened? You were supposed to win that one-on-one tournament," he asked without giving any explanation for why he didn't show up to the college. I thought about asking him why he didn't show up, but I didn't think it mattered, so I just responded to his question, "Man, I couldn't make shots that I normally make. I was rushing my shot too much." He laughed and replied, "You got to play at your own pace and not let the defender speed you up." William was right. I had allowed the taller defender to speed me up as I rushed to get my shot off quicker than usual, negatively impacting my accuracy, resulting in me missing shots I routinely made. The conversation with William lasted less than five minutes, and he was outdoors. It would be weeks before I had another conversation with him about basketball, as my first year was underway at Valencia College. However, several months after the college season began, one of the biggest rivalry games in Orlando high school basketball, Evans Trojans versus Jones Tigers, was scheduled to be played at the "Snake Pit" gym at Evans High School. I came home the night of the game and saw William walking to his room. I didn't see him very often anymore, so I excitedly asked him if he would go to the game with me. "Weo, let's hang out tonight; the Evans vs. Jones game is tonight." He responded by saying he had made other plans. But I was intent on getting him to agree to go to this big game with me, "Come on, man, you know how big this game is; everybody is going to be there." I even offered to pay for his ticket if that was what was keeping him from going to the game. He kept repeating that he had other plans. Finally, he walked back into the family room, raising my hopes that he had changed his mind, and said, "Hey, Tan, can you give me a ride to Bay G's house?" Not what I was expecting to hear, but at least we would have an opportunity to talk during the car ride. I replied, yes, as we walked out the front door. On the drive to 'Old Carver Shores' and Baby G's house, we were weirdly quiet. I recall only a few words being spoken between us before I pulled up at the residence of his friend's house. As he opened the passenger door to get out of the car, he said, "Thanks, Tan. Boy, you are driving too fast," he laughed and exited the car, walking up the driveway to Baby G's house. As I drove off and turned to exit the cul-de-sac, I looked in my rearview mirror and noticed that William hadn't gone into his friend's house. He was walking in the opposite direction of the house. I thought to myself, *where is he going*? But I continued to drive away, not wanting to arrive at the game late, justifying my decision by saying to myself, "I'll ask him about it tomorrow." I truly regret not turning around that night.

As usual, the basketball game was an intense match, and the crowd was large, passionate, and animated. The play was fast and exciting as each team sprinted up and down the court, dribbling and passing the ball incredibly fast and weaving their way through the opposing team's defense. It was a competitive and closely contested game, as each team would hold a lead at one point. The crowd remained on their feet, cheering and shouting encouragement to their team and disagreeing with nearly every official call. But in the end, the home team, the Trojans, won a nail-biting game. It was a thrilling match that lived up to the hype, adding to the rivalry's lore. By the time I arrived back home, it was well past midnight, and I was exhausted. I had plans to get an early start on Saturday morning, mainly so that I could go over to the Southwest Boys & Girls Club to play pickup basketball, something I hadn't done since college season began. As I left home that morning, walking a few blocks from the Boys & Girls Club, I encountered one of my old high school teammates, "Popcorn," a nickname that had stuck with him since childhood. He walked across Lanette Street to the opposite sidewalk in which I was walking, displaying his usual toothy smile, "Hey, Tan, where you are going?"

I smiled as he approached and replied, "What's up, Popcorn? I'm going over to the Club.

"Man, you're not going to believe what happened to me last night," he said with a raised voice.

"What happened last night?" I responded, curious about what wild story he was about to share.

"Man, the police had me downtown questioning me about a murder, talking about how I killed that man in Carver Shores."

"What?" I said with a perplexed look on my face.

Popcorn continued, "Yeah, man, they had five of us downtown in custody, me, Roderick Fuller, Stanley, your brother, Weo, and…."

When he uttered the words "your brother," I didn't hear anything else he said. It was as if I fell into a trance or half-dream-like state of mind. The moment faded as Popcorn said goodbye and ran in opposite directions. I just stood there on the sidewalk, finally turning and walking back home in a surreal, reflective mindset. I don't remember walking past any of the houses I had previously walked past on my way to the Boys & Girls Club. Finally, I arrived back in my driveway. As I opened the front door, I called out to my younger siblings, "Derrick! Sharon!" as vivid thoughts ran through my mind. When they walked into the living room, I repeated the story that Popcorn had told me and asked them if they had seen William. Derrick said he hadn't seen him since the previous day, and Sharon responded likewise. As we all stood there in shock, Sharon recalled a conversation she'd had with her friend, Rayna. "I remember hearing about the death of Mr. Jimmy at school in the middle of the week, either a Tuesday or Wednesday, and even consoled Rayna because the victim was her uncle."

Sharon continued explaining how she expressed sympathy for Rayna's loss: "I said that the person responsible would be caught by the police and held accountable for their actions by the justice system. But when the truth about the crime was finally revealed, and we learned our big brother was involved, Sharon expressed the emotions that ran through her: "I was shocked beyond my wildest imagination; the appalling and inconceivable news that my brother could be involved was unimaginable." Sharon continued to share how she had felt during the week leading up to this dreadful news: "I remember all that day something just not feeling right, but I thought it was because I witnessed one of my best friends at the time going through such a painful ordeal. But I never thought I would lose my relationship with my friend." As we stood in the living room area, I could see the impact on Derrick due to the distressing looks on his face. All three of us were shaken up by the news, but our concerns turned to our mother and how her oldest being accused of murder would affect her. We continued to talk, now focusing on the numbing thought of passing along this news to our mother when, suddenly, the front door swung open. Our mother fell through the doorway crying and screaming, continuously wailing, "No, no, no, William! No. Why, William, no, no, no. Why William, they have my son." The heartbreaking way our mother learned of the news was while driving home from another long day at work, she was listening to her car radio when the music was interrupted by a breaking news report. The radio DJ read the updated police report stating, "The Orlando Police Department has made arrests in the murder of an Orlando man." After spotting the victim's motor vehicle on Interstate 4, a police chase ensued with speeds reaching up to 100 mph, ending when police shot the tires on the vehicle. Two suspects were taken into custody, William Worthington and Stanley Taylor, both residents of Orlando, and both men facing charges of first-degree murder and armed burglary." The breaking news broadcast account broke my mother's heart, leaving her with a feeling of loss, anxiety, and depression that never went away, profoundly altering all of our lives.

My older brother, William, would stand trial for murder! A murder trial is a structured process where a judge and jury listen to evidence and decide if the defendant is guilty of a crime. The prosecutor uses evidence and witnesses to prove to the jury that the defendant committed the crime. The jury is instructed to assume that the defendant is innocent. My brother's murder trial lasted for one week. It included all the routine phases of a criminal trial, including the State of Florida (prosecutor) and defense counsel (my brother's attorney) each presenting their case. The prosecutor presented witnesses and evidence to prove to the jury that the defendant committed the crime. And the defense presented the case for my brother using witnesses and evidence. After each side had completed their presentation, they 'rested'; in the legal world, the concept 'rest' indicates that the prosecution and defense have concluded the evidence each wanted to introduce in this trial stage. The next stage was jury deliberation, where they discussed the evidence presented in the case. During this time, I was still attending college classes and playing on the men's basketball team, but my anxiety and stress level had increased to a level it has never been before. Finally, there was a verdict. After reviewing all of the evidence and facts of the case, the jury reached a verdict. I did not attend the trial on the day of the verdict; my mother was in the courtroom every day; the verdict was not surprising: Guilty!

But, even though not unexpected, the verdict left me with a feeling of emotional numbness and emptiness or disappointment, without an emotional response to situations that would be so impactful that it changed everything for me and my family. After the guilty verdict, the judge scheduled a sentencing hearing in two weeks, where my brother and the rest of us would learn that he would be serving a life sentence without the possibility of parole.

The actual details of the alleged crime were mind-blowing. The trial was scheduled to take place in Orlando about six months after the charges of first-degree murder and armed burglary were filed against my brother, with the co-defendant scheduled to be tried later in the year, facing identical charges. The allegation of the crime stated that the two teenagers went to the victim's house with the intent to burglarize the property; the two young adults entered the home through a side entrance and began to "ransack the home, stealing a credit card, money, and the victim's car," according to the Assistant State Attorney (ASA). At some point during the crime, the victim surprised the two burglars, resulting in him being «hacked, slashed and stabbed in a brutal attack.» The defense attorney for the defendants argued that the victim «burst from his bedroom carrying a machete» which he used to «attack Worthington and Taylor.» The defense attorney further signified that it was during the struggle over the weapon when the victim was injured and died, adding that the two defendants did not plan to kill the victim. However, the ASA countered the defense's argument, stating that the two young men planned to burglarize the home and had devised a scheme to gain entrance into the residence. The final piece of evidence, and in all likelihood most damaging evidence, was the fact the ASA told the jurors that "Worthington confessed to the killing" and that the ASA had a tape recording of the confession— a recording he would play later in the trial.

Initially, I struggled to accept the severity of the situation, questioning the verdict, and hoping for a different outcome with the filing of verdict appeal. A verdict appeal is a legal process that allows a party to request a higher court to review a lower court's decision. Appeals are typically filed after a final ruling has been made... for reasons unknown to me, the verdict appeal filing never happened. But slowly, the realization that this was the outcome, I may never have a "normal" relationship with my brother again, prompted a feeling of profound sadness and mourning for the life that we once knew. The news that my brother was likely going to spend his life in prison was a profoundly devastating and overwhelming experience, filled with a mix of shock, disbelief, grief, anger, and a profound sense of loss, as I grappled with the reality of a future where I would never speak to him again without some restriction on our conversations. My older brother will likely be permanently separated from my life, and our family dynamic would be significantly altered. Everything had changed in just a few short years; four years ago, my brother and his longtime girlfriend, Miranda, were overjoyed at the news of welcoming my brother's first and only child, a baby girl, Che'na Denise Worthington. The two would joggle the complex mix of emotions, including excitement, fear, anxiety, overwhelming responsibility, joy, guilt, and feelings of being unprepared teenage parents. Miranda, who was no longer in a relationship with my brother by this time, would have the added pressure of being a single mother with emotional or physical support from the child's father. The consequences of my brother's conviction and sentence to prison weren't just a loss for me, my mother, and my siblings; he had a daughter, Che'na, a four-year-old preschooler, who was losing her father at a critical stage of her developmental milestones, and anticipation of kindergarten in the not-so-distant future. Explaining a situation like a parent's incarceration to a four-year-old can be challenging. Children may not fully understand complex concepts like jail or imprisonment at that age and often interpret information literally. Children with a parent in prison may experience low self-esteem, depression, disturbed sleeping patterns, and symptoms of post-traumatic stress. In a North American study, separation from a parent through imprisonment was found to be more detrimental to a child's well-being than divorce or the death of a parent. My mother, my niece's grandmother, would become the primary caregiver for Che'na and eventually other grandchildren, including all of Chena's siblings when a problematic situation arose with the mother of the children. This is also known as "kinship care," a challenging role that involves many responsibilities and can cause a variety of emotions; my mother would fill this role for more than two decades.

Adding to the confusion and uncertainty was the reality that my family would have to navigate the complexities of the prison system and the implication for my family of the confusing feelings about an unsure future.

During the weeks of William's trial, I continued to attend classes and play basketball at Valencia College. Still, it was too hard to focus, given the facts of the case and the media coverage. On a few occasions, I overheard students on campus discussing the crime. During a lunch break, as I met up with several friends at the main campus cafeteria, we sat in the upstairs areas with the large round tables and multiple televisions mounted on the walls. While we were eating our lunch, another student walked over to the wall-mounted television and turned up the volume. The loud sound of a midday news broadcast grabbed our attention, and by coincidence, the news report was covering my brother's trial from downtown Orlando. I was guilt-ridden, and, at that very moment, I just wanted to disappear. This embarrassing moment wouldn't be the only one I would encounter; a first-time meeting with the parents of a young lady, Juanita, whom I was picking up from home for a date, became extremely uncomfortable after I answered a question from her mother. Everyone stopped talking, as an awkward silence engulfed the room, it was jarring as if a bucket of ice water had been poured over my head. It was unnerving! Juanita and I would talk about the incident years later, and she recalled it happening in this way: "It was like a scene from the *Leave it to Beaver* TV show. My dad was sitting in his recliner chair, Mom was sitting on the love seat with the Bible in her lap, and you had taken a seat on the side of the sofa closest to my mother. I sat on your other side, careful not to sit too close. The conversation was pretty generic, as the four of us alternated from questions to answers about where you attended high school, what subject your major in college, and whether or not you went to church."

I was prepared for the church question, and quickly responded with, "My family and I have attended Mount Olive AME Church in Orlando since we were kids."

Juanita continued, "Yes, you were polite and confident in your responses." Everything seemed to be going very well until Juanita's mother asked me a series of questions about my family; Juanita said, "Because my mother thinks it's important to know 'who's his people.' You mentioned your parents and your sister and Mom focused in on your last name, 'Worthington,' thinking it sounded familiar, then without hesitation and seemingly unaware of the potential effect, you dropped the bombshell about your brother."

After being asked about my last name and if I was related to a person who had been charged with murder, I responded, "Yes, he's my brother."

Juanita described what happened next: "You could have heard a pin drop; I was mortified. Did you have to mention that at the first meeting? Although I'm sure it was only a second or two, the silence continued forever. I don't recall what else we talked about after that for the short time you remained at our house." But that was the end of the date before we ever left the house. In these situations, it's important to remember that your girlfriend's parents, no matter her age (she was eighteen at the time) want their daughter to be with someone who will keep her safe. In both instances, although not immediately, I noticed people's adverse emotional reactions towards me, whether perceived or imagined. And maybe the perception of how I was seen or thought of was a reason to leave it all behind.

Regardless, I needed to take a day away from school, basketball, and friends and attend a day of my brother's trial. It was the only day during a nearly two-week-long trial I was present in the courtroom for my brother's trial for murder and other crimes. I didn't know what to expect. I had never been inside the Orange County Courthouse building, nor had I ever been inside any other courthouse. But I was familiar with the historically noteworthy building, seeing it on television more than a few times. One of the most notorious murder trials in United States history, the criminal trial of serial killer Ted Bundy, was held in the same building a few years earlier, in the winter of 1980. Now, my brother was on trial in the same courthouse where the notorious serial murderer had allegedly carved his name into the defendant's table.

As I arrived at the courthouse building, the unfamiliar setting created a feeling of anxiousness, fear, and stress. It's hectic, with many people moving in every direction, including lawyers, court staff, police officers, defendants and witnesses, and the media. I walked into the entrance of the double glass doors and immediately noticed the lengthy line of people waiting to go through the security check metal detectors. Once security cleared me, I proceeded directly to the information desk to ask directions to the courtroom for the State of Florida vs. William Worthington case. I was given directions to take the elevator to the fifth floor and turn right, then walk to the last courtroom on the left. As I exited the elevator, I turned right and slowly walked down the hallway. Just before I reached the previous courtroom on the left, a single door to the right of the courtroom opened, and two court officers walked out escorting my brother; he smiled at me as he said my name, and continued to walk as best he could, both his feet and hands were shackled together. Once my brother reached the defendant's table, the shackles were removed before the jury was brought into the courtroom.

The general provision is that defendants should not be shackled or otherwise visibly restrained in the jurors' view, except for major security concerns. A defendant being viewed as restrained can potentially prejudice the jury, making the defendant appear violent or, at worst, guilty. But seeing my brother in restraints did not cause me to see him as more threatening or guilty; I was disheartened. Seeing him shackled made me feel hopeless in being able to assist him, like we had done our entire lives! As I sat in the courtroom, I do not recall much of the testimony from the prosecutor or defense attorneys. My thoughts remained of the visual image of my brother being in what appeared to me to be "slave chains," restraining of your feet or ankles, or both, allowing the person to walk but preventing them from being able to run. This is what it looked like to have your freedom taken away—being able to do what you want when you want was a feeling of freedom he may never experience ever again. I could not bear to attend any more of the trial.

When the jury returned a verdict of guilty, the first-degree murder conviction carried the potential of the death penalty or a life sentence in prison. The conviction left me stunned and in disbelief. William had always been my hero, role model, and motivation for high achievement in basketball, school, and life. Although his excellence cast a large shadow, I never felt hindered by living in his shadow; instead, I embraced it. Although I lived in my older brother's shadow during the transition phase of my life, childhood through adulthood, ages 10-to-17 years old, generally called adolescence, the period was more motivation than intimidation.

The idiom "living in someone's shadow" typically means feeling hidden, like you can never be good enough, and constantly receiving less attention than someone else. A related phrase is to "play second fiddle." But I didn't feel like I was impacted negatively by not having a leading role; sure, I felt like his achievements and abilities seemed to be so great to me that it would be hard for me to be noticed...but it never devalued me; it elevated my efforts and desire to improve my grades in the classroom and skills on the basketball court. Living in William's shadow helped me realize that I am my own person and can pursue my interests even if they are the same ones my brother excels in... But due to this "tragedy," the person who was the most significant motivating factor in my life would no longer be there!

A Life Sentenced

William received a life sentence on March 26, 1986, which in the state of Florida adheres to the rules of Florida Statute, 775 Section 082: "A life felony committed before October 1, 1983, by term of imprisonment for life or a term of at least thirty years; a life felony committed on or after October 1, 1983, by term of imprisonment for life or by a term of imprisonment not exceeding forty years." Some prison sentences allow a prisoner to be considered for parole after serving twenty-five years of their sentence. Nevertheless, in some instances, if the prisoner is denied parole by the parole board at their initial hearing, after waiting a specific number of years, they would be able to be reconsidered for parole. It's important to note that parole eligibility and the decision to grant parole are determined by the laws and practices of the jurisdiction (state of Florida) where the individual is incarcerated. No single consideration "guarantees" a prisoner will be granted parole, as the decision is usually made on a case-by-case basis by a parole board, taking into account factors like the prisoner's behavior in prison, the nature of the crime, potential risk to the community, and whether they have a credible plan for reintegration upon release; however, demonstrating a significant positive change in behavior while incarcerated, coupled with a well-developed reintegration plan, is often considered a critical factor that increases the likelihood of parole being granted. Throughout the years, both my mother and sister have attended parole board hearings for William. Although I have never participated in person, I have provided written statements (personal letters) supporting his early release. When my brother went to prison and I joined the United States Air Force after a year in college, our relationship became significantly strained, marked by feelings of anger, disappointment, and a sense of irreparable distance. I felt as if people were staring at me in college; friends didn't want to hang out with me or go on dates with me; it was a feeling of 'disenfranchised grief,' a term that describes grief that is not acknowledged, validated, or publicly mourned in society.

In a 2016 research study, sociologist Katie Heaton addressed some of the emotional strain siblings can experience due to the imprisonment of their sibling; she described it as 'disenfranchised grief' and that the majority of cases involving this form of grief are the consequences of personal decisions of behaviors made. And this creates a sense of shame or guilt within the individual or that person's family, making it difficult to openly mourn, discuss, or cope with the actions that have created the loss. William and I struggled to maintain a connection with his incarceration due to limited contact and the challenges of navigating prison life; it resulted in a significant weakening of our bond, even with the occasional letters or in-person visits in an attempt to stay connected. I experienced guilt, anger, and confusion about his actions. At the same time, his life of incarceration left him feeling isolated and struggling with the realities of prison life, impacting our ability to maintain a positive relationship. Prison restrictions on phone calls and visits made it challenging to maintain a consistent and meaningful dialogue between William and me, especially when I moved to Germany for several years, with a time difference of six hours ahead of the Florida time zone. After I returned to the mainland United States, at times living in Florida, but most of the time living outside of the state of Florida, there would be sporadic visits and letter exchanges as we attempted to reconnect. While challenging, we have tried hard to maintain a connection through video visits, emails, and telephone calls to work towards rebuilding the relationship bond we shared before his incarceration. If William is ever released, we will seek the resources needed to rebuild our relationship.

As we near forty years since his incarceration, we remain hopeful that he will one day be granted an opportunity to be free again. Communicating with my brother during his years incarnated has changed dramatically over the years. In the initial year, communication was via in-person visits or typically a handwritten letter, which required you to address the envelope with the prison number and address, city, state, and zip code, including my brother's full name. The prison staff can identify the intended recipient based on the prison number. This is a common practice for sending mail to incarcerated individuals in Florida and nationwide. In 2002, JPay began providing services to prisons, starting with electronic money transfers that allowed family members to send money to inmates. JPay's services have expanded to include email, MP3 players, Tablets, and the JPay app. The JPay app has been the easiest way to stay connected and support my brother during his incarceration. JPay lets you quickly send money to a trust account and send and receive emails, photos, eCards, and Videograms. Unfortunately, I have had to purchase a tablet ($99.99 plus tax) more than once to help fund my brother's media account, which is required to use the JPay tablet.

The following is an excerpt from a letter William wrote me in July 2020 in response to a question I asked him about the difficulties of life behind bars for the first time. The time period is after more than thirty years of incarceration in numerous penal institutions throughout the state of Florida. During his many years in prison, my brother has moved around to different prisons throughout the state of Florida, including Avon Park Correctional Institution, Baker

Correctional Institution, Central Florida Reception Center, Hamilton Correctional Institution, Okaloosa Correctional Institution, Polk Correctional Institution, Santa Rosa Correctional Institution, and Tomoka Correctional Institution. The fact that he continually moved around concerned me; I never fully understood why he moved around so much. However, I later learned that inmates have many reasons to move around to different prisons, including changes in their security level, overcrowding at a facility, the need for specific programs not available at their current prison, disciplinary actions, requests to be closer to family, or for their safety if other inmates are threatening them; essentially, transfers often occur to manage prison populations based on security needs, available programs, and individual inmate circumstances.

Hello Tan!

I didn't know how you wanted me to write this up, so I put it as if you were asking me the questions.

The first and only time being in prison…was a shock!!! I say that because I immediately concluded that I would be here for a long time! And every kind of product, illegal product, that could be bought on the streets…you could find here in prison!

The only difference was that everything came with a price, and the 'value' wholesale was ten times higher than what you would pay for the same on the street! You could still buy a 'nickel bag' or 'weed,' but the bag size was ten times smaller and cost ten times the regular street value! So, what I would pay $5.00 for on the street here would cost $50.00, and the 'quantity' would drop to at least 90 percent in weight. There was a 'reefer,' which I just described as a product.

But there were all kinds of pills that I never did, even on the streets, because I was scared of the unknown effects it may have had on me. There were all these other drugs, too, cocaine, meth, heroin, ice, mollie, 'strips' (a form of acid), tech (also called spice or k-2), synthetic marijuana, and, of course, cigarettes.

But to me, k-2 was the most dangerous drug in the system because, for one, it gets you 'higher' than you would have imagined, and two, it doesn't last more than an hour. And thirdly, once you 'come down,' there is a craving that you developed that will strip you of your resistance, your values, and your self-respect, and it changes your mental ability to care for anything or anybody!

There were drugs that I tried and ones that I stayed clear of, especially k-2, because I was so afraid that it would cause me to give up, and stop being who I was… I'd stop caring!

But the only thing that I did, which was a constant for many, many years in my life, was cigarettes and reefer, which I did on the streets. But it's been eight years since I've smoked or done any drugs.

The crazy part about all that mess was, Tan, that I realized that I didn't need it…to live!

Being away from my family, from you all, really had me 'fucked up'…And so I did rely heavily cigarettes and reefer (on family) to cope with a thousand (different) personalities here in these places. But I was also fed up with me…So I talked to myself a lot over the years until I found my heart again (after many attempts to change), and I found that my mind was more potent than any drug that the world had to offer!

Bro, I used to have anxiety attacks all the time, Tan. It was like trying to think of everything at one time and solve each one without coming to a solution! Man, I used to feel so dizzy and sick when it happened. It was like someone else was in control of my body! Bro, you cannot imagine how difficult it was to emerge from one of these attacks! I had 'no' control over these attacks, bro, and it hit when I least expected it to. I used to grit my teeth hard, shaking my head, trying to get free of the attack. Tan, and I rode it out alone, praying that he made it stop! It was that terrifying, Bro!

I used to think I was going to die; I was scared, and this was something I never even told Mama about! I used to worry so much about home, about you all, about being in this place, that I believe this was the reason for these attacks…These episodes happened 2-3 times a month, bro, and I feared the coming of these attacks!

But suddenly, they stopped about a year ago, and I've been blessed without any attacks since. I pray that my mind remains in an 'organized' fashion, where I can feel good about myself and not worry so much about the future, yet I must remain aware of my future and continue to think positively…Because I know that these attacks were brought on my unfocused mind and all the negativity surrounding me day and night.

I am stronger now mentally than I have ever been, with my values and principles intact. Man, I am now fifty-six years old, and I thank God daily for my 'wits,' my heart, and most of all, for sparing me from turning into someone I wasn't! I feel good, Bro…I sat down one day and realized that people were dying off that messed with all those drugs, and everyone said that it 'ain't' going to kill you…But man, they lied!

I realized, bro, that I might be the next one to die, and I made a 'permanent' decision to quit smoking together, even reefer, which you know I smoked on the streets, Tan…even that, I did promise myself to stop, and just like that, I became a changed man…I don't even smoke cigarettes anymore, and I feel very healthy…Thank God!

So yes, Tan, it was tough to adjust behind these bars, but the challenge was not having anyone to share 'personal' feelings and my thoughts with. It's hard trusting in a place like this, man. It's like being welcome behind enemy lines but never knowing who you can trust with your thoughts. There are thieves in here, Tan, not your regular thieves either! Oh no…these thieves approach anyone with thousands of lies. Once you are convinced about one of them, then they have stolen your trust. They are getting you to believe in something that isn't true, and thereby gain your 'belief' that you are sharing knowledge of trust, causing your guard to be let down, and falsehood to be given into your heart. And once that falsehood is found out by you, then it hurts, man.

Because you have let your nature as a man give others a chance, not to be judged by you, according to their face value, causes many vultures to come at you. But I have learned over the years to remain neutral in my contact with other inmates—to be respectful, yet in no hurry to make friends. I know this may sound harsh, but the concept is hard to grasp, Tan. You can imagine that I don't have many friends, yet the few ones I have are enough.…

So yes, it was difficult at first to deal with so many people on so many levels, bro; I was in a new world, with a lot of negativity everywhere I turned. Yet, like so many situations in life, being subjected to certain things or environments for such a long time, you learn to adapt. It's what human beings do, and sometimes it is a harsh reality. Yes, we may suffer, but I believe it strengthens us.

Tan, I have experienced so many things you wouldn't believe, many of which were dangerous. Others that weren't but could lead to life-threatening situations. It is difficult being in prison, bro, but I know that the only reason that I'm not dead now is because my family loves me…and I love you all so much, Tan! I promised myself that I would never leave you all again!

Okay, I will end this for now, bro, but remember how much I love you and that I'm glad you won against me (one-on-one basketball game in 1984) that day! You have heart, Tan; that's what all of us Black Men and Women Need!

Love you, Bro, Weo!

Reading the many letters that William had sent me over the decades since his imprisonment has given me a glimpse at some of what he has had to endure over these years: loneliness, isolation, fear, routine, noise, and bad smells! He has sent countless drawings and cards, displaying his passion and skillfulness as a freehand or sketch artist. Many of his letters also expressed his indifference and distrust for nearly everyone around him and his frequent transfers to multiple correctional facilities due to reasons ranging from adjustments in prison rules and strict enforcement to threats of physical harm, including death threats. Over the years, the tone and tenor of his letters changed as the maladies of old age set in. He now regularly mentions aches and pains, vision and hearing problems, and the inadequate medical care available to him and other inmates. He also expresses concern for the heartache and pains his incarceration has caused our mother over all these years, mainly due to the number of health issues she has battled and the fact that she will be eighty years old in the year 2024.

As my mother's eldest child, William was everything a mother could hope for in a firstborn, and she loved him unconditionally. In his school-aged years, he became her security and anchor through a separation and divorce at an early age from her husband, our father, and his namesake, followed by a long-term abusive relationship with Buddy, mom's "common-law husband" of many years. In his letters from prison, William would write openly about his resentment and ill feelings towards Buddy, our stepfather, with whom he had mixed emotions, and his feelings that our mother would never indeed be happy or safe with Buddy in our lives. In one recent letter, September 2022, he wrote about his conflicting feelings towards the man who had raised us for most of our lives.

Tan, I never intended to leave our family, especially with the situation with Buddy; you know what I'm talking about, man...You know, bro, I never liked Buddy, and I can say that now, man, because I am mature enough to understand what I'm feeling is real. And I am not ashamed to admit that now, but I respect him too because, through all those years, the man provided for us and constantly helped take care of the house. But he was never a father to me or for me, and I know that part of the reason I am here is because I never had (anyone) to look up to. I was a child pretending to be an adult, never realizing that I was leading myself astray.

William's imprisonment was harrowing for Mom, as he had been her umbrella of protection as the eldest son. He felt a sense of honorable duty to be her protector as if he were "Sir Morien," the Black knight of the Round Table, rescuing a damsel in distress. An incident between Buddy and our mother left a deep scar of hatred in William's heart for Buddy. He described the incident by saying that as he, my mother, and step-father were driving in the car about three blocks from the house, in the middle of a heated verbal argument, Buddy abruptly stopped the car in the middle of the road, slammed the gear into park, jumped out of driver side of the vehicle, ran to the passenger door, stanched it open and dragged our mother out of the car, then he physically assaulted her.

At the time, William was a seventeen-year-old, six-foot-one-inch, athletically built teen who jumped out of the vehicle's back seat and ran to the nearby housing. Grabbing the first 'weapon' he could find, a wooden broomstick, he ran back to the car and hit Buddy over the head with the hardwood handle of the broom. The psychological images of that disgusting incident remained in the forefront of his thoughts when he was sentenced to prison, wondering, *Who's going to protect Mom?* As for our mom, no mother wants to go to bed knowing her child is in prison, especially with the knowledge he potentially would never be released. Adding to her agony, the Florida Department of Corrections, which oversees prisons in Florida, prevented her from having in-person visits with William for more than five years due to a violation of a rule she didn't know existed. Once her visitation privileges were reinstated, she was dealing with serious health issues, having suffered a heart attack and some signs of deteriorating health due to aging. The trip to the prison was very taxing, as William had been transferred nearly three hundred miles from his previous prison facility, due to a change in his security-level scoring. The process of going to double locked steel doors, the sound of the gate slammed closed behind you, metal detectors, and physical searching of each person who entered, combined with the ever presence of correctional officers, all added to the stress of older people dealing with the effects of hypertension, arthritis, and heart disease! My mother, a god-fearing woman, has remained hopeful in prayers for all these years that she would one day see her son free again. In a recent conversation with her about how she was after all these years fighting for William, these were her words: "The day my son was sent to prison, words I never dreamed that I'd say about one of my children, never dreamed in a million years. I just prayed that I would be blessed to see my son come home one day." My mother's prayer: "I entrust my son into your loving hands, knowing that your love is unwavering, and your Grace is boundless. Please offer him strength and hope during his incarceration."

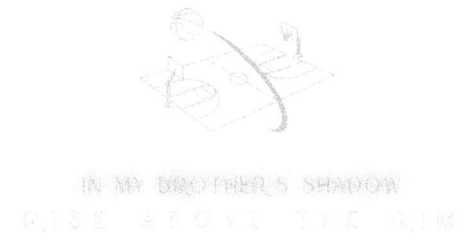

THIRD QUARTER

7
SURVIVING DIFFICULT TIMES BY BUILDING RESILIENCE

I know that family members of individuals convicted in a criminal trial and sentenced to incarceration in prison are often referred to as the "hidden victims" of the criminal justice system. After my brother's conviction and sentence, I didn't feel like a victim of the legal system. Still, I feel the psychological strain and stress surrounding a criminal trial, especially since I was attending college in the city in which the crime and trial occurred. Even before the trial concluded with a conviction, I felt the negative impact of others' judgment, although I had done nothing wrong. But nevertheless, the same year my brother was convicted of first-degree murder and sentenced to life in prison was the same year I left college and joined the United States Air Force, with my first duty assignment taking me nearly five thousand miles away from home, to Kaiserslautern, West Germany.

Kaiserslautern had previously developed into the largest United States military community outside of the United States, with approximately fifty thousand military personnel in Germany in 1986, the year I arrived there. I don't know how big of an impact the personal trauma my family was dealing with played a role in my inability to manage both the athletic and academic responsibilities of college. I underperformed in both, losing my starting position on the basketball team and losing my college eligibility for failing to maintain the National Junior College Athletic Association (NJCAA) minimum grade point average of 2.0 GPA while maintaining twelve or more credit hours. This ultimately led to the loss of my full basketball scholarship! I recall when I realized how much I had lost. Still, at some point, I knew I needed to take an honest look at myself, my knowledge and skills or lack thereof, and acknowledge those shortcomings before coming up with a plan to improve and overcome them every day. All my years of being an athlete have taught me about overcoming adversity, being resilient with the ability to bounce back from a loss on the basketball court or life or thriving during times of challenges or tragedy. I was quite aware that I wasn't the only person who had to deal with life challenges; everyone has to face adversity at one point or another in their lives. But for me, it was an added challenge of getting past the obstacles of losing my brother, friends and family members, and my dream of playing college basketball.

The first person I talked to about my academic dismissal from the college basketball team was my former high school math teacher, Mr. Bailey. "Tan, I know it's not going to be easy, but don't you dare give up. Don't do that," Mr. Bailey said. We talked for hours, like we used to do when I was one of his students, about the failure or withdrawal from classes and losing a basketball scholarship. "Well, Tan, this truly sucks, but you can't feel sorry for yourself because this is a result of you not doing what you were supposed to do." I knew he was right, and I needed to invest time and effort to either regain my college eligibility or follow a different career path. "Do you want to waste the opportunity to get an education?" Without waiting for my response, he continued, "You had best not." Mr. Bailey was someone from whom I always sought advice throughout my years attending

Evans High School and for many years afterward. His final dose of advice was for me to think about what had caused me to find myself in this position. "Tan, take some time and go back and examine what you did and didn't do and make a plan to approach college differently, and you better get it right this time." He was 'my conscious,' a man who truly knew who he was, and where he came from…He was someone who always provided me with a deeper understanding of information or circumstances. "So, Tan, this is the last thing I got to say about it. Get your behind back out there and re-enroll in school or show me some other plans you have for your life." The other plan was the unplanned life-changing decision to join the United States Air Force (USAF). During my first year of college, I met and befriended two local Air Force recruiters, SSgt Diaz and SSgt Hill, as they stood in front of the main cafeteria area on the college main campus seeking to speak to students about the benefits an Airmen in the USAF receive, including housing, excellent food, on-the-job training, and access to educational opportunities. All these benefits got my attention, but the discussion about Air Force basketball teams and the opportunity to have a chance to play against Division I level basketball talent grabbed my attention and stood out as the 'other plan for my life' Mr. Bailey had encouraged me to find.

Initially, I didn't decide to enlist. I began hanging out with SSgts Diaz and Hill at their East Orlando office, helping with paperwork, entertaining recruits, and playing basketball at the local Orlando Navy Training Center gymnasium. During these pickup games, both guys believed I would be a great prospect for the All-Air Force basketball team, allowing me to travel around the world playing basketball and representing the United States Air Force. The possibilities of the USAF fascinated me, but I was still uncertain about taking such a significant step. Losing my basketball scholarship and falling below the required college-level GPA left me with serious doubt about my academic abilities and hesitation in my ability to join the most difficult branch of the military to enlist —the United

States Air Force, with an admissions rate of 16.2 percent. The USAF is the largest air force in the world and the second largest branch of the United States military services. The branch receives thousands more applicants than it can enlist, demands higher Armed Services Aptitude Battery (ASVAB) test scores, and has more stringent physical requirements than other military branches. But, before I could push myself to new heights and follow the US Air Force's motto, "Aim High…Fly-Fight-Win," a call to action, I needed to see my brother to talk with him about my life-altering decision, as he was sitting in jail awaiting his transfer to prison after receiving a life sentence. He would be picked up by the Florida Department of Corrections (FDC) personnel on an unspecified date. Inmates receive no warning when their transfer day happens. Usually, FDC opens the inmate's cell in the early morning hours, instructs the inmate to collect their things, and makes a quick stop to the property room for them to turn in their jail-issued clothing and put on their street clothing. The transferring institution mails all inmates' property and money, and nothing is transported with the inmate during the transfer to prison. The inmate is shackled, belted, cuffed, lockboxed, before being escorted to the bus for the trip to their prison destination. So, finally, I made another trip downtown to see my brother; seeing him was intimidating, emotional, and bittersweet.

The entire process of visiting an inmate can be intimidating from the entry process, which is humiliating, involving lines, body searchers, and metal detectors. In addition, the small area was overcrowded, extremely loud, and distracting. The experience makes you feel every emotion possible: excitement, nervousness, anticipation; the visit time couldn't arrive fast enough. These feelings become more potent the closer you get to being inside the visitation area—a small room with two glass doors, one for the detainee and one for the visitor. The visitation rooms also have obvious cameras and guards who patrol and remind visitors and detainees of proper behavior. Once my brother arrived, the excitement became more robust, with intense love, sadness from missing him, and happiness that he looked healthy and sounded well. He walked into the room wearing a faded blue jail outfit, his hair seemed uncombed, his complexion pale, but his smile was as it always had been —comforting. He spoke in a soft tone once he picked up the phone handle, "Tan, man, what took you so long to come to see me?" I paused before I responded, "I don't know, I been, …I wanted to come sooner," I said, unsure of my words as my eyes locked onto his jail outfit. We talked for nearly an hour. Not once did we speak about his trial or conviction, nor did we speak about my pending decision to join the military. If only for a short while, despite the circumstances, I just enjoyed talking to my brother again.

There was also a little feeling of nostalgia, like a summer visit, as I began making small talk and almost inevitably hit on subjects about events from before William was incarcerated. As the visit came within about one hour of being over, William and I both began to have feelings of sadness. I started missing him before the visit was even over. Years later, William would write me a letter explaining how he felt being taken into police custody and was able to forgive himself for a tragic *mistake* resulting in his prison sentence. Once in the *system*, he moved around to many different correctional facilities, including Avon Park Correctional Institution, Tomoka Correctional Institution, and Quincy Annex Correctional Institution, one of the most significant adult prisons in the region. During his time at Tomoka Correctional Institution in Daytona Beach, which was less than an hour from where I was living at the time, I routinely visited him during this period. The initial visit was the first time I had seen him in more than three years. I was thrilled to see him. He looked great, and it was as if time stood still, after a long hug, we immediately began talking about basketball. We continued to talk. We began walking around the perimeter of the visitation yard when I noticed that there were two fences: An inner fence was installed several feet inside a taller perimeter fence, both with barbed wire on top to prevent inmates from escaping. The gap between the two walls also prevented prisoners or visitors from throwing contraband, slowing down tunneling and allowing dogs to patrol between the walls and catch them. After being somewhat shocked by the environment, I refocused on our conversation, mostly about basketball. "Tan, man, I'm still smooth with my jump shot; we have a prison team that plays against other prisoners." The visit was like the two of us were walking through our old neighborhood of Carver Shores talking about basketball until a loud and long sound of a siren blasted over the speakers, signaling that visiting hours were over. As we said our goodbyes, I suggested he remain motivated in sketching and drawings. "Weo, man, you need to focus on writing your book and creating a portfolio of your freehand drawings." He laughed and responded, "Tan, I'm going to put something together this week to send to you. I'll put it in the mail next week." And he walked away, stopping to wave goodbye one last time.

I was excited to hear that he was thinking about his 'artistic ability,' another talent Weo was blessed with besides basketball. I watched him walk away until he disappeared out of view, entering the same doors he had exited a few hours earlier for our visit. I routinely visited him in the coming months and years, each visit having a recurring theme: basketball. Initially, I didn't mind having those conversations, since playing 'b-ball' was one the foundations of our relationship for as long as I could remember. However, whenever I tried to talk about him staying vigilant, not giving up, and staying positive as we continued seeking ways to gain his freedom, his primary focus always seemed to be on the game we grew up loving— 'roundball.' He'd talk about how he was the best player in the prison facility basketball court, how many games his team won, how his 'prison team' easily won a game against another visiting prison team. Everything revolved around what was happening on the prison yard basketball courts. I was becoming quite irritated by what I perceived as his carefree attitude to discussing his freedom, resulting in me speaking frankly to him: "William, man, you're not thinking about your life when you get out of here." And although I felt bad about my sounding off on him, I didn't understand why he wasn't contemplating life outside of the prison. I would later realize his dispassionate state of mind was his way of adapting to the environment he was now forced to survive discreetly in the face of danger or risk, and live every hour, day, month, and year!

It was a realization that caused me to feel remorse for getting angry about my perception of his lack of caring; it was easy to say, since my life didn't require me to be wary of every person I encountered daily. Besides, basketball was his last connection to freedom. It was what he loved most in life, his only coping mechanism. He told me years later he had nothing else; the game of basketball freed him for a few minutes each day: "It's what I had when I came in here, and I don't want to let it go." He would also write about self-forgiveness, letting go of guilt, and liberating himself from shame. In describing the thirty years (at the time of the letter) that he spent in prison, William wrote:

I was shocked! Apart from me, I died inside that very day because the one thought that was foremost in my mind was the fact that I was leaving my Mama without doing everything I told her I would do for her. That was my biggest shock, and I was devastated, and knew the action would be the source of everyone's distress. I thought about my Mama, then I thought about Tan, and then everyone that I loved…my thoughts began to become a blur as if God himself was closing my eyes and the rest of my thoughts lacked clarity of meaning. Yes, and no! I'm going to explain first by saying No! Because I KNEW what I was doing was going against EVERYTHING I EVER WANTED TO DO FOR MY FAMILY AND MYSELF…And yes! I've forgiven myself because I realize I'm NOT A BAD PERSON! My family loves me because they have forgiven me…And so has God. Therefore, it's only appropriate that I find forgiveness in my heart for myself…. I know the action that got me here was not being me; I needed to give myself some grace, be less critical for becoming someone else, and get back to being ME. It's not difficult to describe the time I've spent in prison—it's another world, and adaption is a part of the human trait. I accepted my fate, you see, and it became easy to cope with the injustices, prejudices, and violent confrontations that are there daily. It's the same on the streets and out in society. You learn to cope, or you don't. I've always been athletic, and my art means a lot to me; it's a mental stimulant that soothes the everyday suffering and frustrations.

As the years turned into decades following William's conviction for murder, our entire family has had to deal with some good and bad times, peaks and valleys on the journey toward forgiveness. William had to realize that he deserved to be happy or to move on with his life, even as he remained behind bars. His journey towards self-forgiveness became his coping mechanism to help him overcome the trauma of not living up to his expectations. Some have argued that forgiveness interventions for prisoners should include modules that reduce self-punitive attitudes. However, others say that self-forgiveness is a complex concept that can take a long time. Many prisoners find it harder to forgive themselves than being forgiven by others, but accepting responsibility, expressing remorse, and treating yourself with compassion are all steps towards forgiving yourself.

The family has continued to support William as the impact of incarceration can cause a person's psychological well-being to suffer hypervigilance, interpersonal distrust, alienation, compromised self-worth, and PTSD. Even after nearly four decades in prison, our family remains steadfast in supporting and showing love to William. We understand the significant psychological difficulties his time in prison has inflicted on him and our family, and we have all visited him, spoken with him over the telephone, and exchanged written letters over the years so that he knows he has the full support of his family. As dreadful as the prison environment can be, life outside of the penitentiary continued for the rest of us, the good and the bad. But coping with a public tragedy can be particularly challenging because not only are you grappling with a range of emotional, physical, and cognitive reactions, but also the public scrutiny as a consequence of your relationship. Within the span of five years after graduating high school, I had to cope with several public tragedies, including the unexpected death of a good friend, the staggering murder conviction of my brother, the untimely death of my Uncle Bobby (Robert E. Gaulden, 1955 – 1990)—1 of 472 murders in the nation's capital of Washington, DC in 1990, a decade where homicides in the city peaked at more than five hundred murders per year. Although not a public tragedy, but no less painful, my maternal grandfather Clarence Gaulden (1986) and Grandmother Claudia Mae Kennedy (1997, at the age of eighty) would pass away during my emerging adulthood years. My grandfather's death occurred the week after I returned from taking my first steps towards launching my military career: United States Air Force (USAF) Basic Training for eight weeks and USAF Technical Training school for an additional eight weeks. I returned home to the news that my maternal grandfather, Clarence Gaulden (1916 – 1986), had passed away at the age of seventy, the man I had affectionately called "Daddy" in my early childhood, during the time my grandparents were raising me. In those formative years, my grandfather played the "father" role even more so than my biological father.

I relied on him and my grandmother for many of my social, emotional, and physical needs during those years. The news of his death was intensely painful, and I remember attending his funeral service as the start of my healing process. The opportunity to participate in his homegoing allowed me to experience my grief and embrace my feelings. The time-honored celebrations of my grandfather's release from this life and a reunion with God, a custom among the African American community, were comforting for my grief. During his homegoing service, many of our family members, neighbors, friends, and church members offered prayers and gave eulogies that honored his life. My grandfather's homegoing was the last time I would ever speak to my Uncle Bobby. He gave me advice on the responsibilities of having a family and avoiding the seduction of life's temptations, in particular, as a young Black man.

A few short years later, during my second military assignment at Hurlburt Field Air Force installation located in Fort Walton Beach, Florida, I received a phone call from my Aunt Cookie (Uncle Bobby's wife). My initial enthusiasm was quickly dampened by the tone of her voice, one of desperation and despair. "Tan, someone just killed Bobby!" I felt a tingling anxiety-related numbness, like "pins and needles" prickling all over my paralyzed body, before I suddenly responded, "What, what happened?" with my mouth remaining open, eyes widening and tearing up in disbelief as if a sudden jolt of electricity had moved through my body leaving me temporarily stunned! "What?!" I repeated.

Aunt Cookie, sobbing, continued speaking while crying, "I don't know what happened; someone shot him, and his body is still lying in the street." I'm not sure what was said in the remaining phone conversation, but afterward, I immediately called my mother and shared the shocking and devastating news with her that her baby brother had been murdered. In no way are we the only family who has had to deal with traumatic experiences. People around the world go through the emotions of loss, helplessness, and troubling memories from losing a loved one. According to studies, roughly half of all Americans have had an immediate family member incarcerated, meaning a significant portion of families are impacted when a loved one goes to prison; this translates to around 113 million adults in the United States having experienced this situation with a close family member. Nearly 50 percent of Americans have had a family member incarcerated at some point in their lives.

I still have vivid memories as a young boy living with my grandmother in Hinesville, Georgia in the early 1970s, the first time I witnessed a family member go to 'jail,' my Uncle Bobby (my mother's youngest brother) was convicted of a crime at age fifteen and placed in a juvenile detention center. This outcome disproportionately placed Black boys in these facilities at a rate nearly five times higher than other races. I believe that people who have experienced this feel similar to how I felt: a profound sense of emotional loss, feeling like they've lost a significant part of their life, characterized by feelings of grief, sadness, isolation, anxiety, anger, and sometimes even a sense of guilt, as the relationship they once had is drastically altered and limited by the constraints of incarceration; essentially grieving the loss of their family member's physical presence and the life they shared before imprisonment. And I'm sure others may feel sympathy for their loved one—you still care about them. Being in jail sucks. If their family member is facing a long sentence, like my brother, they are likely grieving the loss of the relationship they once had and thinking about how they may never get those days back... it's a feeling I share with all of them!

Dealing with loss isn't the only challenge in life; coping with a changing world—whether within the confinements of prison or in everyday life—presents unique challenges. Society has undergone significant changes over the past forty years. The world has changed in dramatic and unprecedented ways since my brother was given a life sentence following his conviction for murder in the 85th year of the 20th century, where today he's entering his 23rd year of the 21st century incarcerated, a period that represents nearly 68 percent of his life on earth, indeed a life spent in prison. It is tough for me to conceptualize a life confined behind bars—how William's incarceration has subjected him to degrading treatment, inhumane conditions, and abusive interactions. The cognitive trauma from these experiences would certainly handicap him if he were ever given the chance to be reintegrated into society.

I had often wondered how anyone who served forty-plus years in prison could make the transition back into society, even with family support. After four decades of adaptation to the extreme structure of prison life, experiencing mental and emotional anguish, making a successful transition into society would likely result in feelings of shock and deep distress in an attempt to manage all of the freedom of life in the free world. If the former inmate entered prison in their twenties, now walking out of prison in their sixties, the change that has taken place the past forty years…Prison rules decide when lights go on and when they go off. Every moment of the day is scheduled. When you have been in the prison system for the majority of your life, how can you be expected to function as a member of society? This statement highlights the significant challenge faced by individuals who spend a large portion of their lives incarcerated, as the highly structured prison environment, with strict schedules and controlled routines, can make it incredibly difficult to adapt to the autonomy and flexibility required for functioning in everyday society once released; essentially, "prison takes away the ability to make personal decisions about your day, so when you leave, you don't know how to manage your own time or make choices," according to The Marshall Project (nonprofit journalism about criminal justice).

Because of my family's personal experience with long-term incarceration, William is entering nearly four decades of imprisonment; I and other family members have become increasingly motivated to help prisoners once they are released while also hoping that one day, the released prisoner will be my brother. In addition to family members' involvement, I have also realized the experience and counsel of a particular friend, Jimmie G, who overcame a twenty-seven-year prison sentence after a wrongful conviction; the conviction was overturned, and he was ultimately acquitted of the crime. Today, he is a recent college graduate and a motivational speaker who uses his experience to assist other formerly incarcerated men. Jimmie and I spoke about his time in prison and how both he and my brother had spent decades in the Florida prison system. I later introduced him, via an email message, to William. Jimmie suggested that William should get more involved with available organizations that focus on prisoner reentry programs, offering support like housing assistance, job training, mental health counseling, life skills development, and connecting them with community resources to help him successfully transition back into society. Here are a few ways you can help former prisoners:

- Volunteer with reentry organizations; many non-profits work directly with recently released individuals, providing mentoring, job placement assistance, and essential needs support; mentor programs, sharing your life experiences and guidance to help former prisoners navigate challenges like finding housing, managing finances, and reconnecting with family.

- Advocate for policy change, supporting legislation that aims to improve reentry programs, reduce recidivism rates, and address issues like access to employment and housing for formerly incarcerated individuals.

- Educate your community and raise awareness about the challenges faced by people returning from prison and dispel stereotypes to foster understanding and support; offer skill development workshops where you can teach practical skills like resume writing, computer literacy, or essential financial management to help former prisoners become more competitive in the job market.

- Support transitional housing programs, like volunteering or donating to organizations that provide temporary housing for recently released individuals while they get back on their feet.

Connect with local businesses, encourage businesses in your community to consider hiring formerly incarcerated individuals, and provide opportunities for job training.

Important considerations when helping former prisoners: respect their boundaries, understand that they may be hesitant to share personal details, and respect their privacy; Focus on empowerment, avoid treating them as helpless, and instead, focus on building their confidence and self-reliance. Be patient; reintegration takes time, and there may be setbacks along the way. Collaborate with professionals; work with social workers, therapists, and other experts to provide comprehensive support.

Although many of the programs mentioned are not widely available at every Florida prison system facility, they are obtainable in many correctional facilities. Unfortunately, large numbers of inmates do not take advantage of the resources and services available to most prisoners, including my brother, William. Although I had not consistently visited with my brother after he had been sent to prison because I had joined the United States Air Force and no longer lived in Florida, we continued to communicate through letters. He would always ask me when I was coming to see him in person. In early 1993, I received military orders. I was assigned to Patrick Air Force Base (recently renamed Space Force Base), renowned for its critical support to the Space Program, including managing all launches of uncrewed rockets at Cape Canaveral Air Force Station (Space Force Station), which is located between Satellite Beach and Cocoa Beach, Florida. This new military assignment and my residence placed me within two hours of Avon Park Correctional Institution, where William was housed. It was the first time in nearly a decade that he and I were living our lives within hours of one another, and it allowed us to have consistent and frequent in-person visits. In-person prison visits in Florida are governed according to Rule 22-601.723, Florida Administrative Code which lays out the visiting check-in procedures, number of allowed (five) visitors, age limits of visitors (children eleven years or younger do count against the five approved visitors) allowed to visit an inmate in the visiting area at one time.

William and I would usually greet one another in the limited space visiting room area before going outside into the recreation yard, a fenced area with tables and chairs allowing family visits outside of the usually crowded visiting room. This allowed him and I to have our conversation in as much privacy as possible; as we continued to walk along the fence line in a circle, our discussions would cover all topics from his life inside prison and my life outside in the real world. However, he never wanted to discuss programs or services to improve his chances of receiving a board-approved early release from prison. During one visit, I insisted that we discuss his chances of being released instead of discussing playing basketball in prison or my basketball coaching career or training business. It did not go well, and our typical hour-long visit lasted only about half the time of our previous visits. I never understood why my brother seemed reluctant to help himself by taking advantage of prison programs and services. Still, it became incredibly frustrating and disheartening to me, as I felt powerless to intervene directly while also wanting to see him take positive steps towards rehabilitation and a better future upon release, so I thought the best approach was to offer support and encouragement through our regular communication, suggest available programs within the prison system to him, and suggest that he consider seeking guidance from a prison counselor or family support group to navigate the complexities of this situation; it was essential for me to understand the sensitivity of the matter and not to try to force him to change, but I wanted him to know that what he had been doing wasn't getting the results we wanted, him closer to being a free man again!

So, after speaking to him about the potential benefits of participating in prison programs and taking responsibility for his actions, the next challenge was to convince him to seek professional guidance. He was surprisingly receptive to reaching out to a prison counselor or a family support group specializing in incarcerated individuals to gain insights and strategies for support during his incarceration. But I was also careful to respect the fact that all these actions were his choices, and I had to respect that boundary and understand that I could not control his actions. If he wasn't willing to make the most of his time in prison, like actively participating in programs or opportunities available to him to improve himself while incarcerated, including education, vocational training, counseling, or rehabilitation programs, which could significantly improve his chances of successful reintegration into society upon release…there wasn't anything I could do about it! For many former inmates, it's a nearly impossible adjustment to make! The family members who have been supporting the formerly imprisoned inmate, although not living a physical life of confinement, have endured an emotional and psychological incarceration, which has a significant impact on the mental and, in some instances, bodily health of family members.

Reset, Refocus, and Restart After Coping with Tragedy

Joining the United States Air Force (USAF) soon after leaving college was a desperate attempt to cope with my grief and reestablish a sense of direction in my life. As a military brat and child of a retired military sergeant, I always had the utmost respect for the men and women of the armed forces. Although I was the son of a Vietnam veteran (United States Army) and was born in a military base hospital, I didn't enlist in the United States Air Force out of a sense of honor or duty to serve my country. Joining the military was a way to reset my life after dealing with tragedy, as it provided me with a structured environment with significant life changes, including a new routine, skills development, a sense of purpose, and the opportunity to build a new identity, intending to lead to personal growth and a fresh start, after the major life shift of losing my brother and college scholarship in the same period.

Becoming a member of the USAF not only reoriented my life but also assisted in the recovery of my self-esteem, confidence, and undeveloped emotional state of mind. My early experiences in the aviation service included my first flying on an airplane, my first-ever shooting an M16 rifle, and my first being outside of the United States, a ten-hour international flight to Frankfurt, Germany, the major financial hub in Europe. The decision would allow me to experience the military's unique culture with its emphasis on commitment and follow-through; in addition to training, the idea of learning new skills to be more successful in life resonates within the military community. I was keenly aware that significant preparation would be needed to reach the level of acceptance into the Air Force, but enduring the training also required a higher level of preparation and provided me an opportunity to redeem myself from my failed attempt to be a college student-athlete. However, I was cautious not to become entangled in memories of the past to the detriment of embracing my potential military future with enthusiasm. In January 1986, I arrived at Joint Base San Antonio-Lackland Air Force Base in San Antonio, Texas for Basic Military Training (BMT), eight weeks of extensive physical training, including running, calisthenics, marching, classroom education, with instruction on Air Force history, customs, courtesies and military protocol, and weapons training. After graduating from BMT, it was off to Technical Training, up to fifty-two weeks long, where you receive the specific training for the career you have been assigned. Next, I took a brief "leave" of absence, to visit my family back home in Florida, prior to boarding an international flight to West Germany for my first duty assignment, Sembach Air Force Base near Kaiserslautern. I would serve the next eleven years on active duty and an additional six years in the active reserves—a career that allowed me to travel internationally to both West and East Germany before "the fall of the Berlin Wall" (the wall divided communist East Germany from West Germany) in 1989.

I visited other European countries in Germany, including France, the Netherlands, Luxembourg, the United Kingdom, and Spain. Other international travel destinations included Mexico, Panama, and Japan. I also traveled to several US territories, such as Puerto Rico, Guam, and the Northern Mariana Islands. In addition to world travel adventures, I completed training and began a new career as an air traffic controller. This rewarding profession plays a vital role in ensuring the safety and efficiency of our air travel. However, the job also comes with high stress levels, demanding schedules, and the need for unwavering focus and attention to detail. Becoming an air traffic controller involves grueling training that normally spans 18-to-36 months. The requirements include a series of tests, skills assessments, physical and psychological examinations, and an extensive background investigation to obtain a secret security clearance. The security clearance process includes a comprehensive examination of your criminal record, credit history, personal conduct, and other details to verify that you are "reliable, trustworthy, of good conduct and character, and loyal to the United States." The Federal Aviation Administration (FAA) has air traffic control facilities in every state, including Puerto Rico, the US Virgin Islands, and Guam (a facility where I worked as a controller for three years). It was the best job I've ever had, and the requirements to make quick decisions, be detail-oriented, concentrate, and work always reminded me of playing basketball (although any mistakes could have much greater consequences). Basketball has remained the one thing that has been consistent in my life; it has taught me how to be a better athlete and a better person. My love for this game has significantly influenced so many of the decisions I've made in life; and that didn't change during my years in the military. The Air Force and other military branches offer opportunities to play intramural sports to foster teamwork, increase squadron cohesiveness, and build esprit de corps. Improving unit morale worked, but winning the base championship became more about the bragging rights of being the best team on the military base. The competition wasn't the best, but in addition to the intramural teams, many military bases have a 'base team.'

These teams require players to participate in tryouts and, if selected, to travel to other military installations both on mainland

United States as well as military bases located internationally. The competition was much higher, and many teams consisted of players who had played college basketball before military service. Another level available for military, active duty, and academic attendees is the All-Air Force basketball team; members are selected from among the best United States Air Force basketball players and compete against similar teams from the Army, Navy, Marines, and Coast Guard. Being invited to participate in the All-Air Force training camp was one of the most competitive basketball events with the most talented players I have ever played in and competed against. I played numerous games worldwide during those years, scoring many points and leading many of the teams I played for in scoring and making three-point field goals. There were also game-winning baskets and a streak of six consecutive forty-point games.

I had the opportunity to compete against players on the Russian national basketball team and players from Germany, Spain, and China. However, the most memorable game I played allowed me to get a little revenge. During my tour of duty at Hurlburt Field Air Force Base, I was a member of the basketball team for several years. I regularly played home and away games against players from the Naval Air Station Pensacola, located in southwest Pensacola. As my teammates and I entered the Naval Station's gym and looked around for the visiting team's locker room, we noticed Navy team players on the court shooting and sitting in bleachers behind the team chairs. I noticed a familiar face among their players—it was one of my old high school rivals, Anthony Shorter. He had been a member of the 1983 Orlando Boone High School team, whom we played four times that year (1983), winning the first three games, before they upset us in the fourth game.

They then began their run at the Florida High School State Basketball Championship, a title I still believe we should have won to this day. Although I couldn't change the past results of that final game, I needed to prove to Shorter that I was a much better player than I was in that losing game all those years ago. I didn't feel any personal animosity towards Shorter; I felt strongly about needing vengeance against anyone who played on the team that "stole our championship." That wasn't necessarily the truth, but I needed someone to blame for that 1983 Orange County District boys' basketball semi-final loss. On this day, my USAF basketball team would win a less-than-competitive game versus Shorter and his Sailor teammates. I was leading scorer for the team, as I had been all year, scoring a game high forty-three points.

The victory against my old competitor, Shorter, and his teammates didn't make me feel any better or remove the bitter feeling inside of me from that loss nearly ten years ago; the Boone Braves remain the 1983 boys' basketball state champions. Although it was years before I would actually admit it, they (Braves) were worthy and deserving champions. They made the necessary adjustments in that fourth and final game against us and won the remaining games in the district and state tournament to claim their legendary coach, Wayne Rickman, his second state basketball championship; he also led the Braves to a 1977 state championship. We were confident that we would win a fourth game against Boone. We beat them relatively easily in the previous three games, but the fourth would have a surprisingly different outcome. The Braves upset us, the second-seeded team, in the semifinal district tournament game led by an outstanding performance by senior wing player Lennie Grace, who poured in thirty points, and an exceptional team shooting performance, shooting better than 93 percent from the free throw line; as a team, Boone shot 26-of-28 from the foul line in the win.

On a visit back to Orlando, more than thirty years after high school, I am sitting down eating breakfast and talking with Lenny 'Tank' Grace, the star of the Boone state championship team, and losing that final game to them came up...Lenny, whom I've known since elementary school, looked up from his plate and said "Tan, you need therapy," just as he said when we were in high school. We both laughed. But at that very moment, I had an epiphany: All of those times competing against one another, that shared experience of overcoming obstacles not only built resilience and strength within us but also forged a bond that lasted long after the final buzzer of a game, creating friendships that remained intact long after our playing days were over.

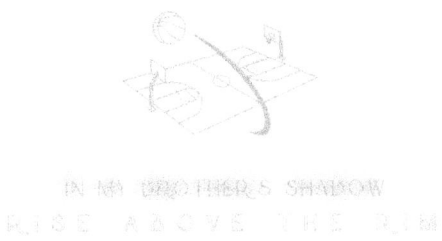

8
BECOMING A COACH

Becoming a coach was not a culmination of a grand plan to stand on the sideline yelling at players. Still, due to an unfortunate sports injury, I found my passion and calling for coaching. Reflecting on my own career journey, skills, and knowledge I've learned over the years what could help others achieve their goals. The injury, a torn rotator cuff of my right arm, occurred while I was playing in a flag football game and required a minimally invasive arthroscopic procedure to repair the injury. The recovery time was estimated to be between 4-12 months, effectively ending any chance I had of playing basketball for the base team for the season. Although I had always fancied myself coaching on the floor as early as I was playing YMCA youth basketball, it took an injury to get me to try coaching for the first time. Once I decided to give coaching a try, I didn't know how to go about establishing my coaching philosophy and priorities. So, I headed back to my old high school to speak with former basketball coaches Tapia, Gordon, and Lingelbach, each of whom was generous with their time and advice. Much of what they shared with me was similar—remember the "Trojan" way, focus on fundamentals, teamwork, commitment, and character—with a consistent emphasize on defense, rebounding, passing the ball, and taking good shots. Their guidance and suggestions would become the pillars of my coaching philosophy.

At basketball practices, I relied on much of what I had been taught as a player in high school. However, I certainly continued to learn valuable lessons from the other coaches who gained a wealth of knowledge about basketball over the past thirty years. In keeping with the tradition of the "Trojan way," the first few days of practice set the tone for the entire basketball season, introducing new players and new aspirations, and establishing habits that would become the tradition of the basketball program. It's during the initial days of practice when you assess the talent level of your players, get a feel for who is passionate about the game, and then evaluate the fundamental skills of players using drills to determine who's the best ball handler, shooter, defender, rebounder, and who are your hustle players. Hustle is a mindset that sets a player apart from another player who may be more talented, allowing players to find within themselves a fire to engage in every play, even the monotonous ones; to be a player who always gives you the best version of themself. All of this, in theory, seemed like a great play; now, as a coach, I needed to make it all work.

The first time I can remember "making a coach's decision" was when I was in the ninth grade. During a junior high school basketball game at Memorial Junior High School, I was the captain and leading scorer for the team, and the game closed when the opponent went on an 8-0 scoring run to take a two-score lead in the final minutes of the fourth quarter. Without waiting for our coach's signal for a timeout, I took it upon myself to go up to the referee and ask for a timeout, with my fingers pointing into the palm of my other hand in making the shape of the letter T. As we walked towards our team bench, our head coach asked who had called the timeout. I responded that I had done so, and the coach said, "Good call!" I didn't have a strategy for calling timeout in that game; we needed to take some time to regroup. Since timeouts are used primarily for strategy, they play a key role in every basketball game and are extremely crucial at the end of a close game. Therefore, they should be used wisely to get the maximum benefit. Whenever a timeout is called, players should run to the bench, especially in the case of a twenty- or thirty-second timeout. We came back to win the game, so the results proved the timeout was a prudent call. The next day in school, my coach, Coach Stanley, applauded my leadership, basketball IQ, and insightful use of the timeout in a critical game phase. He also gave me additional advice that would prove very valuable when I became a coach, including the following: "Be sure you have all players' eyes on you; eye contact is a must. Ensure every player is listening before you as the coach begin speaking." Years later, as I was developing my coach's philosophy, I remembered Coach Stanley's advice and combined those words with similar advice from dozens of coaches I would play for and coach over the years. The most important consideration is to understand yourself, what motivates you, why you are coaching, identify your style, and what you want to achieve. In addition, prioritizing your values, identifying objectives, understanding your athletes, developing team culture, being respectful and disciplined, and developing your skills was the type of advice I received over the years. But through all of the advice and conversations I've had with coaches, the most significant impact on my coaching philosophy, core values, ethics, and beliefs for guiding my approach to practices and games came from my years of playing basketball in the Snake Pit, Evans High School legendary gym which had no central air conditioning or heating. But Evans teams were virtually unbeatable in the gym well into the 2000s under coaches Fred Pennington, Richard Hulette, Rudy Tapia, and Calvin Lingelbach, combining for a record of 775-234 over thirty-four seasons. The Snake Pit was replaced with a new gym in winter 2021. The new facility has a capacity of 2,100 and has both central air conditioning and heat.

Still, the tradition of excellence and memories of celebration in the Snake Pit will be retold for years to come. And the Trojan basketball tradition will always stand above all other influences in how I go about building a culture in my sports programs. These principles formed the foundation of my coaching philosophy, but I still needed coaching experience in an actual basketball game. The start of the military basketball season would provide that opportunity weeks after I became the coach of the team. I had previously been the star player, and I was presented with a coaching challenge I didn't see coming. The PAFB men's basketball team's first game of the season was a road game at MacDill AFB, in Tampa, FL, against a veteran team with an experienced coach. By contrast, we had a team of new players, many of whom were competing in their first Armed Forces level competition. Of course, I was not just inexperienced on the bench, it was also my very first game as a coach. The game was 'sloppy,' with both basketball teams showing inexperience at the start; the players were careless and lazy with the ball, leading to turnovers, needless fouls, and slow gameplay. Both teams had multiple offensive possessions without attempting a single shot, losing possession of the ball repeatedly. We turned the ball over twelve times in the first half, and MacDill's team wasn't much better at protecting the basketball. In the second half, I made a lineup change, substituting two reserve guards—both talented but inexperienced—to change the game's momentum by bringing fresh legs, energy, and hustle to our offense. The discussion to make a change wasn't received well by the two players who were relegated to the bench at the start of the second half of the game. I had hoped the players would take the opportunity on the bench to observe the game and take notes of the opposition's defensive weaknesses, offensive threats, and what we could exploit to our advantage. Instead, they both just sat on the bench pouting. The two reserve players didn't play badly, certainly not as bad as our guard play was in the first half of the game. But to my astonishment, just five minutes into the second half, one of the players who didn't start the second half got up off of the bench and walked towards the scorer's table to 'self-check' himself into the game! I shouted at him to get back to the bench. As I watched him slowly walk back and sit at the end of the bench, I thought this was my first time dealing with a player who challenged my authority as a new coach. I didn't take it personally, but I knew I needed to clarify players' roles and responsibilities better to help players understand their roles as teammates.

As the game continued, we never got closer than six points, and I began my coaching career with a loss! Post-game locker room meetings erupted into shouting between players and, eventually, between players and coaches. When cooler heads finally prevailed, we all had a long conversation about what had happened. Several players thought I was substituting players fairly, and others thought I was showing preferential treatment to one group of players over another group. The bottom line was that the players on the team didn't view me as a coach, but another player telling them what to do or not do. If I were going to be successful, I would need to change that perception. Because I was a recent teammate of most of the team, accepting me now as a coach required me to set some boundaries. First, as the team's new coach, I was willing to earn the players' respect as a coach by being professional, organized, on time, and using a consistent and reasonable approach. Once mutual respect is established, players are less likely to challenge the coach's authority.

The goal was to have players not see me as one of their peers or a former player, but as a coach who should be respected. To achieve this goal, I decided to spend more time being a coach than as another player at the gym. I would volunteer to coach youth basketball at the military base's youth center, host and work at different youth basketball camps, and attend as many basketball coaching clinics as I could fit into my schedule. The increase in coaching enhanced my understanding of the court with effective communication and anticipation of player movements as I learned new teaching methods for some of the top coaching from high school and college programs around the country. The first coaching clinic I attended was held in Jacksonville, Florida, and was attended by more than 150 coaches nationwide. The camp's headline coach was University of Florida men's basketball head coach Billy Donovan, a two-time NCAA Champion, and three-time SEC Coach of the Year. Coach Donovan's presentation focused on building up the Gator's offensive and defensive styles of play. His attention to detail in developing his team's offensive set and defensive rotations was indelible. He provided a detailed practice plan with breakout drills for a set of three practices; below is an excerpt from the All-Access Florida Basketball Practice with Billy Donovan DVD set:

Practice 1

- Includes drills that work on closing out and on one-on-one perimeter defense from a variety of locations.
- Set plays to initiate the Spread Pick and Roll that will create motion in the defense and take away help, putting the defense in disadvantageous situations early in the possession.
- Drills for converting defensive rebounds into transition offense.

As Coach Donovan prepares his players for their first exhibition game, he does a lot of teaching and building up their style of play. He demonstrates the various offensive actions that lead to their motion high offense and their spread pick and roll action. He starts with five-person offensive drills (actions). This 5-on-0 situation has the team running through various actions for each player, beginning with the big men in the post through a pick and roll followed by a double screen. After going through their set plays and motion offense, Donovan builds his defensive style with a driving line drill. His defense continuously works on closeouts and squaring up on the ball to contain dribble penetration. Donovan moves to transition drills that combine getting back in transition and disrupting the fast break.

The second half of practice focuses on the offensive end. He uses a Circle the Wagon Drill to train his players to get the ball into the post to score. He wants to take advantage of his post players scoring opportunities and establish an inside presence that will lead to open shots on the perimeter.

The practice ends with a full-court press attack. Donovan emphasizes the importance of getting into the press right after a bucket is scored and sprinting back when the press is broken.

Practice 2

- Learn transition drills to improve passing and scoring in advantage situations.
- Use the Gator Scramble Drills to train your team to recover on defense in a scramble situation.
- Learn how to use scrimmages to determine how sound players are translating practice skills into game situations.

Coach Donovan spends much time during the second practice going 4-on-4 or 5-on-5. He runs a 4-on-4 shell defense to create competition, run offensive plays and sets, and teach his players how to defend the screening actions they will see.

He builds his players' help-side defense using a Scramble Drill that teaches his defenders to protect the basket when a defender gambles for a steal or is beaten off the dribble from the wing. Players learn how to stunt and get back to their man while also learning how to read the offense and take charge.

In 5-on-5 situations, Donovan uses end-of-game transition posting to teach his players how to get the ball into the post off a transition set or a secondary break opportunity. In this setting, the focus is on the post, but he still wants his players to understand that they need to create without forcing off the spread pick and roll offense.

Coach Donovan finishes his second practice by working on the defensive end of the floor. He practices falling back into several defensive alignments, including a 2-3 zone defense and an aggressive pressuring man-to-man defense.

Practice 3

- Learn to use a shell defense to work on different actions from different types of offenses.
- Use game-like drills to develop your post players.
- Beat defensive overplays by running the "floppy action" set and counters.

Donovan continues to emphasize defensive principles. He teaches his players how to defend various offensive actions, such as the UCLA and Flex Offense, and protect different screening actions from every floor angle.

Coach Donovan finishes with a great post player/guard breakdown drill set that fits right into his offensive tactics. With these great breakdown options, you will have your guards and post players working together and on the same page. He ends the practice with "Circle the Wagons Live," which takes the transitions lessons and puts them in-game context in a controlled scrimmage.1 (1. Source: Championship Production Author: Billy Donovan.)

Coach Donovan's practice plans are not necessarily an endorsement of his Spread Pick and Roll or Motion High Offenses, but more as a helpful model to break down a program-specific practice for any system a coach uses. I like the tenets of the five-out motion offense, particularly for youth basketball players, as the offense is "position-less" and has all five players executing basic movements and floor spacing. This allows all players on the team to develop their ball-handling and court awareness skills, leading to well-rounded basketball players. An added benefit of the motion offense is that it allows the coach to teach fundamentals while working on the team offense simultaneously, making for efficient use of practice time…and the offense helps players learn how to play. This is especially helpful at the youth basketball level because coaches get an opportunity to see players improve rapidly as those young basketball players are at the beginning stages of learning the game. Because most military bases usually only have one facility dedicated to youth athletics (Youth Center), for those athletes aged 6-13, both the boys' and girls' youth basketball teams are required to share the basketball courts, usually a single full-court gym. This results in having limited practice time on the court and increasing the importance of coaches maximizing the limited practice time they have with players.

Nevertheless, working with youth basketball players in camps, clinics, and leagues became a passion I would continue being involved with for over twenty years.

The next step, and perfect opportunity in my coaching development, came about during a friendly conversation after playing pickup basketball games at the base gym. One of the young ladies, KC, who regularly played pickup basketball at the base gym with the guys, asked me if I had a few minutes to talk. She had recently been hired as the new head women's basketball coach at the local community college, Brevard Community College (now Eastern Florida State College). KC spoke for several hours about her new head coach role, returning to coach at her former college, where she played point guard for the winning small college program for two years.

She was honest and direct, asking if I would be interested in being her assistant coach, tasked with developing an offensive system for a young team with only two returning players. The Lady Titans program achieved moderate success and established a good tradition under the previous coach, completing four consecutive winning seasons, winning multiple Central Conference Championships, and participating in the NJCAA Region VIII State Championship Tournament. So, KC was taking her first coaching job with the added pressure of replacing a coach who'd achieved respectable success with the program and the expectation that the next coach would surpass the previous accomplishments. After a few days of thinking about the positives and negatives of Coach KC's offer, I accepted the offer to become the team's lead assistant coach on her staff for the women's basketball team.

The tremendous opportunity to coach on a higher level was too good to pass on, and I would have another chance to help develop young players on and off the basketball court. Although there were some drawbacks to taking the position, the pros outweighed the cons. What made me reluctant to accept the job and caused me the most concern was that I had never coached girls or women's basketball before and college-age athletes. The physical differences between genders are much greater. The structure of the game was similar for both, but the speed and athleticism were vastly different. Also, the female players used a slightly smaller basketball, 28.5in (size 6) for women and 29.5in (size 7) for men. The college men and women played two twenty-minute halves of basketball, though this was changed before the 2015-16 basketball season. The National Collegiate Athletic Association (NCAA) and National Junior College Athletic Association (NJCAA) Oversight Committee approved a rule change, switching the women's game from two twenty-minute halves to four ten-minute quarters. The proposed rule change was intended to improve the flow of the game by reducing timeouts and free throw attempts, plus the expectation of a faster-paced game resulting in teams scoring more points. I was excited about the new opportunity I was offered and looked forward to my role as assistant women's basketball coach, using my experience and skills in this unfamiliar position to see what I could achieve.

After deciding to accept the college coaching job, the next weekend was my scheduled visit with my brother William. I couldn't wait to share the news with him. On Saturday, I left my house in the wee hours of the morning for a nearly 2.5-hour drive from Melbourne to the Avon Park Correctional Institution—a drive that lasted longer than my actual visit with my brother. Upon arrival at the correctional institution, the security procedures prior to visitation included presenting a government-issued photo ID, walking through metal detectors, and having my person searched to ensure I did not have any prohibited items (keychains, tobacco, lighters, large bills of money, and personal gifts for the inmate) before being allowed to interact with the inmates. Certain clothing is also prohibited, including attire resembling facility staff or inmate uniforms, offensive graphics or language, and revealing or tight clothing. In addition, the visitors and inmates' behavior are closely monitored during the visit. Any inappropriate conduct, loud or disruptive behavior, inappropriate physical contact, or not following the instructions of the facility staff at all times, could result in the visitation being canceled and future visitation rights being suspended. After a decade apart, seeing my brother in a prison setting was an emotionally complex experience, filled with a mix of feelings like relief at seeing him again, sadness about the lost time, curiosity about how he's changed, and some apprehension about the prison environment itself. We both significantly changed our appearance due to aging and the prison environment. Each of us had gained significant weight from days when I was a 150-pound college freshman, and he was maybe fifteen pounds heavier than me.

However, the two most notable differences were that neither of us had hair on our heads, and his skin tone appeared much darker. I didn't ask if he had shaved his head due to stress, hair loss from male pattern baldness, or, like myself, done so because basketball icon Michael Jordan had made bald heads cool, especially among basketball players. Many see a shaved head as a self-confident act.

GQ (Gentlemen's Quarterly) magazine once described Jordan's bald head as making him look like a hairless Hercules, a superman with a noble plate. As for his skin color appearing darker, I didn't know if his skin tone was darker or if my mind didn't accurately recall his darker skin tone. But it's commonly believed that prisoners' skin color may appear darker during incarceration due to a combination of factors, including limited sun exposure, poor diet, lack of exercise, and stress, which can all contribute to increased melanin production in the skin, leading to a darkening effect, particularly noticeable in individuals with darker skin tones; this phenomenon is often linked to the concept of "colorism" within the criminal justice system, where darker skin tones can be perceived more negatively and may even lead to harsher punishments.

As our visit ended, we had spent the entire visitation catching up on life events, asking about his experiences in prison, and talking about basketball inside and outside of prison. After spending years in prison, I still looked up to my big brother. Our bond was no longer as strong, but I was still hoping that he would redeem himself and start his life over after being released; however, the experience of incarceration can create complexities that might affect the dynamic of your sibling bond, requiring open communication and understanding to rebuild trust.

William and I embraced and sat on one of the benches inside the visitation area before entering the yard and walking around the fence line area for a private conversation. I told him I had accepted a new coaching position as a women's college basketball coach. He was excited for me: "Tan, I like watching women's college basketball. We watched the Tennessee team play this week, and that girl, Chamique Holdsclaw, can play! And they can shoot the ball better than a lot of the men college players." I laughed and told him we did not have anyone near the level of Holdsclaw or the other tremendous players on the Tennessee roster. Still, we had young ladies who were passionate about the game and eager to play college basketball. "Tan, boy, you better keep me updated on how the team is doing when y'all start playing games." I promised him that I would regularly update him with the team's progress. Then, out of nowhere, he got excited, as if he remembered something significant. "Oh man, Tan, boy, I almost forgot to tell you. We are getting our basketball team here at Avon Park. The public information officer for the prison system told us the news last week." The public information officer had noticed how important playing basketball was to many inmates. To many of them, including my brother, playing basketball was more than a game. William explained how he and other inmates had been reading the local newspaper and sports section. He had noticed an article from a staff writer who had interviewed the prison facility's recreation director, who described the plans for starting a basketball team.

In the article the recreation director said, "Sometimes a basketball isn't just a basketball. An inmate learns valuable lessons playing a game with a team—how to practice, show up, accept responsibility, humility, to accept guidelines and rules and to accept the objective authority of a coach and on and on." The director told the staff writer that several state universities had donated more than two dozen basketballs and other sports equipment. Because Florida State law prohibits most direct donations to prisons, the basketballs and other equipment had to be directed to the Corrections Foundation, a nonprofit direct support organization for the Department of Corrections managed by a former prison secretary. The same laws also prohibit any sum of the prison budget from being used on leisure or hobby items for the inmates. At one time, faith-based groups and local groups in the communities near the prisons would send a few items to prisons but never enough basketballs or other sports equipment to keep hundreds of inmate basketball players engaged.

William was overly excited about the news and shared that he would transition into coaching the prison team after playing for the team during its first season. He previously shared with me in one of his letters that he had hoped to become a high school basketball coach one day after his playing career. This dream was reignited in his mind when the "Sports as Rehabilitation for Prisoners" program highlighted by the NBA's Golden State Warriors began visiting the San Quentin Prison (2013) in San Quentin, California, to play basketball games against the inmates. This rehabilitation center is one of the leaders in the sports-as-therapy philosophy. The professional players began playing against the inmates because they realized the participation was bettering the inmates' social interaction and making the inmates feel human. The Warriors players have been playing basketball with inmates ever since.

When the horn sounded, indicating the visitation time had ended, William and I felt like we had been talking on the basketball court. It was the best visit I'd had with him in a very long time. As I left, William walked off to check back in. I continued to look back into the yard in hopes of catching a glance of him, and fortunately, I did. I could see him through the prison fence, and he could see me. I heard him say my name, and we both waved goodbye. As I began to turn away, one last lingering glance over my shoulder, a final breath held, then slowly turning away to walk back to the parking lot and my vehicle, leaving the previous image of him waving goodbye in my mind!

Once college classes began and we had our first team meetings, I was excited and a little uncomfortable meeting the players, many of them for the first time. But after a brief introduction, followed by a team meeting, it was time to get to work. As mentioned, the Lady Titans only returned two players. The best player on the team, Robin, was a six-foot wing who was a fantastic athlete with a versatile all-around skill set. She had been chosen as a pre-season all-conference player who lived up to that hype for the team. The other returning player, Kelly, was a 5'8" shooting guard recovering from an MCL injury, requiring her to wear a hinged knee brace with metal or carbon fiber rods on either side of the brace. She was also our team's designated three-point shooter when we needed to make a long-range shot in critical phases of the game. Coach KC believed she would be one hundred percent recovered by the beginning of the season and would be a solid and experienced contributor to the team. The remainder of the roster was made up of first-year freshmen players who had never played in a college basketball game.

I was familiar with two of our freshmen guards, Nuria Butcher and Shawnta Price, both local high school players who routinely played basketball at the military base gym with the guys. They were both very competitive players who allowed themselves to be coached, made eye contact, listened, and welcomed coaching in an effort to be better basketball players. I was less familiar with the other players on the team, but they were all very coachable and respectable former high school players. However, none of the players on the team were top basketball recruits, and the team had only one player taller than six feet. We would have to realize fundamentals and have high basketball IQs if our student-athletes were going to have a successful season. Our lack of height and strength was glaring as the average female center in college basketball is usually six-foot-five while guards are typically five-foot-eight. Only our all-conference guard-forward, Robin, measured at the college-level average height of six feet, for her position. But even with our young team's limited physical size and strength, the lack of experience was our biggest impediment to having a successful season—not only the players but also two first-time college coaches. Our first fears came to pass: the team won only two games all season and had significant problems scoring against defenders at the college level. But to the ladies' credit, they played hard throughout the entire season, even while many lost more games in that single season than in their entire high school careers. At the end of the season, it was apparent changes needed to be made. KC and I discussed the players on the roster, the fact we were losing our best player, and what recruits we needed to bring for the next season to be successful. We discussed strategies to attend summer camps and showcases, looking for players with the skills that would improve our team for the upcoming season, and decided that in addition to attending camps, we would reach out to coaches by email or phone to express interest in their program and specific players.

KC and I also agreed that I would be the lead recruiter for three schools in particular, two in Orlando, Evans and Jones High Schools, and Astronaut High School, located in Titusville, Florida. All three schools were perennial powerhouse girls' basketball teams and boosted some of the best female basketball talent in the Central Florida area. The trio of teams had a total of four players, two wing players, and two combined guards, whom we had identified as the key to our recruiting class. After weeks of calling the players' coaches and visiting with the players, attending some of their final high school games, I was successful in getting three of the four players to agree to a college visit and participate in a summer workout with returning players (this workout including drills, 3-on-3 and 5-on-5 basketball games). After the workout ended and all the players had gone home, KC and I sat in the gymnasium and talked about the excitement that was on display in the gym and the potential impact these recruits could have on next year's team. But the pending resignation as the team's head basketball coach should have been discussed and caught me by complete surprise. The Monday following our weekend workout, I arrived at the school at my regular time, looked into the gym to see if any players were doing skill work, and walked towards the coaches' offices. KC walked out of Don Smith's office, the college's Athletics Director (AD) and head boys' basketball coach; just as I was about to enter the colored double glass doors to the coach's office, she immediately called out me, "Hey, Rob, let me speak to you for a minute." I smiled and started walking towards her, anticipating she was about to tell me Don's approval of our recruiting event; she shocked me instead: "Rob, I wanted to be the first person to tell you that he resigned today and will not be returning as the team's coach next season." When a head coach resigns, the impact on the assistant coach or coaches can range from increased responsibilities to the loss of their jobs. But, once word of the coach's pending departure is communicated, it can quickly spread around the campus, including to student-athletes and the media. To control the accuracy of communication, a plan was developed to inform the team's current players, potential recruits, and the local news media.

Coach KC's husband, a military member, had received an order (military change duty location) to another military base requiring the family to relocate to South Florida. We met with all the players on the team, and they each thanked Coach KC for giving them an opportunity to play college basketball, and for her leadership, and for being a mentor. Although KC recommended me to be her replacement, due to other circumstances, another head coach was hired, and my first season of coaching women's college basketball was also my last. But it was not the last college basketball game I would coach. After a year away, I returned to the sideline at Brevard Community College as the men's assistant basketball coach. Brevard Community College's Athletic Director/Head Men's Basketball Coach, Don Smith, called me unexpectedly in what I thought was an afternoon phone call of small talk. What he had in mind was to ask if I was available and willing to accept an offer to be his top assistant coach for what he believed was the most talented college team he had in his fifteen years at the school. I didn't need to think about it, I agreed immediately, as I desperately wanted to get back into coaching college basketball. But I did have one demand: in exchange for accepting the coaching job, I wanted a paid membership to both the National Association of Basketball Coaches (NABC) and the Black Coaches Association (BCA), including attendance to both of the organization's annual conventions each year with the college paying for all of the expenses. The BCA, formed in 1988, has been steadfast in improving the employment opportunities and professional development of minority coaches at the college level.

In addition to releasing reports on minority coaching hires, the organization hosts several career development events for minority coaches, including its annual convention. Coach Smith agreed to my request and thought it was a great idea. So, I decided to continue my professional development by attending events that enhance a coach's understanding of Xs and Os, leadership, ethics, and the critical issues impacting the game.

A Weekend in Dallas at the BCA

After finalizing travel arrangements for a round-trip flight to Dallas Fort Worth International Airport, I booked my hotel and rental car reservations. All that remained was to pack my luggage and call and check in with the other coaches and friends attending the convention. As a second year NJCAA basketball coach, I was attending my first Black Coaches Association (BCA) National Convention and was unfamiliar with the convention agenda filled with meetings, breakout sessions, coaches' clinics, and an annual banquet. Since the convention was being hosted within the 'Big D,' Dallas, Texas, I was hoping to do some extra activities in the city, including exploring the Dallas Arts District, African American Museum, Tenth Street Historic District, Freedmans Town, and the Texas Black Invitational Rodeo which features black cowboys and cowgirls competing in bull riding, calf and steer roping, and barrel racing. I was looking forward to exploring as much of Dallas as I could. The BCA was formed in 1988 with the primary purpose of "fostering the growth and development of ethnic minorities at all levels of sports, both nationally and internationally." The group's leadership included such college basketball heavyweights such as Georgetown University John Thompson who built the Hoyas into a perennial powerhouse; the University of Arkansas Razorbacks Nolan Richardson, who's famed 'forty minutes of hell' pressure defense was ranking havoc on the college basketball world; and, George Raveling, a three-time Pac-10 Conference Coach of the Year, who won the award at three different universities. As a young coach, I was beyond excited about attending the event. The BCA had made some positive things happen for minority coaches around college basketball, and being a member would increase my opportunity to advance my career in the profession. The BCA event featured a coaches' welcome luncheon, on-court demonstrations, coaching clinics, committee meetings, coaches' social, cocktail hours for networking, and a Black-tie formal dinner.

I looked forward to attending all the seminars, workshops, and meetings scheduled for the convention, but I didn't want to attend the Black-tie dinner alone. I didn't know who I could invite who would accept my invitation on such short notice and who would enjoy spending hours at a basketball coaches' conference for an entire weekend. One person came to mind immediately: Paolina. She was very intelligent and elegant, loved basketball, and had this unique ability to take an otherwise meaningless conversation and transform it into an unforgettable moment of chitter-chatter. We had met nearly a decade earlier, and through shared beliefs and experiences, a strong feeling of friendship formed. Our bond connected through military service, a love for basketball, and African American theatre, and our secret fascination with reading erotic stories by Zane. Paolina would be the perfect companion for the weekend. Although we lived in different parts of the United States—she was on the West Coast, and I was on the East Coast—we regularly talked over the phone through the years, visiting each other on occasion and constantly supporting my basketball career. A late request to fly out to Dallas on my dime was no different; she accepted the invitation and would join me at the BCA convention in Dallas.

I arrived at the Dallas/Fort Worth International Airport on a busy Thursday morning. The airport was overcrowded as usual (DFW is ranked the world's third busiest airport), with its five terminals and more than 160 gates, creating long-distance walks and puzzled passengers hurrying through the unfamiliar terminals. I eventually found my flight's baggage claim area, collected my luggage, and headed to the car rental to pick up my rental vehicle. I had several hours before Paolina's flight arrived, so I rushed to check into the hotel where I now had reservations for two rooms, picked up my coach's pre-registration package, and headed down to the coach's social gathering in the hotel lobby.

One of the first coaches I encountered in the lobby was the University of Miami's first-year head coach, Perry Clark. Coach Clark would become the only Hurricanes coach to take the team to the postseason in each of his first two seasons. Clark's second season would see his Canes set a school record for wins. All those accomplishments were impressive. Coach Perry welcomed me as I introduced myself to him and reminded him that we had previously met. He greeted me enthusiastically saying, "Hey, Coach, great to see you again. What do you guys look like for next season?" I responded respectfully, "Coach Clark, nice to see you. We have an experienced and very talented group, potentially could be the most successful team in school history, with championship aspirations." Coach Clark smiled and responded, "Coach, all successful teams that I've ever seen have three characteristics: they play unselfish, they play together, and they play hard." I maintained eye contact and said, "Coach, this team checks all those boxes." He tilted his head, then nodded in agreement, before responding, "Okay, I'm looking forward to seeing how you guys do this year; good luck." I thanked him and continued walking through the hotel lobby. Various basketball coaches and athletic directors were walking through the lobby, equipment exhibits, team uniform manufacturers, and coaching training aid demonstration of the ample floor space.

I made a mental note of what exhibits I wanted to come back to visit later. It was time to drive to the airport to pick up Paolina as her flight would be landing within the hour, and with the myriad of interstate highways, maneuvering the rush hour traffic would take patience to get to the airport before her flight arrived. I arrived at the DFW arriving flights curbside about five minutes after Paolina's flight had landed, hoping she wasn't already waiting for me. As I parked at the curbside, she emerged from the terminal wearing a white button-down top and blue jeans. Her hair was flawless, and her shade perfectly flattered her almond skin tone. As she gracefully walked out of the baggage claim doors, I called out to get her attention. She waved and smiled as we greeted one another with a hug. I grabbed her luggage and placed it in the rental car's trunk, and we drove away, heading back to the hotel. Paolina and I talked as if we had just seen one another a day ago; we never seemed to lose our connection, no matter how long it had been since we last saw one another. Once we arrived back at the hotel, as we walked through the hallway of the hotel lobby, I pointed out the exhibit with its vendors for the weekend basketball event, and I handed her the room key and told her unfortunately, our hotel rooms were on different floors. She responded with, "What's up with that, man? You couldn't get us a suite with two beds?" I laughed before I replied, "No, not at that last minute; I was lucky that I was able to get you a room in the same hotel." She smiled and said that I screwed up by waiting until the last minute to invite her and make the travel plans: "Man, you messed this up. Your business trip planning skills need work." I agreed with her! We laughed and walked over to the elevators. After getting Paolina into her room, I told her I was heading back down to the lobby. She said that she was going to take some time to freshen up and would meet me in the lobby for dinner. We decided to have dinner at one of the area's Italian restaurants. We had a great conversation then headed back to the hotel. As we returned to the hotel and walked towards the elevators, our small talk was around the BCA breakout sessions scheduled at 8:00 a.m. Paolina was quite clear: "Do not wake me that early." I laughed and said, "I will not. I'll check in with you after the morning sessions go on a break." She nodded, smiled slightly, and said, "thank you."

I was so exhausted from the excitement of the day. After getting out of the shower, I don't remember anything after my head hit my pillow, well other than the buzzing sound like a bee with laryngitis awaking me in what seemed like ten minutes after I fell asleep. I had a full day attending breakout sessions, including the first scheduled "Professional Development Series" (PDS) clinic, a continuing education program designed for coaches of all levels, with topics such as leadership, ethics, and Xs and Os. NABC and BCA required coaches to attend at least five clinics to become NABC PDS certified. The first day's full schedule included the following types of events:

Day 1(Friday)

- 8:30 a.m.: Professional Development Series Clinics
- 11:00 a.m.: NABC & BCA Executive Committee Meeting
- 11:30 a.m. – 12:00 p.m.: Classroom Clinic – The Current and Future Landscape of Collegiate Athletics
- 12:30 p.m.: NABC & BCA Board of Directors Meeting
- 1:00 p.m.: Marketplace
- 2:00 p.m. – 3:00 p.m.: Classroom Clinic – The Coach's Guide to Student-Athlete Mental Health
- 3:00 p.m. – 4:00 p.m.: Classroom Clinic – Transition Game
- 4:00 p.m. – 5:00 p.m.: Classroom Clinic – First Timers Meeting
- 5:00 p.m. – 6:00 p.m.: Classroom Clinic – Transition Game
- 6:00 p.m. – 7:00 p.m.: On-Court Clinic – Gymnasium TBA

Day 2 of the convention followed a similar pattern: breakout sessions, classroom clinics, and networking opportunities. The days' events were bookended with the annual banquet featuring renowned networking oracle Dr. George C. Fraser as the keynote speaker. Dr.

Fraser is the chairman and CEO of FraserNet, Inc., a company he founded almost thirty years ago with the vision to lead a global networking movement that brings together diverse human resources to increase opportunities for people of African descent. Many considered him to be a new voice for African Americans and one of the foremost authorities on economic development, networking, and building effective relationships. In addition, Dr. Fraser is the mastermind behind the revolutionary Power Networking Conference and stands as a beacon of innovation and empowerment within the African American community. Paolina and I thoroughly enjoyed all the activities of the Black-tie event. We engaged in fascinating conversations with other attendees and debates among us about some topics discussed during the evening. The next day, our final full day in Dallas, we were heading out early for some sightseeing and shopping in the 'Big D,' including a visit to the Art District and a surprising favor event, the Black cowboy/cowgirl rodeo. The next day, we rode back to the airport together, I dropped off the rental car, and we grabbed a quick breakfast before boarding separate flights back to our respective cities. I thanked Paolina again for supporting me and promised to return the favor one day. Once I arrived back in Florida, I called Coach Smith and told him about the trip and that I was ready for the start of the season. He laughed and said, "Robert, I truly believe this may be the best team I've had here." I told him I would remind him of that bold statement at the end of the season, as we both laughed and hung up the telephone.

Coach Worthington's Six Key Points to Positive Communication with Athletes

Two fundamental principles that sports can teach are positivity and healthy communication. Although every coach has their style and method, most agree that positivity and communication are critical for a successful team. I used the following six key points to guide my youth basketball camps, Hoops Drills for Skills Camps, over the years, providing a non-threatening environment for youth of all ages to develop competence in basketball and life skills.

These keys for positivity and communication resonate in any field of play. The coaches who dedicate their lives to teaching young athletes what it means to be a winner on and off the field will benefit from the wise words of a seasoned coach and mentor.

1. **Build trust from day one.** Emphasizes that it's essential for coaches to send the message that they care. It's also crucial that they build confidence from the moment athletes walk into the gym or onto the field, and coaches need to reinforce character building and values, not just the fundamental skills on the basketball court.

2. **Engage players on and off the court**. Coaches should start the season by asking the athletes to describe what they believe are the strongest and weakest parts of their game. Stand or sit with your players during water breaks and engage them in conversation about the workout. Active engagements by coaches can improve communication and create a dynamic relationship between the coach and the athlete. In addition, coaches should design practices and drills that keep starter and non-starter players engaged and focused. Players' development programs can include competitive games, challenging drills, interactive coaching techniques, and summer workouts.

3. **Create an emotional link**. My years of experience have taught me that teams with a shared emotional link always work better. Coaches should be empathetic, understanding, and accepting of their players. They should also be available as tutors or advisors and host events outside the athletic program. If a team has weaknesses, which most do in some way, they can overcome them by working together

and avoiding the pitfalls of negative language. A positive approach is far more effective than yelling profanities at players, although sometimes a more authoritative voice is needed to make a point!

4. **Recognize the power of non-verbal communication**. Not all communication is verbal. Coaches must understand how non-verbal communication, such as eye contact, posture, and body language, can impact athletes. Coaches can convey their attitudes and feelings through their body language. For example, standing tall with shoulders back and making eye contact can help create a positive impression. On the other hand, crossing arms, leaning back, or turning away can signal disinterest or boredom.

5. **Communication is more than just a head coach-player exchange.** All coaches at all levels can foster positive, healthy communication. It's more than just how the head coach talks to players. Coach-coach communication, coach-parent communication, and coach-official communication are all critical—and players observe and notice all of them. Worthington's three keys for engaging with different groups: Be consistent, honest, and straightforward.

6. **Remember why you coach.** There are many reasons why coaches coach, including paying it forward for the people (coaches) who have influenced their lives. Coaches can feel called to support underserved groups of people and be positive role models for their athletes, which can help them develop strong relationships. It's about your passion for being out on the court, the field, or the ice.

9
THE HEART OF A CHAMPION: REFLECTIONS ON THE 2000 BCC MEN'S BASKETBALL TEAM

"The best team we've ever had here." This was the main appeal long-time Brevard Community College (BCC) Head Men's Basketball Coach Don W. Smith made to me when he offered me the position as his top assistant coach for the 1999-2000 men's basketball team. It was a bold statement, but one he felt strongly about. "I tell you, Robert, this is probably the best group we've ever had here," Coach Smith said. "We have size, length, experience, and athleticism; and most importantly, they're a resilient group who trusts one another and appreciates the unique skills of each other." I told Don that I would give his offer sincere consideration and get back to him in a few days, although, in my mind, I already knew I would accept it. I wanted to learn more about the college, the level of competition, and the players for whom Don had such high praise.

I didn't take long to decide; I called Don on the phone later that evening and accepted his offer. Brevard Community College is located in the center of the Florida Space Coast, the home of Kennedy Space Center, a vital part of the United States space program since 1962, and the home port for the retired Space Shuttles Atlantis. In addition, Cape Canaveral, and Patrick Air Force Bases (later renamed Space Force Installations) are also a nature lover's paradise with the white-sand beaches of Cocoa Beach. The college was established in 1960 as Brevard Junior College, but less than three years later, it merged with Carver Junior College. This institution provided educational opportunities to African American residents of Brevard County. The college was renamed Brevard Community College (BCC) in 1970 when the state of Florida established a two-year college system. After the state expanded the mission of many of its community colleges in 2013, providing bachelor's degree programs, the school changed its name once again to Eastern Florida State College (EFSC). But nearly fifteen years before the significant expansion of the school's educational mission, it had the good fortune to have perhaps the best team in school history, or at the very least the most successful team in school history—the 1999-2000 men's basketball team. The team competed in the National Junior College Athletic Association (NJCAA), more commonly known as JUCO. JUCO is particularly beneficial for athletes who want to sharpen their skills and improve their academic standings before attending a four-year university. The harsh reality is that only 6 percent of high school basketball players will play their preferred sport at the NCAA level, resulting in many playing in other leagues, such as the NJCAA and NAIA colleges. The competition format in NJCAA is the same as that of different divisions in the United States. Each college or university team competes in a conference, a league comprising of 6-to-15 local college teams typically within bordering states. During the season, the JUCO schools compete against the other conference members to try to win the conference. The best-performing programs will advance to the regional stage of the NJCAA national tournament (state championship), where they will compete against the best team in the neighboring conferences for the right to compete in the NJCAA national tournament. Winning conference and regional titles are an achievement, but it is the NJCAA national title every JUCO team wants to win.

The national game is prestigious; thus, the competition is fierce as it will contain the best JUCO teams around the United States competing against one another at the Hutchinson Sports Arena in Hutchinson, Kansas. From our very first basketball practice of the season, the goal for the team was to end our season in Hutchinson at the NJCAA Men's National Division I basketball tournament, a singular goal and focus used to unify and inspire the team around a common purpose. Coach Smith's practice plan included players getting their individual work before our one-hour team practice, starting with a routine warm-up of stretching, light jogging, backpedaling, and shuffling before a half-court layup line drill. The rest of the practice schedule included a combination of conditioning, shooting, defensive and offensive set drills, fast break/press defense drills, and special situations drills. Our practice drills were as intense and competitive as any that I had ever been around, and the excitement grew when it was time for our team defense pressure drills. This fifteen-minute block is where we built the foundation for our 3/4 court diamond press. Our 6'6" athletic small forward with a wingspan of a seven-footer made him unstoppable at smothering and forcing the ball handler to the sideline, allowing our trap to occur, and setting up our help defenders rotations.

The typical trapping spots were either just before or after the offensive player crossed the half-court line, and with our length and athleticism at nearly every position, it was devastating in creating turnovers by opposing teams. After our pressure defensive drills, depending on whether or not it was pre-game practice (the day before we played a game) or regular practice, we spent time practicing special situations like sideline and baseline out-of-bounds plays, quick hitters, tip-off plays, free throw plays, and buzzer beater plays. If it was early week practice with no schedule for more than a few days, we added a half-court shooting contest to end practice early and skipped the end of practice conditioning if someone made a half-court basket, usually in less than three attempts. If we were having a pre-game practice, some drills would be replaced with reviewing the opponent's offensive and defensive sets and how we would attack them during the game. We would have our second unit guys run the plays of the opponent, and we'd go through a meticulous breakdown of all the ways to attack their defense with our offensive sets and how to defend against their offensive system.

The final segment of our pre-game practice was usually an intrasquad, starters versus backups, full-court scrimmage. The practice games served primary roles, helping our guys better understand the game strategy for the upcoming game and assisting coaches in determining which reserves players to use in specific matchups at different positions for the game. These intrasquad scrimmages were routine throughout the season. However, as we entered conference play, we changed the routine by scheduling a more structured scrimmage, or more like an exhibition game in a slightly less formal setting than a regular season game. As coaches, we wanted to allow the team to test themselves against different competitors and evaluate players' performance and our game strategy against a top-level team. Therefore, to assess our team's strengths and weaknesses, build team chemistry, and adjust before the official conference games began, we welcomed a national ranked powerhouse program, Vincennes University Trailblazers, to play us at a home gymnasium in an exhibition game with officials and fans in attendance. Vincennes, a junior college out of Indiana, was not only a three-time national champion with thirty-four national championship appearances, more than any other junior college in the nation, but they also held the record for the most consecutive tournament appearances in the modern era of junior college basketball. The team that took the floor against us included the All-American combination of Aaron McGhee and Ronnie Griffin, both outstanding players. It was typical for the Trailblazers to reload with talent year after year. The previous season, the team featured perhaps the best players in school history in their 6'7" two-time All-American Shawn Marion, who was averaging 23.5 points and 13.1 rebounds per game.

Several years later, Marion would be the ninth overall pick in the NBA draft, play in the league for sixteen seasons in the NBA, win an NBA championship, and earn four NBA All-Star game selections. Because both McGhee and Griffin were widely viewed as JUCO "studs" playing with a team regarded as one of the best programs in the country, it was excitedly the type of challenge we wanted for our players and team. Our guys embraced the challenge and showed no signs of intimidation at the prospect of facing such an accomplished basketball team. A few of our players, led by our unofficial team "enforcer," Marshall Sanders, even arrived at the gym well before game time to scope out the competition. They were eager to see if the Trailblazers' two standout players were as good as advertised so that we could measure ourselves against greatness! The pace of the game was fast and exciting, with each team going on scoring runs to take the lead at different points of the game.

Both teams played with confidence, but in the end, the Vincennes University team made some critical shots in the final minutes of the second half to win the game, 86-81. Although we didn't come out on top, the game provided our players and coaches with the belief that we were as good as any team in the country, and we planned to prove that the next opportunity we got.

Coach Smith called our team a "makeup of a bunch of gym rats with a strong work ethic, great attitude, and good meshing of personalities and willingness to play assigned roles, each unselfish, and that's contagious." His assessment was reasonable. Still, he did leave out that they were a very talented group of basketball players. The team comprised of eight sophomores and seven first-year student-athletes with great length, athleticism, and experience, as well as outstanding shooters, defenders, and two solid point guards. But the cornerstone of the team was the talent, leadership, and competitiveness of the team's three best players: 6'6" small forward Norman Cain, whose length and speed allowed him to move quickly and change directions swiftly to attack and defend every inch of the basketball court; 6'3" shooting guard, Joe Gordon, a smooth, free-flowing sharpshooter whose consistent accurate shooting was nearly unstoppable at times; and, 6'6" power forward, Marshall Sanders, whose athleticism and strength allowed him to rip through taller defenders on offense as a reliable double-figure scorer. And an impactful defensive disruptor as a tenacious rim protector with timely momentum-changing 'rejections' (defensive block shots), seemingly out of nowhere. Sanders' unique strength and athleticism allowed him to 'front the post,' a defensive technique where a defender stands between the post player and the perimeter player with the ball in a way that disrupts the low post effectiveness of the opposing team's post players. In fronting the post, it minimizes the number of inside post passes and, as a result, limits the number of offensive touches and shots in the low post area.

The other two starters were two former high school teammates, 6'0" point guard Andre Jenkins, a coach on the floor, who was a quick ball-handler who used a pass-fake shot-fake to set excellent passing lanes and had the ability to change direction fast to guard and press the other team's ball handlers; and 6'2" combo-guard, Andre McFall, a scrappy high energy player, who was a pesky defender who usually guarded the opponent's best perimeter scorer. Freshmen Michael Phenizee, a 6'8" post player who was a force within the key on both ends of the court; and 5'11" point-guard, Bobby Ferrer, who had won a state championship in high school, provided the team with another ball handler and distributed the ball to teammates, with the added benefit of leadership and championship attitude. Other key role players for the team included 6'4" multiple positions player Marvis Christian, who could adapt to different game situations and excel in various skills; 6'2" tweener Sam Santiago, our team's "utility player," who could play wherever he was needed based on matchups, injuries, or player hot streaks; and, 6'8" low-post power forward, Brian Donlon, who played a crucial role in helping us defend the low post, an essential part of our team's defensive scheme. The remaining players on the roster, Tim Phillips, Joe Cowen, Oviedo Gonzalez, Phil Puckett, and Michael Butler, all saw game action throughout the season, and even in limited action, they remained engaged and answered the call whenever their number was called to enter the game.

The 1999-2000 Brevard Community College men's basketball team was a juggernaut by nearly every measurement. We did not lose a game in the Southern Conference, compiling a record of twelve wins and zero losses, with most of the victories by double-digit margins, becoming the first team in conference history to complete a perfect record (12-0). As the Southern Conference champions, we qualified for the NJCAA Region VIII State Tournament (Florida Junior College Basketball Championships) in Marianna, Florida. The final practice before boarding the charter buses for the seven-hour bus ride to the Florida Panhandle was when Coach Smith held a pep talk with them. As we gathered around the centerline of the court, he recanted a conversation with a sportswriter from the area and someone who had seen all of the best JUCO basketball teams in the state play that season. Coach Smith said that the sportswriter had told him he believed we were the best team in the state! Don continued, "So, if he's seen everyone play and thinks we are best, then let's go win a state championship!" The players erupted in cheers and applause, and we were confident that we would be the winners when the tournament was complete! We went on to defeat three nationally ranked teams during the week, culminating with victory in the title game over the state's number one ranked team and 1995 NJCAA National Champions, Okaloosa-Walton Community College, in a win of 66-62. Winning the NJCAA Region VIII State Basketball Championship title allowed us to advance to the NJCAA Division I National Basketball Championship Tournament in Hutchinson, Kansas for the second time in school history. After the team traveled back home to our college campus, after all of the hugs and congratulatory slaps on the back had ended, and nearly everyone had gone home, I walked out of the office door and reflected on the journey. I thought of the tremendous pressure, the hours of hard work, the moments of on-court brilliance, winning the state championship, something I had dreamed about for decades.... Still, I felt empty as I walked toward my vehicle. I needed to share this moment with my brother, William, this state championship victory was the culmination of a dream we shared together since we were kids! Next up was the chance to compete for a national championship in Hutchinson, Kansas.

NJCAA Division I Men's Basketball Championship

By the spring of 2000, we were on our way to play for a national championship, excitedly where we thought we would be, preparing for a trip to participate in NJCAA Men's Division I Basketball Championships scheduled to be hosted at the Hutchinson Sports Arena in Hutchinson, KS. We checked off our team goal checklist two of the three primary goals we set to achieve at the beginning of the season: first was to win our conference championship; second, to win the state championship; and third, to play for a national championship in Hutchinson, a location with which I was not familiar. Our theme for the season was "Vision and Faith on The Road to A Championship!" Hutchinson, Kansas first hosted the NJCAA National Championship in 1949 and has hosted the championship tournament ever since. The format has changed many times throughout its history, and until 2013, it was a false double-elimination tournament. The event was a single elimination and consisted of twenty-three games over six days. The NJCAA had only one division for men's basketball until the 1986–87 season when division 2 was added. A third non-scholarship division was formed, starting with the 1990 tournament. The NJCAA is divided into twenty-four regions that form sixteen districts. The sixteen District Champions receive automatic berths in the National Championship, and eight at-large bids are extended. This format has been in effect since the 2017 Championship. More than 200 NJCAA Division I men's basketball teams each year target the ultimate prize—a trip to Hutchinson, Kansas, and an opportunity to compete for a national championship.

Following our flight arrival at the airport in Hutchinson, Kansas, about fifteen hundred miles from Cocoa, Florida, we had several chartered buses waiting to take us to our hotel before a late evening workout in preparation for our first-round championship game.

We were met at the hotel by our assigned team host. Each team has a primary contact for activity coordination and assistance, including scheduling practice sessions, both before and during the championship tournament week. In addition, as coaches, we were tasked with reviewing prior to submitting the official team roster and picking up team party coaches, players, cheerleaders, team manager, and academy advisor admission badges before game day. The team host also accompanied us to the Sports Arena, and our first team practice was scheduled at an off-site practice facility, memorable because of its old-time red brick walls and white metal backboards.

All practices had to be scheduled through our Team Host, and official NJCAA basketballs were required for all practice sessions. Teams were not allowed to bring their basketballs to the Sports Arena. After practice, we returned to our hotel. Then after a short team meeting, players were given the remainder of the afternoon to rest or hang out before everyone met in the hotel lobby at 5:30 p.m. for team dinner that was scheduled for 6:30 p.m. The team returned to the hotel just before 10:00 p.m., which was the time Coach Smith had destinated as the team curfew for all players to be in their rooms for the night.

We had scheduled a meeting the following morning at 8:30 a.m. before leaving for the Sports Arena at 10:00 a.m. for our first-round game at 12:15 p.m. Coach Smith and I discussed the next day's plans, and he asked me to make sure players' room checks began one hour after curfew and for every other hour for four hours after curfew (until 3:00 a.m.). The players' room checks began at approximately 11:30 p.m. Our team's academic advisor, Annie Hannah-Khan, accompanied me to every room because we also had to perform room checks for the cheerleader squad. Each of us stood at the door as the other went inside the hotel room. I would enter the rooms of the players, and Mrs. Khan would enter the rooms of the cheerleaders; it was pretty routine for the first two rotations of checks. But the next set of room checks was anything but routine. We walked through hotel hallways casually talking as we approached the next room, this one being for the cheerleaders.

I stopped at the door and leaned back against the wall as Mrs. Khan knocked on the door and entered the room. I don't recall how long Mrs. Khan was inside the room, but I noticed it was longer than previous room checks had taken. At that moment, she stuck her head out of the room and said, "Coach Worthington, one of your players is hiding in the bathroom shower [of the cheerleader's hotel room]." I didn't immediately respond; I had to let it sink in a moment. Then I said, "What, who, which one, who the hell is hiding in the shower?" As I began to walk into the room, Mrs. Khan stopped me, raising her arm with her palm towards me and all five fingers, before whispering, "Coach, she needs to put some clothes on." I yelled at my player while still standing outside of the room, "You better come out of that damn shower!" Mrs. Khan laughed and walked out of the room into the hallway, slightly holding the door open, whispering, "Coach, he said that he can't come out of the bathroom because he left his clothes on the floor near the bed." I looked at Mrs. Khan with my raised eyebrows and eyes widened. "I can't believe this shit; we're playing for a championship tomorrow." Mrs. Khan and I stayed just outside the room door as my player came out of hiding and retrieved his clothes before getting dressed and exiting the room. I don't remember even completing the remaining checks of player rooms. It was nearly 3:00 a.m., and we were about to play the most significant game we had ever played in less than twelve hours.

My morning alarm was blaring in what seemed like a blink of an eye. It was time to get out of bed and start preparing for our first national tournament game. Still, first, I needed to brief Coach Smith about what happened with one of our key players, and make sure that our team manager, Kimo, had checked that all of the players' uniforms and equipment were packed and loaded on the team bus, and that we had a meeting set up for our players/coaches. The next stop was Coach Smith's room to inform him about the unfortunate violation of team rules the night before the season's biggest game. After a brief discussion about the matter, Coach Smith decided that the breach of team rules, even by a superstar player, warranted a punishment that any other player on the team would receive. We continued to speak about how rules and consequences should be applied consistently to all players, regardless of their status as superstars. Although we were about to play a crucial game, we decided to sit our starting big, a critical key player for team success, for the first half.

While winning the upcoming game was of great importance, the long-term impact of the decisions on the team's culture, values, and reputation was the ultimate reason for the decision. Upholding ethical standards and promoting a culture of accountability and fairness can contribute not only to the team's success in the long run but also to the player accepting responsibility for his actions, allowing him to grow as a player and young man from the experience. During our pre-game meeting, the pep talk was short, and the team was informed about the decision to change the starting line-up and focus on the mental preparation to play their best game. Next, we reviewed the timeout rules—media timeouts and team timeouts. There were four media timeouts, at the first dead ball under 16 minutes, 12 minutes, 8 minutes, and 4 minutes in each half. When a timeout is granted or charged, or the officials elect to use instant replay and either create a dead ball with thirty seconds or less before the media marks or create the first dead ball at or after one of the 16-, 12-, 8-, and 4-minute marks, that timeout or the dead ball will become the electronic-media timeout for that specified media mark time. As for team timeouts, there were three thirty-second timeouts for each team per regulation game.

Teams may carry up to two thirty-second timeouts into the second half; one sixty-second timeout for each team per regulation game that may be used at any time during the game. Finally, each team shall be entitled to one additional thirty-second timeout during each extra period in addition to any unused timeouts it has not used previously. The players sat quietly, listening intently to every word. Finally, Coach Smith ended the meeting with, "Now, let's go win this game!"…the players erupted, clapping their hands and shouting, "We got this!" It was time to board the bus for the short drive to the Sports Arena.

Once we arrived, all teams were required to enter the facility through the Northwest side of the Hutchinson Sports Arena at the designated entrance gate. The locker rooms for the teams are located north of Sam Butterfield Court, where all NJCAA Division I National Championship Tournament games were played. Teams are permitted to use the locker room assigned to them after the conclusion of halftime of the previous game. Once the teams returned to the court, we immediately headed to our locker room. After the games before us, we waited until the official scorekeepers permitted us to enter the main court since rules prohibited teams from taking the main court earlier than thirty minutes prior to their game. Additional warm-up rules were as follows: All games will start at the scheduled time. Each team will be allowed at least fifteen minutes of warm-up time before the first and second-round games start. A minimum of twenty minutes of warm-up time will be allowed for all games. The horn sounded to signal game time. We huddled in regular pre-game gathering, hands raised high, final game instructions, and a final "Titians!" before breaking the huddle and taking the court. From the opening tipoff, we struggled; we turned the ball over several times within the first two minutes of the half, and we seemed to be lacking focus; this was unusual for a team that had been "locked in" all season, being fully attuned and in synch with one another as if reading each other's thoughts, resulting in playing superbly and rarely committing mental errors. But at that moment, being on the big stage with the brightest lights, we were not playing our best game.

At halftime, we talked with the team about turnovers, shot selection, and defensive responsibilities for our low-post defensive rotation. But for various reasons, our play continued to be uneven in the second half, and we lost our first game in the tournament. It was a deflating loss, but one which we had to put behind us and get ready for the next game, scheduled for the next day as the mid-morning game. We bounced back and won our second tournament game as players responded as they had all season by refocusing, correcting the mistakes from the earlier game, and shooting "light out" from the field and free throw line. Our uneven play would return the next day, in game three of the tournament, and we would suffer our second loss in three games, second ending our tournament and season.

After advancing to the NJCAA Division I National Championship Tournament for the first time since 1979, we finished with a disappointing 1-2 record. The ending of the season was especially disheartening because we wholeheartedly wanted and believed we could win a national championship, and we didn't get the job done. But it was undoubtedly a championship team that achieved incredible success that more than twenty years later remained unmatched at school. In addition, our second loss in the NJCAA National Championship tournament proved to be the final game Coach Don Smith would coach. He announced his retirement shortly after the most successful season in school history ended; arguably, the greatest coach in school history decided to hang up his coach's whistle for good. In his final season with Brevard Community College, Smith set a then-program record with twenty-nine wins and his second state tournament championship in the 1999-2000 season.

Overall, Coach Smith finished with 288 wins at Brevard Community College, the second most in school history, a career winning percentage of .610, and averaged more than nineteen wins per season. Coach Smith's success at the college earned him the distinguished honor of being inducted into the Space Coast Sports Hall of Fame. Most of the team would move on as well; our five starters, Cain, Jenkins, McFall, Gordon, and Sanders, all received offers of athletic scholarships at four-year colleges, and several of our reserve players were also offered opportunities to continue playing college basketball at smaller four-year schools. I wondered if I would return or not for another season; not only was the college looking for a new men's basketball head coach, but also a new athletic director who would oversee the hiring of a new coach. The college decided to promote the school's baseball coach, Andy Russo, as the new athletic director and hired former Florida A&M (FAMU) men's basketball coach and future hall of fame inductee (2017) Ajac Triplett as the basketball team's next head coach. After meeting with Coach Triplett, to discuss my role, strategies, and player development ideas, we agreed I would return as his lead assistant coach. But replicating the success and talent of the 1999-2000 team would be a very tough task, even if you replaced one hall-of-fame coach with another!

1999 – 2000 Men's Basketball Team Roster

No.	Name	Position	Year	Hometown
43	Butler, Michael	Guard	Freshmen	Orlando, FL
40	Cain, Norman	Forward	Sophomore	Melbourne, FL
50	Christian, Marvis	Forward	Sophomore	Cocoa, FL
45	Cowen, Joe	Guard	Freshmen	Melbourne, FL
42	Donlon, Brian	Center	Freshmen	Rockledge, FL
15	Ferrer, Bobby	Guard	Freshmen	San Juan, PR
44	Gonzalez, Oviedo	Guard	Freshmen	Melbourne, FL
24	Jenkins, Andre	Guard	Sophomore	Eau Gallie, FL
34	McFall, Andre	Guard	Sophomore	Eau Gallie, FL

No.	Name	Position	Year	Hometown
33	Gordon, Joe	Guard	Sophomore	Palm Bay, FL
55	Phenizee, Michael	Forward	Freshmen	Pittsburgh, PA
14	Phillips, Tim	Guard	Sophomore	Willeton, AU
22	Puckett, Phil	Forward	Freshmen	Lexington, KY
54	Sanders, Marshall	Forward	Sophomore	St. Petersburg, FL
30	Santiago, Samuel	Forward	Sophomore	Stockbridge, GA

Team Accomplishments

- School Record twenty-nine wins in single season; overall 29-7 record
- Southern Conference Record 12-0 (first undefeated season in conference history)
- Won Southern Conference Regular Season Title
- Won NJCAA Region VIII State Tournament Championship
- Advanced to the NJCAA Division I National Championship Tournament (second time in school history)
- The team ended the season with a top ten (ranked ninth) national ranking

Top Players Individual Achievements

Joe Gordon

- First team NJCAA All-America (27.5 ppg. 5.3 rpg. 2.4 apg.) (Scoring average was tops in the nation among Division I junior colleges and ranked No. 2 in the country in scoring among all junior colleges)
- Named the Southern Conference & Florida Junior College Player of the Year in 1999-00

- Set school single-season scoring records for scoring average and three-point field goal percentage.
- Scored over fifty points on two occasions.
- Signed with The University of Miami

Norm Cain

- Named first-team All-Southern Conference
- Named to the NJCAA Region VIII All-Tournament Team
- Signed with The University of Tennessee Chattanooga

Marshall Sanders

- Named to the NJCAA Region VIII All-Tournament Team
- Signed with Kentucky Wesleyan College
- Won 2000-01 NCAA Division II National Championship with Kentucky Wesleyan College Men's Basketball Team
- NCAA Division II National Championship All-Tournament Team
- 2001-02 NCAA Division II National Champion runner-up (Kentucky Wesleyan College)

1999-2000 State Championship Men's Basketball Team Honored

On Saturday, January 22, 2022, Eastern Florida State College (ESFC)—formerly Brevard Community College—hosted the 1999-2000 Men's Basketball State Championship team during the halftime of its home game against Florida State College at Jacksonville at the Titan Field House gymnasium in Melbourne, Florida. It was the first time in more than twenty years that arguably the most successful basketball team in the school's history had all stepped on a basketball court together. The last time this group of players was on the court together, they set a single-season record by winning twenty-nine games, completing the first undefeated season (12-0) in the Southern Conference history, winning the conference regular season title, before advancing to the NJCAA Region VIII State Championship Tournament, where the team added another championship to advance to the NJCAA Division I National Championship for only the second time in school history. It was a fantastic experience to be back on the EFSC college campus. Visiting with the current EFSC basketball team players in the locker room for a pre-game talk was great, as was finally taking court together with the members of the 1999-00 men's basketball team. The spectators, players, and coaches from both teams stood and cheered as the accomplishments of the great 2000 team were read over the loudspeaker. An unexpected and wonderful chance reunion happened, as the former players and I sat in the spectators' bleachers directly behind the Titans team seats, awaiting the halftime program to begin.

I noticed a familiar figure walk past, a short, older white man with gray hair and a strong resemblance to Woody Allen. He stopped next to the Titans team seats and briefly spoke with EFSC head coach Jeremy Shulman before slowly walking off and taking a seat in the bleachers a short distance away from where we were sitting. I was sure I knew who this guy was, so I immediately walked over to Coach Shulman and said, "Coach, the short guy you were just speaking with, is that Coach C?" Coach Shulman smiled and replied, "His name is Toody. He's a big supporter of the program. Do you know him?" I replied, "Yes, that's Coach C or Toody; he was a part of the coaching staff for the 1999-2000 BCC men's basketball team; I thought that was him." Coach Shulman and I exchanged a fist bump, and I walked back over to where the year 2000 players were sitting to give them the surprise news, that Coach C was seated just a few feet away from where we were sitting! I told the players to hold on for a minute, and I walked back over to where Coach C was sitting. He looked at me, unsure if he knew me, and then suddenly blurted out, "Robert, Robert, hey, how you are doing? You've gained weight!" I laughed before responding to his comments, "Coach C, it's good to see you. I have a surprise for you. Most of the 1999-2000 basketball team guys are here tonight." I motioned for the guys to come, and they all came running over, each exchanging hugs with Coach C. Coach C seemed at a loss for words, but the expression on his face was of overwhelming joy! Later, during the halftime ceremony, Coach C joined the players and me on the court to be acknowledged by the fans and take a team photo. The halftime celebration was made even more special with the unexpected reunion with Coach C— Tom "Toody" Cirincione—a Pittsburgh native, as well known in the college basketball circles as anyone after his relentless pursuit of coaching opportunities in a career that has spanned more than forty years.

After the game, Coach C and I exchanged telephone numbers and promised not to lose contact again; he asked me how long I would be in town and if we'd come in just for the game. I explained to him that I arrived in Florida the day before, and we had begun the celebration of the 2000 team's achievements on Friday night at a banquet hosted at the EFSC campus conference room. All of the guys who attended the game also participated in the Friday night event, which included Coach Ajac Triplett and former players from the 2001 team, Manny Clifton, and Michael Leggett. EFSCs administrators, past and present, were in attendance, as were members from the college's academic advisor and support staff. In addition, Cocoa, Florida Mayor Michael C. Blake presented each team member with a "Proclamation" in recognition of their outstanding accomplishments. The Proclamation read:

> *WHERES, the Brevard Community College Men's Basketball team holds a school record of twenty-nine wins in a single season, with an overall 29-7 record; and*

WHEREAS, the Brevard Community College Men's Basketball team holds the first undefeated season in conference history with a Southern Conference record of 12-0; and

WHEREAS, the team victoriously won the Southern Conference Regular Season Title; and

WHEREAS, they also won the NJCAA Region VIII State Tournament Championship; and

WHEREAS, the men's basketball team advanced to the NJCAA Division I National Championship Tournament which is the second time in school history; and

WHEREAS, the team ranked ninth in the national ranking at the end of the season.

NOW, THEREFORE, I, Mayor Michael C. Blake, on behalf of the City Council of the City of Cocoa, Florida, do hereby acknowledge and celebrate the outstanding achievements of the Brevard Community College Men's Basketball team.

The proclamation was completed with the signature of the mayor and the seal of the City of Cocoa affixed to it. The players and their families were thrilled with the respect and recognition shown to the historic team and its accomplishments. The local media from the Florida Today newspaper and the Space Coast Daily sent reporters to interview players and coaches attending the event to ask how they felt about the reunion after more than twenty years. "It's still surreal," Sam Santiago said. "I still can't believe that the guys are here and that we even had this opportunity to make this happen." He continued, "If you asked us today what was unique about our team, we'd all say our practices. Our practices were more challenging than the games, and we pushed each other daily. That's always been something I carry with me throughout my career in telecommunications, even more so in the military."

We were from all different walks of life, but if there is a common goal, there's nothing a Titan can't do!" Santiago was joined by teammates Marshall Sanders, Tim Phillips, and Joe Gordon who also provided some personal insight into the team for the reports. Sanders added to Santiago's statement, speaking about the team's competitive nature and the bond all players and coaches shared as the main ingredients that make the group unique. "We all got along and meshed well," Sanders said. "We had no one ego tripping, which made good chemistry for the team on and off the court." I agree with Marshall's assessment. The players on the 2000 championship team never sought to focus on individual importance or accomplishment. As was the case twenty years earlier, Sander's best friend on the team, Tim Phillips, echoed a similar opinion: "I don't think any of us thought that far ahead. We had aspirations for sure, but at the start of the season we were just trying to come together as a group, intending to win a championship." And even while being the team's most decorative players, he acknowledged what made the team so special was "These guys were so talented," Phillips said firmly. "They were talented, they were passionate and motivated to win, a key factor in our athletic performance on the court, and the essential ingredients to reaching our potential, allowing them to work hard even when they're tired, bored, or in pain. And it's what made us special."

I was overjoyed with the outcome of the reunion. I am not sure it could've gone any better, with the exception of maybe if more of the formers players and Coach Smith could have attended, to otherwise a very successful twenty-plus years reunion of the Brevard Community College Titans, the 2000 NJCAA Region VIII State Champions, the last championship the college has won in men's basketball. Nearly twenty-five years later, what this team accomplished continues to be the standard of greatness for men's basketball at the college. It was a fantastic team. The record speaks for itself. We had very competitive practices, but our competition in practice prepared us for our season. I think that is what carried us through and allowed us to have the success that we did. What does it mean to be called the best team in school history? It means the team should be more than just another group of players. They should perform in a manner that ensures their goals are consistently being met, effectively and efficiently. This was done, all of that and more. It's the best team I've ever coached!

FOURTH QUARTER

10
A JOURNEY OF PERSONAL GROWTH

After completing one final season of coaching the Brevard Community College men's basketball team, I felt like we had done some great work over the past two seasons, but I had reached a point where I believed it was time to move on. I didn't come to a decision quickly as I felt a sense of commitment to the current players on the team, many of whom I recruited to the college, and I truly enjoyed working with and learning from a Hall of Fame coach, Ajax Triplett. On my last day on campus, the athletic director organized a team meeting with all the players, team managers, and coaches in attendance. I told the team that I had decided not to return for the upcoming season. I continued to express that I wanted to pursue a different career path as an air traffic controller (ATC) in the aviation industry. The profession was familiar, as I'd previously worked as a military air traffic controller for nearly ten years. Air traffic controllers are primarily concerned about safety. They are also tasked with directing aircraft efficiently to minimize delays and manage the flow of air traffic into and out of the airport airspace, including the crucial duty of guiding pilots during takeoffs and landings. Air traffic controllers work in various types of facilities, including control towers—tall structures with a control room used to direct and control airport traffic—approach control facilities, or en route centers. They often work rotating shifts, usually in semi-dark rooms, using radar or manual procedures to track airplanes entering their airspace. Controllers must maintain a high mental focus and concentration for extended periods, which can be challenging, especially during late-night shifts. Some have argued that air traffic controllers should be calm, calculated, and confident, with a type A personality (traits including ambition, drive, and competitiveness) and a willingness to be challenged. While working as an air traffic controller can be demanding and stressful, I found the career choice incredibly satisfying and critical to my growth. The profession requires intense concentration and constant vigilance because you control the skies, guiding hundreds of aircraft to safety and keeping the aviation industry operating as seamlessly as possible. An added benefit of the job was the opportunity for ongoing learning, development, and growth.

The experience is highly regarded, as controllers develop into experts at communicating under pressure, and their attention to detail, decision-making, and teamwork make former air traffic controllers' ideal candidates for senior roles in planning and policy, project management, and logistics positions. The journey of personal growth is not linear; it's complex and dynamic, and it's a lifelong process of self-discovery and self-improvement that involves understanding yourself and challenging yourself to reach your full potential. Personal and professional development usually involves setbacks, challenges, and unexpected detours. The journey can also be unpredictable, with periods of exponential learning and development where you experience significant leaps in skills, knowledge, or understanding. It's about being open to change and growth, acknowledging your strengths and weaknesses, and embracing the potential for transformation. Reaching new heights can mean something different for everybody. Some may take it literally and want to climb a mountain or go skydiving. Others might want to pursue a lifelong goal, like starting a business, writing a book, or learning a new skill. The process for me, likely due to my years being involved in athletics, started with goal setting, which involves taking risks, trying new things, and stepping outside of one's comfort zone—all of which can result in failure and setbacks.

Before leaving to pursue a new career path in the 'Land of the Chamorro,' I visited my brother William at the Avon Park Correctional Institution, in his fifteenth year of incarceration. In prior visits William and I never discussed how he felt about being in prison for such an extended period; mostly, we talked about his basketball exploits within the prison. But during this particular visit, it was different; he and I both sensed a need to have a deeper conversation, maybe because I was about to leave the continental United States or the fact that he had reached a milestone of fifteen years on a life sentence with the possibility of parole, "fifteen years to life." It would be years later before I learned that a life felony committed after October 1, 1983 (nearly three years before my brother's conviction) requires a term of imprisonment for life or a term of imprisonment not to exceed forty years in prison. As we began my usual routine of walking around the perimeter of the yard in an attempt to talk in private, I asked William how he was coping and if there was any news about the possibility of him being paroled. He responded by saying, "Tan, man, it sucks in here." He continued by saying that you could never get too comfortable or be trusting of anyone in prison. He explained what is known as a 'convict mentality,' a term used to describe an inmate's mindset and behavior. An inmate with a 'convict mentality' doesn't allow any form of disrespect or perceived disrespect, regardless of how minor the infraction is, and there will be consequences on every occasion. Now in his fifteenth year, William was recognized as a convict due to the 'unwritten rule' that after serving a long sentence, he had enough time to know what was happening and what to expect. However, although he had learned from years of experience what to do or not do, in other words, how to do his time, he had not made much progress in personal growth. He described the time spent in prison over the previous fifteen years as "like being frozen in time." William had entered prison as a nineteen-year-old adolescent, the phase of life between childhood and adulthood, from ages 10-to-19. More than fifteen years later, in the early stage of middle age (ages 35-44), he was still emotionally in the development stage of a nineteen-year-old. As our visit ended, just as we had done at the beginning of our prison visit, we embraced once more. I told him to be safe, and he told me to do the same, and we each walked off in separate directions. After going back through the exit process, I continued to look back to see if I could catch one final glance of my brother. I could see him, and I yelled his name. A twelve-foot-tall security fence separated us, but we could still see one another through the "prison mesh." We both continued to wave until he entered a set of doors, disappearing out of sight.

I was scheduled to board a flight in less than a week from Orlando International Airport (MCO). The flight departed at 9:20 p.m., Thursday, September 13, 2001, to AB Won Pat International Airport (GUM) in Guam—16 hours and 56-minute flight, which could be as long as 20 hours and 45 minutes depending on the number of stops en route and the speed of the commercial airliner. But in less than 72 hours on the morning of September 11, 2001, the deadliest terrorist attack in American history occurred, also known as 9/11.

Solidarity After 9/11 Attacks

09.11.2001

Credit: Getty Images/iStockphoto

On the morning of September 11, 2001, after working a mid-shift at the Patrick Air Force Base Control Tower from 11:00 p.m.-6:00 a.m. I had to remain for an additional hour due to an unexpected incident. This threw off my body's circadian rhythm, or internal clock, which left me feeling excessively sleepy, a little cranky, and mentally slower than usual. When I arrived home, I proceeded with my routine of taking a shower and doing a final check of messages before getting into bed for a few hours of sleep, but my usual routine was disrupted just as I was in the transitional phase between wakefulness and sleep, known as the hypnagogic stage. Hypnagogic is the transitional state of consciousness between wakefulness and sleep. Research studies have found that shift workers are far more likely than the general population to meet insomnia or excessive sleepiness criteria. So, as I slowly opened my eyes to the auditory sound of my phone ringing, for a few seconds I didn't know if I was awakening or experiencing a 'false awakening,' believing I needed to begin getting ready to go back to work. But the phone was ringing, and once I answered it, I received shocking and fearful news; the quivering and frightened voice of a close friend, Adrienne, was on the other end asking if I was watching cable news. Without waiting for an answer, and in a harsher voice she shouted, "Turn on your TV right now! We just got attacked by terrorists! A hijacked airplane crashed into one of the New York City high-rise towers." I asked her to repeat what she'd said, "What happened? What are you talking about?" as I sat in bed and reached for my TV remote control. I told her that I was awake and would call her back. As I clicked the button on the remote, there was no need to change the TV channel as nearly every network was broadcasting the news of the worst terrorist attack in the history of the United States, 9/11.

American Airlines Flight 11 was the first plane to hit the World Trade Center's North Tower on September 11, 2001, at 8:46 a.m. Eastern Time (ET). The plane's impact killed everyone on board and trapped people on the upper floors of the tower. The second aircraft, United Airlines Flight 175, struck the South Tower of the World Trade Center at 9:03 a.m., and at 9:59 a.m., the South Tower collapsed. The North Tower collapsed at 10:28 a.m. after burning for over an hour and a half. Two other hijacked passengers, American Airlines Flight 77, crashed into the west side of the Pentagon at 9:37 a.m.; and United Airlines Flight 93 crashed in an empty field near Shanksville, Pennsylvania, at 10:03 a.m. as onboard passengers attempted to retake the aircraft from the terrorists. The plane was the fourth airliner to be hijacked on that day and was initially headed towards Washington, DC. The twenty-four-hour news channels like CNN, HLN, CNBC World, and BBC News 24 covered the attack non-stop. As soon as the news broke that the first plane had hit the World Trade Center's North Tower, all programs and commercials were suspended, and networks began broadcasting uninterrupted news coverage.

Some twenty-four-hour news channels aired footage almost immediately, and CNN had a live feed of the Twin Towers at 8:49 a.m., just three minutes after the first plane hit. Other channels used news coverage to share information, with VH1 and MTV using CBS's material and ESPN and ESPN2 using ABC's. The 9/11 attacks on September 11, 2001 had a lasting impact on the United States, the individuals who personally experienced the tragedy, people who witnessed it through network broadcasts, and the country as a whole. In the aftermath, Americans came together in many ways to respond to the horrific events of the 9/11 attacks. The nation's sense of grief and loss endures to this day; an estimated four hundred thousand people were exposed to harmful substances or experienced physical or emotional stress during the attacks and the nearly year-long recovery operation. People reported suffering from chronic illnesses, including respiratory diseases, mental health issues, and numerous types of cancer. The United States' response included pursuing terrorist and terrorism around the world, rebuilding the World Trade Center, and restoring the damage to the Pentagon.

More than two decades later, the American public still harbors concerns that another 9/11 attack could happen, even as the country underwent a nationwide effort to secure infrastructures from another attack.

The 9/11 attacks triggered a secondary trauma effort for me and my family, a vicarious effort of experiencing stress from being exposed to horrible images and stories of victims of the 9/11 attacks. The stress reaction can be just as intense as those experienced by someone who directly experienced the trauma. The traumatization of seeing the images of 9/11 caused me to relive the same stressful reactions I had the day I shockingly learned my brother, William, nineteen years old at the time, had been arrested for murder! A nineteen-year-old is still considered an adolescent. Technically, a person is still an adolescent until their neurological development is complete, around age twenty-four. A study found that African American adolescents who were indirectly exposed to the attacks experienced significant symptoms of post-traumatic stress disorder (PTSD). The study also found that anger and hostility were correlated with PTSD. Terrorism is intended to provoke collective fear and uncertainty. This fear can spread rapidly and is not limited to those experiencing the event directly—others who are affected include family members of victims, survivors, and people who are exposed through broadcast images. Psychological suffering is usually more prevalent than physical injuries from a terrorist event. Understanding these psychological consequences is critical to the nation's efforts to develop intervention strategies at the pre-event, event, and post-event phases that will limit the adverse psychological effects of terrorism. My mother was dreadfully afraid of me traveling overseas after the 9/11 attacks as I was scheduled to take a twenty-plus hours long-distant flight, crossing the Pacific Ocean, and at the boundary of the Philippine Sea, to the island of Guam on an 'international flight' days later after the attack. Although Guam is not considered overseas travel because it is a US territory, meaning you are technically still traveling within the United States when you go to Guam, some government agencies may define "foreign travel" to include US territories depending on their specific policies. The attacks induced substitution away from air travel generally and caused a shift in travelers' preferences for particular destinations. The United States experienced an immediate and precipitous drop in arrivals of international visitors, particularly from those flying to and from overseas or long-distance domestic destinations.

Days after the attack, the Pew Research Center conducted a series of public polls and surveys, and nearly all Americans expressed feelings of sadness (92 percent) and depression (71 percent).

Twelve months after the 9/11 attacks, in an open-ended question posed by the Pew Research Center, a majority of Americans (80 percent) referenced 9/11 as the most important event that had occurred in the country during the previous year. Strikingly, a larger share also volunteered it as the most important thing that happened to them personally in the prior year (38 percent) than mentioned other typical life events, such as births or deaths. Again, the personal impact was much more significant in New York and Washington, where 51 percent and 44 percent pointed to the attacks as the most essential personal event over the prior year. (Source: A survey of US adults was conducted from June 16 to July 4, 2016.) But the impact was also still being felt by my family, especially my mother, who was not welcoming to the news that I would be boarding a flight for more than twenty hours over the largest ocean basin in the world, the Pacific Ocean, also known as the "peaceful sea," and at the boundary of the Philippine Sea, to the island of Guam on an 'international flight' days later after the attack.

In 2016 – 15 years after 9/11 – the attacks continued to be seen as one of the public's top historical events

In an open-ended question in 2016, % who named ___ as one of the top 10 historic events that occurred in their lifetime that had the greatest impact on the country

Sept. 11	76
Obama election	40
The tech revolution*	22
JFK assassination	21
Vietnam War	20

*Technology includes mentions of the internet, computers, cellphones, smartphones and social media.
Note: Open-ended question
Source: Survey of U.S. adults conducted June 16-July 4, 2016.

PEW RESEARCH CENTER

Two days after the 9/11 attacks on the United States, I was boarding an airplane for a twenty-hour-long flight across the western Pacific Ocean to the island of Guam, an unincorporated territory of the United States. During the days following the 9/11 attacks, many Americans, including Black Americans, were not only fearful of flying but other potential negative consequences, marked by a sense of shared national trauma alongside concerns about possible racial profiling and increased surveillance due to the heightened focus on individuals of Middle Eastern descent, which sometimes impacted Black Americans as well, even though the attacks did not directly target them; this led to discussions about the intersection of race and national security in the post-9/11 era. In particular, concern was the potential increase in police racial profiling of Black men, a traumatic experience I share with more than 40 percent of Black Americans who share that they have been stopped or detained by police because of their race.

In addition, the Patriot Act and increased surveillance measures implemented post-9/11 raised concerns about potential infringements on civil liberties, disproportionately impacting marginalized communities, including Black Americans. Many of the nation's civil rights groups have asserted that the Patriot Act violates Constitutional rights and allows the government to spy on individuals without due process and search their homes without consent, actions particularly sensitive to Black America due to a long history of government monitoring and suppressing of Black Americans. The history of the US government spying on African American leaders is deeply rooted in the Civil Rights era, primarily through the FBI's "Counter Intelligence Program" (COINTELPRO), which involved widespread surveillance, infiltration, and disruption tactics aimed at discrediting and weakening prominent Black activists and organizations like the Black Panther Party and the Southern Christian Leadership Conference, led by Martin Luther King Jr., and leaders of the black militant movement during the 1950s and '60s, specifically the Nation of Islam national spokesman and leader, Malcolm X, who had been surveilled and monitored by the FBI until his assassination in 1965.

In the immediate days after the attacks, there was a general shift away from air travel and a decrease in international visitors to the United States. Some studies have found that the circumstances of the situation can constrain people's responses to terrorism-induced fear of flying. I was more than just a little uncomfortable about flying; my response was to be more defiant than fearful of thoughts of air travel. As I walked through the airport terminal, cleared through the airport security checkpoint by TSA, and finally handing the airline agent my boarding pass, I refused to give in to any harboring fears of flying. Even as the aircraft disconnected from the terminal ground equipment and prepared to begin taxiing to the runway, thoughts of the 9/11 attacks remained. Finally, the pilot made a flight announcement to prepare for takeoff. As the ground roll began, the airplane acceleration speed picked up, providing enough lift for the aircraft to become airborne. As the ground gradually gave way to the sky, a feeling of calmness came over me.

"Hafa Adai" Welcome to Guam

Credit: Getty Images/iStockphoto

My flight from Orlando to Guam included several stops; the first stop was a routine four-hour flight to the George Bush Intercontinental Airport in Houston, Texas. Next was an extended nonstop eight-plus-hour, 3,919-mile flight to the Daniel K. Inouye International Airport located in Honolulu, Hawaii. And finally, another nearly eight-hour, 3,817-mile flight to Guam's Antonio B. Won Pat International Airport. The total straight-line flight distance from Orlando, Florida to Tamuning, Guam, is 8,213 miles. Still, because the Pacific Ocean is such a massive body of water that requires aircraft to use a considerable amount of fuel, most commercial flights fly a curved route, which is shorter than flying straight across the ocean. The small island spans 8.5 miles wide at its widest point and is thirty miles long, it sits around sixteen hundred miles west of Manila, the capital of the Philippines, and thirty-eight hundred miles west of Honolulu, Hawaii, in the Pacific Ocean.

Guam has a long history with the US military and has been home to many military units over the past sixty years—it was especially active during the Vietnam War as a waystation for US bombers. My biological father, William Worthington Sr., had done two tours of duty to Vietnam; he was awarded the "Bronze Star" with two "V" devices and had several stopovers at the island of Guam. The "Bronze Star" was awarded to US service members during the Vietnam War to recognize acts of heroism or meritorious service in combat situations, often signifying actions above and beyond normal duty expectations; while serving in the Vietnam Theater of Operations, my father also had two "V" devices added to his prestigious medal signifying acts of bravery in combat. After his death in November 2017, the prestigious military decoration he earned during a tour of duty in the Vietnam War, signifying his significant achievements in combat situations, was given to me by his wife. I had the certificate, and the "Bronze Star" framed, and it hangs in my work office as a reminder of his bravery and exemplary performance of duty.

During the Vietnam War, Guam primarily served as a vital staging point for the US Air Force, with Andersen Air Force Base acting as a significant hub for B-52 Stratofortress bombers launching bombing missions over Southeast Asia; essentially, Guam was a critical refueling and departure point for operations in Vietnam, with large numbers of military personnel including my father rotating through the island as well.

I was excited about the opportunity to explore all the island had to offer and experience the culture of the Chamorro people. But before I could explore all the gratification of island living, I needed to contact my Guam Air Traffic Control Tower supervisor and advise him that I arrived safely on the island and would report to work on Monday morning. Next I got checked into my hotel and went to the nearest rental car agency to rent a vehicle for the next thirty days. After previously spending more than a decade as a military air traffic controller, I wasn't overly concerned about learning air space and runway configurations as the airport's newest tower air traffic controller. Tower air traffic controllers typically communicate with aircraft within a radius of 3-to-30 miles from the airport, which is the primary area of responsibility for a tower controller; they manage takeoffs, landings, and taxiing movements within this range. Air traffic controllers give pilots taxiing and takeoff instructions, air traffic clearance, and advice based on their observations and experience. Pilots will typically initiate contact with the tower controller within a few miles of the airport and maintain communication until they are well beyond the airport's immediate airspace.

In addition, as a tower controller, I was responsible for giving pilots taxiing and take-off instructions and communicating with other vehicles operating within the airport's movement and nonmovement areas. One of the unique parts of being an air traffic controller is using standardized phraseology to communicate with pilots airborne or on the ground, as well as all vehicles seeking permission to operate in airport movement areas. Air traffic controllers' (ATCs) standardized phraseology reduces the risk that a message will be misunderstood and aids the read-back (pilot or vehicle operators repeat the instructions given by ATC) process so that any error is quickly detected. Examples of ATC phraseology include: "(aircraft call sign) taxi to runway number" or "taxi via." Additional instructions may include a time and a hold short of or crossing a specific runway. Guam control tower operations at the Won Pat International Airport were not a particularly busy facility, managing slightly more than three hundred flights weekly; by comparison, the world's busiest airport, Atlanta Hartsfield-Jackson International Airport (ATL), averages twenty-one hundred arrivals and departures daily. However, despite its limited number of flights, Guam was not exempted from aviation accidents, which can be caused by various factors, including mechanical failure, adverse weather conditions, pilot or controller error, and sabotage. During the three years I worked at the Guam control tower, like most airports, we had several minor incidents, including aircraft and vehicles crossing the runway without ATC approval. This unauthorized crossing or entering a runway safety area is known as a runway incursion. It happens when an aircraft or vehicle crosses an active runway to complete a ground movement. This can happen if a taxi clearance has a taxi limit that goes beyond the runway or if a vehicle or aircraft doesn't stop at the limit of its taxi clearance. According to the Federal Aviation Administration (FAA), there are four categories of runway incursions:(1) Category A is a serious incident in which a collision was narrowly avoided; (2) Category B is an incident in which separation decreases and there is a significant potential for collision, which may result in a time-critical corrective/evasive response to avoid a collision; (3) Category C is an incident characterized by ample time and distance to avoid a collision; (4) Category D is an incident that meets the definition of runway incursion such as incorrect presence of a single vehicle/person/aircraft on the protected area of a surface designated for the landing and take-off of aircraft but with no immediate safety consequences. In addition, we had a slightly more serious incident involving a small (less than 12,500 pounds) aircraft sliding off the runway after a landing, causing the runway to be closed temporarily, but with no serious injury to the aircraft or pilot.

By good fortune, we did not have any accidents nearly as serious as the infamous Korean Air Line (Flight 801) Boeing 747 airplane crash in 1997, where the jetliner impacted the top of Nimitz Hill and slammed into a canyon before erupting into flames, a fatal accident resulting in the death of 226 people, the deadliest plane crash in Guam's history. Throughout the time I lived on the island, we were blessed with good luck concerning any major aircraft accidents; the most noteworthy disaster occurred on December 8, 2002, when super typhoon Pongsona passed over the island with strong winds gusting up to 175 mph, with sustained winds of 65 km (40 mph) as it crossed the northern portion of the island, leaving the entire island without power for months and destroyed nearly thirteen hundred houses with a total cost of the damage over 730 million dollars (USD). Because I had only been on the island for several months, the night of the typhoon was my first time working a mid-shift (10:00 pm until 6:00 am) in the Guam tower. Because the storm's wind was so strong and sustained, we had to plan for an evacuation of the control tower in the interest of personnel safety, a requirement when wind gusts reach 75 mph (65 knots). Typhoon Pongsona was my first experience with a super typhoon, equivalent to a strong category four or five hurricane. I had been told before arriving on the island that Guam was hit by a typhoon every 4-5 years and that I would likely not experience one during my three-year assignment there. This prediction was proven wrong within my first few months on the island as Typhoon Pongsona became the third most intense storm ever to hit Guam, knocking out communications and electrical power, including 65 percent of the island's water wells inoperable, leaving much of Guam without water services for months. The experience of taking nightly cold showers was not a pleasant one for me. I prefer relatively hot showers, and adjusting to the initial shock of getting into a cold shower triggered an adrenalin surge, rapid breathing, and a sense of fear.

I would stand outside the shower with the water running and 'psych myself up,' mentally preparing myself for the shock of the cold water before I could get into the shower. I could never control my uncomfortable feelings about cold showers; some people said that their discomfort would be replaced with a sense of calm after they got used to the cold water…that never happened for me! As I prepared for my first typhoon experience just two months after arriving on the island of Guam, I reflected on my growing up in Orlando, Florida, where we were constantly (about once every three years) under the threat of a hurricane. The storms would bring heavy wind and rainfall, falling trees, street flooding, poor drainage, leaving debris scattered, and the dreaded power outage due to power lines being down, resulting in no lights or television at home. So, unaware of the danger of contaminants such as sewage and chemicals in the standing flood water, my brothers, William, Derrick, and I would join other kids in the neighborhood running in the water for fun. The main difference between hurricanes and typhoons is where they occur; hurricanes often affect the United States East Coast and the Caribbean, while typhoons usually hit Guam, the Philippines, and Japan. But they are both tropical cyclones with similar characteristics, including damaging winds, heavy rainfall, flooding, and damage to homes, buildings, roads, and powerlines. But one of the most noticeable differences in my experiences with tropical storms in both Florida and Guam is the significantly different time it takes to restore critical services; for example, restoring power and water services to residences in Florida would take a few days maximum, while in Gaum restoring these services to the entire island could take months.

I passed the time by writing letters to my brother, William, describing in vivid detail the sounds, smells, tastes, images, and feelings of Guam's white sand beaches, crystal clear waters, and tropical climate. I also sent my postcard featuring the island's beauty, culture, and history to my mother and friends back in Florida. But what I did most was play pickup basketball at the US Air Force Base, Andersen Air Force Base, Guam. Because I was a federal employee as an air traffic controller, I was allowed to play on one of the intramural men's basketball teams. During the season, we won the base basketball championship. Although I was no longer an active-duty member of the Air Force, spending so much time on the base felt normal and allowed me to bond with people who had similar experiences.

We had to continue to manage the flow of air traffic in the coming days after the storm to ensure the safe and efficient takeoff and landing of aircraft. But one of the reasons I feel such a connection to being a controller is the teamwork that the job requires; similar to being a member of a good basketball team, one air traffic controller after another takes responsibility for a specific portion of the aircraft's flight path to ensure that the plane is safely separated from another air traffic or vehicle traffic. A typical shift includes a supervisor position, a flight controller position, a ground controller position, and a local controller position. The air traffic control tower supervisor oversees operations related to position assignment positions, coordinates with other air traffic control facilities, and manages facility records and logs. The initial communication between the pilot and controller usually begins when the pilot files a flight plan with the flight service station, which will require the controller to work the flight position to give the flight plan instruction to the pilot; this plan outlines the route the aircraft will take, plans for an emergency or weather-related problems, before taxiing, the process of which the aircraft moves from one location to another after landing or before taking off.

Once the pilot has received approval of the flight plan, the next step is to contact the ground controller for taxiing instructions. The ground controller is also responsible for approving vehicles and personnel entering or crossing the runway. After coordinating with the flight controller position, the ground controller determines the aircraft's position before issuing taxi instructions to a runway. The local controller assumes control before the aircraft departs the runway or enters the air traffic pattern for landing sequences. In some countries, all air traffic control is performed by the military. In other countries, military controllers are responsible solely for military airspace and airbases; civilian controllers maintain airspace for civilian traffic and airports. As a civilian air traffic controller in Guam, I managed aircraft movement at the Antonio B. Won Pat International Airport and in controlled airspace. In contrast, Andersen Air Force Base (Guam) military air traffic controllers manage aircraft at military airfields as the main point of communication for aircraft on the flight line. In addition, military aircraft may follow different rules and procedures than civilian aircraft, varying from minor differences to a lack of regulations.

The local controller's final communication with the pilot typically issues a takeoff clearance and change of frequency instructions, "Continental 1528 Runway 24R Cleared for Takeoff – Wind Calm."

The Impossible Journey

After more than three years of Guam's tropical island lifestyle and pristine white beaches, I returned to the US mainland, transferring to Brown Field Municipal Airport in San Diego, California, known for its beaches, parks, and warm climate. The airport serves general aviation aircraft, including charter, air ambulance, law enforcement, flight training, sky diving, and airships. Brown Field Airport is just 1.5 miles north of the United States – Mexico border. Less than one month after I began working at the facility, a fatal accident involving a Learjet air ambulance happened just before my day shift in the control tower. The air traffic controller working the night shift gave instructions to the pilot of the jet, which was a contributing factor; the controller gave the crew a heading (direction of flight) towards high terrain, resulting in the pilot crashing into a mountain. According to the US National Transportation Safety Board (NTSB) preliminary report, the controller's instructions, 'cleared to fly into a mountain,' allowed the aircraft to move towards the mountain. All five people on board the plane were killed. Six months after this accident, I relocated to my home state of Florida and the Orlando Sanford International Airport in Sanford, Florida, where I worked for nearly five years. During this period, I was offered another opportunity to coach basketball, this time at the professional level with the Brevard Blue Ducks, a minor league men's professional basketball team in Melbourne, Florida, as a United States Basketball League (USBL) member. The developmental league for players to move up to the National Basketball Association (NBA) was founded in 1985 and ceased all official basketball operations in 2008. Working with the Blue Ducks was my last coaching stint and was one of the most rewarding of my basketball coaching career. During my first year with the team, I was ecstatic to be hired to work with the legendary "Tiny" Archibald, one of the all-time great NBA point guards and the first player in history to lead the NBA in scoring and assists in the same season. Tiny was a member of the Naismith Basketball Hall of Fame Class of 1991 and National Collegiate Basketball Hall of Fame. During my second year with the team, I also gained invaluable experience coaching with former NBA Player and 2005 American Basketball Association Coach of the Year Brian Rowsom. Coach Rowsom was inducted into the UNC Wilmington Hall of Fame. The opportunity to work with and learn from two incredibly knowledgeable basketball minds with a wealth of experience was unbelievable. Through the shared coaching experiences, the three of us developed a bond that grew into a lifelong friendship that continues to this day through numerous ventures, including professional basketball showcases, youth basketball developmental camps and training, appearance at the Central Intercollegiate Athletic Association (CIAA) Women's and Men's basketball tournament, and the unlikely participation in a celebrity golf best ball tournament in Miami, Florida. I am grateful for the time I spent on the sideline with Nate (Nate "Tiny" Archibald) and Brian; our mutual respect for each other created a lifelong bond.

Following my second season with the Blue Ducks, I was presented with another remarkable opportunity to work at the Mike Monroney Aeronautical Center (MMAC) in Oklahoma City, Oklahoma, where the mission is to impact every aspect of the United States national and international aviation systems. The MMAC is also home to the Federal Aviation Administration (FAA) Air Traffic Control Academy, where all FAA air traffic controllers receive sixteen weeks of instructions followed by the Air Traffic Skills Assessment exam. Taking this exam is a crucial step to becoming an air traffic controller, but a very challenging task, as only 2.5-to-6 percent of candidates pass the ATC test. I enjoyed working at the MMAC and received merit awards for my performance. Within two years, I was offered a chance to relocate back to the East Coast at the National Flight Data Center (NFDC), a facility located within the Federal Aviation Academy HQ in Washington, DC, established to operate a central aeronautical information service for collection, validation, and dissemination of aeronautical data in support of the federal government and the aviation community. I was overjoyed with the opportunity and began searching for a community within the District of Columbia, Maryland, and Virginia (DMV) areas to live. By telephone, I contacted my friend, Brian Rowsom, who had lived in the area during his NBA playing career and sought his opinion about the area. He enthusiastically endorsed moving to Columbia, Maryland, Howard County; with its top-ranked public school system, a thriving arts and cultural scene, a plethora of pristine parks, trails, outdoor activities, and lakes, and a focus on sustainability, Columbia is a community that blends nature, culture, and innovation.

After weeks of Google searches, speaking to realtors, and seeking the opinions of friends and co-workers who live in the area, I found the perfect community for my family: Columbia, Maryland. The Howard County community ranks as the safest county to live in Maryland, the number one school district in the state, and one of the best places to live in the US. Columbia is a planned community of nearly a hundred thousand people between Baltimore and Washington, DC. Money magazine called the community "much more than your average suburb" and highlighted its multicultural population, safety record, and variety of activities for families and adolescents. Columbia has been an extraordinary place to raise my family with its diverse population and enduring appeal, with houses between wooded bike paths and creeks.... It just feels like home!

But like the rest of our home lives were disrupted by a once-in-a-generation outbreak, the COVID-19 pandemic dramatically changed all our lives and relationships in America and around the world. The economic impact was estimated to be twice the size of that of the Great Recession of 2007-2009, when economies worldwide experienced deep decline. The COVID-19 economic costs were twenty times greater than the terrorist attacks of 9/11 and forty times greater than the toll of any other disaster to occur in the United States in the 21st century. The international health crisis sparked national and state responses regarding economic and fiscal policies that increased funding for scientific research, treatments, and new vaccines. In addition, every state implemented mandatory wearing of facial masks and ordered nearly all public schools closed for in-person attendance, forcing all students to attend school virtually from home. This unexpected and rapid disruption to our lives created anxiety. It concerned me as it likely did every other person in the country dealing with this sudden and unanticipated change, new routine in our daily lives, loneliness, and financial pressure from not knowing if we would have a job waiting for us when we returned to work, rumors and misinformation contributing to the fears and panic of the nation. These concerns were on my mind when I discussed with my family that I wanted to use this crisis as an opportunity for personal growth and transformation, one that would require a shift in my perspective, resilience, and adaptability to achieve one of my life goals, earning a doctoral degree. Earning the Doctor of Business Administration (DBA) degree would be an achievement of the highest academic degree and is an intellectually challenging and emotionally rewarding journey. Because we were amid the COVID-19 pandemic, one of the requirements for a doctoral degree program would be one that could be earned virtually. The journey would include authoring a research proposal, conducting a literature review, and collecting data through experiments, interviews, or surveys. After a few days of research, I quickly decided that Walden University's DBA program was the best choice. The university offers a virtual online learning community that is highly respected as a reputable online university. In addition, Walden's reputation is highly regarded among employers, graduates, and others in the academic community. Most importantly, it would allow me to achieve the personal growth and intellectual challenge I sought. Walden's DBA program provides a deep dive into complex business problems, offering an intellectually challenging environment to satiate one's thirst for knowledge. Walden University also has a unique addition for its doctorate candidates, pursuing a consulting capstone doctoral study, an increasingly popular way for doctoral candidates to implement their research findings. Walden University's consulting capstone project allows doctoral candidates to collaborate with a nonprofit organization or small business; I was assigned to work with a nonprofit healthcare think tank organization to gain valuable real-life and real-time experience. Walden doctoral candidates follow the Baldridge framework and criteria for performance excellence and a comprehensive approach using a systems perspective that aims to "improve [an] organization's performance and get sustainable results." The consulting capstone project allows participating doctoral candidates to gain a solid foundation and experience in consulting and coaching while also delivering valued insights into how they might achieve strategic objectives to the leaders of client organizations. Small businesses and nonprofit organizations often lack human and fiscal resources to address specific initiatives; the consulting doctoral candidate helps bridge a gap from current operations to potential organizational change and future sustainability.

The journey through the DBA consulting capstone program is marked by rigor. It demands a high level of personal commitment in time and effort to ignite the academic mindset and capabilities. The more than three journeys forced me to be resilient and recover quickly from difficulties and various challenges in my personal and professional life. As I headed into year three, it was time to begin working on my consulting capstone project, enabling doctoral candidates to function as researchers and unpaid consultants who regularly confer with the leaders of their client organizations and deliver a final report. The consulting capstone project journey can be transformative for both the doctoral candidate and the client organization. According to Dr. Peter Anthony, my doctoral program chair and faculty member in the School of Management, "Walden's DBA consulting capstone project provides doctoral candidates the opportunity to complete their doctorate while simultaneously honing consulting skills. This consultant-scholar combination produces doctors who apply their experiences to assist global organizational leaders in achieving sustainable and socially responsible results." The DBA journey was an experience that challenged me in a variety of ways, helping me learn more than I thought possible in a relatively short period.

When I walked across the stage in San Antonio, Texas for the hooding ceremony (commencement) that recognized doctoral candidates had completed their doctoral program, I became one of only 2 percent of people with a doctorate, and it was the only time during the three years that I felt nervous emotions. I'm grateful to my program director, committee chair, and members for their support and encouragement, especially during the two oral defenses of my capstone (dissertation). I've included my dissertation abstract, which is a short, well-structured summary of the most important points of my dissertation's research. It presents all of the major elements of my research work in a highly condensed format.

Abstract

Healthcare Organizational Strategies for Designing and
Implementing Economic Think Tanks

by
Dr. Robert Worthington

Abstract

A lack of focus on organizational strategy impedes the development of successful healthcare think tanks. Healthcare leaders are concerned about the lack of strategies and their importance in combating fraud, reducing errors, enforcing practice guidelines, and improving patient healthcare services. Grounded in the four trajectories of industry change theory, the purpose of this qualitative single case study was to explore strategies healthcare management leaders use to develop successful healthcare think tank organizations. The participants were three healthcare professionals in senior leadership positions for a healthcare think tank organization. Data was collected using semi structured interviews, a review of organizational documents, and review of organizational websites. Through thematic analysis, five themes were identified: the importance of various stakeholders, understanding politics and current federal and state regulations, driving innovations in healthcare, focusing on low-and-moderate income families, and networking and connections. A key recommendation is for the organizational leaders to incorporate the voices of as many stakeholders as possible throughout each process, which is vital for establishing trust in the organization and its services or products. High involvement in the process by various stakeholders enhances a deeper understanding of think tank initiatives and their effect on public policy, healthcare innovations, and patient outcomes. The implications for positive social change include the opportunity to address disparities in healthcare access, affordability, and the quality of care received by low-and moderate-income families.

"IT ALWAYS
SEEMS
IMPOSSIBLE
UNTIL
IT'S DONE"

-NELSON MANDELA

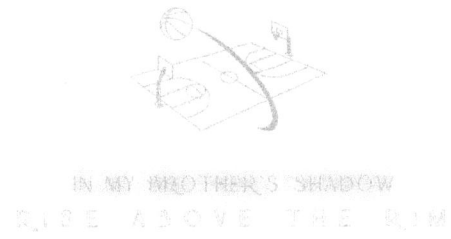

11
NO MORE EXCUSES: TAKING
RESPONSIBILITY FOR OUR CHOICES

A s I pondered addressing such a complicated, difficult topic, I reflected on my own experiences. These included conversations with friends, family members, educators, psychologists, and organizations that support the Black community. Although grateful for all shared points of view, most conversations ended with no consensus on the causes or solutions to the problems many Black communities face today. Ultimately, we agree that opposing ideas can exist, allowing seemingly opposing facts or perspectives to exist simultaneously. In psychology, these coexisting opposites are called 'dialectics' (the coexistence of opposite truths). Some believe that accepting dialectics can lead to a greater truth about oneself and others, allowing us to continue to move forward despite our discomfort with a particular topic or situation. Obviously, the views shared on the pages of this will not resolve all of the issues facing Black people in America, nor address the nearly five hundred majority-Black cities in the United States, with the largest populations living in Detroit, Michigan (639,000), Memphis, Tennessee (633,000), Baltimore, Maryland (586,000), New Orleans, Louisiana (384,000), and Cleveland, Ohio (373,000) (Source: The Brookings Institution). But I felt a need to, at the very least, reflect on my personal experiences and journey from a little black boy from a Central Florida housing project (Griffin Park) with average grades in school to walking across the stage at the Henry B. Gonzales Convention Center in San Antonio, Texas at the commencement ceremony after earning my doctoral degree. I'm living proof that the saying "It doesn't matter where you start but how you finish" is not just a famous quote but a mission statement for achieving whatever goals you're willing to work towards. According to a 2022 Pew Research Center survey, 63 percent of Black Americans view racism as a serious problem, 60 percent say police brutality is a significant problem, 54 percent view economic inequality as a major obstacle, and several other issues are viewed as severe dilemmas facing Black Americans including affordable health care, voting limitations, and quality of education in school grades K-12. Other polls show concern for violence and crime, economic issues, and housing issues.

All these issues are not only affecting Black communities. Still, the Black experience has proven that many of these issues are born of systemic racism and discrimination in the United States. If we examine recent events, like the COVID-19 pandemic, it disproportionately affected Black communities, continued efforts to place roadblocks that obstruct minority voting rights, a growing movement throughout the country to "ban books" and remove anti-racist curricula out of our nation's public schools. These are all events that indicate how extensive structural, institutional, and systemic racism is in the United States. However, acknowledging the centuries of discrimination and bias in America does not absolve us of the accountability and responsibility for resolving the problems that we have perpetuated within our communities. A study published in Social Psychological and Personality Science presented research that established that Americans like to hear messages about 'personal responsibility,' mainly if those messages were directed towards Black audiences but were less receptive when given to a white audience. A group of Stanford University college students conducted experiments where of the three included between 100-150 participants, with 68-to-75 percent of participants identifying as white and the remainder identifying as African American, Asian American, American Indian/Alaskan Native, or other. The experiment focused on beliefs about the equity and impartiality of American society and how various ethnic groups responded to messages about individual blame or systemic blame as the cause of these issues.

The results of the research weren't a total surprise: the majority of the participants believed that Black people are more likely to feel that American society is equitable, and the majority also felt that Black people need to hear more messages about personal responsibility for their failings instead of blaming society or 'white people' for their problems (Social Psychology and Personality Science). Another part of the experiment involved all participants being presented with an excerpt from a 2008 Father's Day speech given by President Barack Obama. Not all participants received the original text of the speech, where Obama emphasized themes about personal blame and responsibility. Instead, some received edited copies that placed the primary emphasis on missing Black fathers from the home. Here's the original excerpt from Obama's speech: "We need fathers to realize that responsibility does not end at conception. We need them to realize that what makes you a man is not the ability to have a child – it's the courage to raise one" (Sen. Barack Obama (D-Ill., June 15, 2008, at the Apostolic Church of God in Chicago, Illinois). The third experiment (the use of edited copies of Obama's speech) of the research study conducted by Phia Salter and her college at Texas A&M University edited versions were as follows:

- "Individual blame"—"But we also need African American fathers to realize that responsibility does not end at conception. We need them to realize that what makes you a man is not the ability to have a child—it's the courage to raise one. We need families to raise our children."
- "System blame"—"But we also need people to realize that the breakdown of African American families is due to a broken system. As a nation, we must create a fairer playing field and foster an environment where all fathers can raise their children. We need families to raise our children."

All participants were asked to rate their agreement with the speech overall, how much they liked it, and how vital the speech's message was. The results showed that the participants who identified as white had favorable views of the speech when it was given to a Black audience and a less than favorable view if given to a white audience. The researchers explained that the results could not simply be explained away by saying the majority group (white) was expressing their belief in personal responsibility. Otherwise, the other groups (of minority participants) would have had the same results. Although the study cited here is exciting and well-intended, it is just one study of research that doesn't answer, nor does it pretend to do so, all of the questions these complicated issues ask of all of us. Some may suggest that the opposing opinions presented in the research study are a dialetheia. Regardless of a person's point of view, we can all agree that there are issues within our communities that we need to improve.

As someone who wasn't born into wealth or an established upper-class family of 'old money,' I relied on self-motivation and intense passion to fuel my drive to achieve goals, even when the journey was difficult. My passionate personality traits have given me the power to adjust to overcome life's challenges. Being born with a strong passion has been my 'superpower' and the source of my ability to overcome obstacles in pursuit of personal and professional goals. But it's also important to understand that achieving success in life is not a straight line; setbacks and failures are a natural part of the journey. However, we cannot ignore research that shows children who grow up poor (an estimated 333 million children live in extreme poverty around the world) have a more challenging time escaping poverty and are likely to be inadequate as adults. According to numerous studies on social issues like poverty, particularly childhood poverty, including studies conducted by the United Nations International Children's Emergency Fund (UNICEF), being born into poverty can have long-lasting effects on a person's life, including their health, education, and ability to find employment. In the United States, one in five children live in poverty, and nearly two in five will be poor for at least a year before they turn eighteen. Half of babies born into poverty will remain inadequate for at least half of their childhoods, and the racial gap is significant, with 40 percent of Black children experiencing persistent poverty compared to 5 percent of white children. These statistics are concerning to all groups of people for different reasons, but for Black Americans in particular, the continuous encounters with racial discrimination and its impact remained at the forefront of their concerns; in fact, nearly 8 in 10 Black Americans say that they had personally experienced racial discrimination (79 percent), and most also say racial discrimination is the primary (not the only) reason many Black people made progress to be successful in society at a higher rate (68 percent).

Hip-hop Music Both Positive and Negative Effects on the Black Community

Does rap music influence positive or negative behavior in the Black community? The answer is a paradox with two contradictory truths, with examples of both positive and negative effects on the Black community. Hip-hop can help young people of color find their identity and a voice to challenge social constructs and oppressive systems. It can also foster a sense of unity and belonging and provide a way to express experiences and emotions. On the other hand, there have been some negative effects, such as promoting violence and misogyny. In the '90s, some people were uncomfortable with the controversial lyrics, which frequently portrayed or even glorified ghetto life, hypersexuality, and violence. But with that said, the responsibility for how rap music lyrics and messages influence our behavior says more about the individual's personal choices than it does about the rap music they are listening to. As I was growing up in Griffin Park (GP), Orlando, Florida's first public housing project, in the 1970s, my siblings and I never thought about the fact we were living in low-income housing or the ghetto; in fact, I never heard anyone call Griffin Park the hood or ghetto until years after we had moved away. As my family and I reflected on the years we lived in the historic housing project, we realized that the memories were mostly happy memories shared with family and friends. I affectionately remember movie nights at the local drive-in theater, playing 'ball' at the park, and watching some older boys 'play the dozen.' The nostalgic memories of growing up in GP are personally meaningful and are triggered by various things, such as the smell of exhaust fumes, an old '70s song, or seeing one of the guys from the old neighborhood. Reminiscing about those years and the friendships built always makes me smile. Perhaps the one unpleasant memory that's conspicuous was the constant smell of exhaust fumes and the continuous sound of passing cars and trucks on the East-West Expressway. But once we moved out of the Griffin Park projects, although the memories were fond ones, we were excited about the opportunity to improve our lives, and our living conditions.

The first house, a four-bedroom, two-bath house with more than 1,289 square feet of living space, was a major upgrade size from the "matchbox-sized" apartment units in the GP housing complex we moved out of after six years. By the beginning of the 1980s, how we viewed housing projects had changed, largely because of the introduction of hip-hop music to a wider audience in the United States. The song "Rapper's Delight" by the group Sugarhill Gang is credited with the wide-scale influx of hip-hop to the larger market, not that it was the first rap song released. I can vividly recall the summer of 1979 as we moved into our new home at 4845 Lescott Lane; we were sitting in the space, we did not move any furniture at that time, of the dining room as the carpet installer measured, cut, and fitted carpet to the floor space in our living room. "Rapper's Delight" was blasting from my brother Derrick's boombox, as we all attempted to rap along with the popular hip-hop song, 'I said a hip-hop, the hippie, to hippie the hippy, the hip-hip-hop, and you don't stop the rocking to the bang-bang to bang to boogie to be' or something like it. It always sounded much better the louder the music was playing on the boom box! Derrick's boombox was a suitcase-size multi-band radio cassette tape player/recorder, allowing you to record directly onto cassette tapes. It had a power cord allowing it to be plugged into a power outlet in the house; it was also powered by six D-cell batteries and included a handle for on-the-go carrying, allowing you take your music on the go! In the late '80s, most of us listened to rap music, also known as hip-hop, which is Black American music. It originated in the early 1970s in the Bronx, New York, in African American and Latino communities as a fusion of various cultural influences. It began as an anti-drug and anti-violence genre, and some say it also formed as a cultural response to racism and oppression and a way for Black communities to communicate.

Hip-hop culture has influenced music, fashion, and more around the world. As the influence of rap continued, some began referring to it as 'ghetto' music. Creditable hip-hop artists were chief among those describing rap as ghetto music. "I have found that all music has originated from the ghetto, and this is why I call the album 'Ghetto Music: The Blueprint of Hip Hop.' Only ghetto consciousness will understand it, and only ghetto consciousness will enjoy it," declared a noted American rapper from the Bronx, New York. "If you ain't never been to the ghetto, don't ever come to the ghetto." Another prominent American hip-hop group promulgated this message in one of their songs, "Cause you won't understand the ghetto. So, stay the fuck out of the ghetto." These opinions vary on the positive messages or negative influence of glorifying the ghetto or hood in rap music. Still nevertheless, negative stereotypes became common to associate with the genre, like heavy drug use, violence, crime, sexism, and laziness. Unfortunately, some people embraced these stereotypes with their attitudes and behavior. In expressing the school of thought that music can influence negative behavior, it is certainly not solely to blame for issues facing Black communities throughout the US. However, some studies show that music can impact our mood long-term, increasing depression and anxiety. On the other hand, rap music can have a therapeutic effect in helping people cope with depression and anxiety, improve emotional expression, and help people learn to communicate and relate to others. It can also help build self-esteem and learn coping skills, personal growth techniques, and self-empowerment. Yet another example of coexisting opposites (dialectics) is the coexistence of opposite truths. Some theories put forth the idea that music can affect our behavior negatively or positively, and the impact has long-term effects. The ethos theory hypothesizes that music has a long-term effect on an individual's character, in particular, to encourage them to show kindness, compassion, and display helpful behaviors toward their fellow man. Many believe hip-hop made Black culture mainstream in the '70s and '80s, providing Black youth of that time a microphone, a platform, and a world stage for their outspoken lyrics against injustices many other people in the country were overlooking.

Ghetto/Hood Culture

The term ghetto usually refers to any urban area exclusively settled by a minority group, primarily African Americans, a group that was constrained and bullied into living in the ghettos because of legal and illegal discrimination and economic and social pressure in the United States. Hood culture is a subculture that developed from these lower social classes of neighborhoods. Housing segregation has a long history in the United States; in 1933, amid the most prolonged and deepest downturn in US history, 'The Great Depression,' with one-quarter of the American workforce out of work and the country facing a housing shortage, the federal government began a program explicitly designed to increase... and segregate American's housing market. According to the author of *The Color of Law*, Richard Rothstein, the early stages of 'redlining' began under President Roosevelt's "New Deal" and were the equivalent of a "state-sponsored system of segregation." The term redlining would be devised years later and described how US banks categorized undeniable neighborhoods of color as 'hazardous' or underserving of financial investment due to the racial makeup of their residents. In the 1950s, every state in the United States had laws mandating residential district segregation. The policies of redlining laws were devastating to African Americans, excluding many of them from new suburbs being built, exacerbating problems with air, water, and noise pollution in the neighborhoods where they were allowed to live. Finally, the 1968 Fair Housing Act outlawed racially motivated redlining and designated federal financial regulators, including the Federal Reserve, to enforce the new legislation. This is the history of how racially discriminatory practices created the neighborhoods that would become the ghettos and hoods of America where ghetto/hood culture was born.

This culture of speaking Ebonics, stupidity, ratchet behavior, sagging pants, referring to one another with the N-word, and gangbanging, all of which at one time or another has been blamed on rap music, movies, and politics pandering to the people who embraced this type of conduct. Hood culture comes from the people in Black communities who are in favor of this type of behavior. In addition, these same people considered a Black person who was educated, well-mannered, and well-spoken, and despised gang activity as corny, nerdy, or acting white. "Go into any inner-city neighborhood, and folks will tell you that government alone can't teach kids to learn. They know that parents have to parent, that children can't achieve unless we raise their expectations, turn off the television sets, and eradicate the slander that says a Black youth with a book is acting white." ~Barack Obama, Keynote Address, Democratic National Convention, 2004. This type of attitude is a critical source of hindrance in many of our Black communities to this day, a complication to achieving more success for many more Black people... admittedly, this is not the only stumbling block we face. However, whenever someone among us rises to the occasion and says, "We can be better than this," the surprising response of many is to talk that person down, telling them to 'stop acting white' or 'You ain't black enough'... "you need to go back to the hood or ghetto where you came from." This is hood culture, and it is holding many of us back.

Hidden rules of economic class

America's lower, middle and upper classes view basic issues in different ways, according to social scientists, Here are some typical assumptions by members of the three economic classes.

	POVERTY	MIDDLE CLASS	WEALTH
POSSESSIONS	People	Things	One-of-a-kind objects, legacies, pedigrees.
MONEY	To be used, spent.	To be managed.	To be conserved, invested.
FOOD	Key question: Did you have enough? Quantity important.	Key question: Did you like it?	Key question: Was it presented well? Presentation important.
CLOTHING	Clothing valued for individual style and expression of personality.	Clothing valued for its quality and acceptance into the norms of middle class. Label important.	Clothing valued for its artistic sense and expression. Designer important.
EDUCATION	Valued and revered as abstract but not as reality. Education is about facts.	Crucial for climbing success ladder and making money.	Necessary tradition for making and maintaining connections.
WORLD VIEW	Sees world in terms of local setting.	Sees world in terms of national setting.	Sees world in terms of an international view.

SOURCE: aha! Process Inc.   **Todd B. Spidle**/SUNDAY NEWS

Why are Black Men Associated with Physical Threats and Violence?

Black men's association with threats and violence has been viewed through numerous factors, including socioeconomic standings, exploring false stereotypes, and the consistent arguments made in an attempt to manufacture public dislike and mistrust, a character assassination. Nevertheless, I wanted to explore what statistical data tells us about ourselves and whether data, although accurate, is misleading. According to historian Michael B. Katz (2013), throughout history, America has associated people with poverty and unworthiness, all self-inflicted conditions. Therefore, they are unworthy of public sympathy and support. When an entire group of people are perceived as unworthy, it has powerful social consequences.

In 2022 (various sources), *about* 43.4 million of 334 million US citizens are Black, about 13 percent. So, about 6.5 percent (**21.7 million**) of the US population is Black males. If Black males who commit murder did so at a rate proportional to their percentage of the US population, Black males would commit 6.5 percent of the murders committed in the US (i.e. 1,285 of 19,776). But that's not what we see. In 2022, there were *about* 19,776 murders in the US. Black males committed 9627 of those, which is 48.9 percent. This is 7.5 times the 6.5 percent expected rate if the Black male rate was proportional to its population share. And about 54 percent (10,679) of murder victims are Black males! This is the greatest threat to Black males in the US, not other threats coming from racism or other kinds of malice. It's not even close.

About 58.9 percent of the US population is non-Hispanic white. That's about **98.4 million**. In 2022, they committed 40.1 percent (7704) of the murders. The other kinds of males commit the other 6 percent of murders. About 12 percent (2107) of murders are committed by females, leaving 88 percent for males. This difference has nothing to do with *race*. So, we can conclude with high confidence that males are more dangerous (far more likely) than females when it comes to killing citizens in the US.

In the chart below about police shootings in 2022, we see that 34.5 percent (389) of police shooting victims were white, 20.5 percent (225) were black. The expected rate for Black people would be 6.5 percent (71.3), 3.15 times the predicted rate.... if no other factors were affecting the data. The white male rate was only 60 percent of their expected rate of 58.9 percent (646), which means that whites are shot at a lower rate. So, based on the data, police shot Black people disproportionately at a higher rate.

So many people jump to the conclusion that the police are trying to kill Black males just because they are Black. The thinking goes something like this: Whites have oppressed Black people in the past, and a significant portion continue to want Black people to be victimized in the US society. And if the opportunity arises where they can kill a Black male in some police encounter, whether justified or not, they will do it.

The above conclusion does not follow from the data. A more rational conclusion is that Black males are the *most violent* citizens (males are more violent than females by far by sex/gender), more likely to kill citizens, and therefore, more likely to have encounters with the police that lead to deadly force resulting in higher killings by the police. And this is bad whether the police are wrong or not. The police threat is far less of a threat to Black males than is the threat of Black males murdering other Black males. Just look at the numbers: **9627** murders by Black males (10,679 murdered Black people total) vs. **225** killings of Black people by the police. And since more white males (**389**) are killed by the police than Black males (225), it does not follow that killings are always due to racism. That's to say, it's not the proximate cause.

The behavior (malice) that ought to have the most attention and urgency to reduce…is the tendency of Black males to kill citizens in the US. This notion that Black people kill Black people and whites kill whites (a deflection from the point) as a mitigating factor is misguided and not relevant. *All of us* in the US (citizens) care most about NOT being harmed…being killed intentionally, which is probably the ultimate harm! Sure, we have other harms (stealing, assault, etc.). And, of course, being killed due to a disease or accident is not in the same category as murder, which causes more deaths of citizens. But what we care about here *in this analysis* is intentionality (malice). So why do Black males murder citizens at a rate over seven times their expected rate? "Black homicide rates are seven to eight times those of whites though blacks have a rate of poverty only four to five times that of whites" (Office of Justice Programs).

Perceived Threat Associated with Police Officers and Black Men

Racial disparities in policing in the United States, in particular, the recent high-profile incidents resulting in the death of Black men and women, have ignited a national debate in households of both white and Black families about policing policies. The list includes Daunte Wright, Andre Hill, Manuel Ellis, George Floyd, Breonna Taylor, Atatiana Jefferson, Aura Rosser, Stephon Clark, Botham Jean, Philando Castile, Alton Sterling, Freddie Gray, Tanisha Fonville, Eric Garner, Michelle Cusseaux, Akai Gurley, Gabriella Nevarez, Tamir Rice, Michael Brown, Tanisha Anderson, and Sonya Massey. These names represent just a few of the Black Americans killed by police, there are more! Taking into consideration evidence that both Black men and police officers are associated with threats, three research studies examined the impact of those noted threats and their correlation to the support for or against legislation to reform policing policies across the country. The researchers found that the evidence showing police officers as threatening resulted in increased support for police reform legislation that limited the use of lethal force and ensured harmonizing police force demographics in communities of color. In contrast, the perception of Black men has been threatening, resulting in a reduction of support for police reform. This theme of resistance to policing policy reform when Black men were the perceived threat was consistent throughout.

Moreover, research findings show that even publicizing racially charged police encounters with Black people could reduce support for policing policy reform. These adverse precautions of Black men are just one of the challenges to why police reform is so difficult. Another is determining which institutions to work with and work through to enhance justice and police responsiveness, accountability, and effectiveness. And yet another major challenge, and maybe the most difficult to overcome, is the fact that police reform has become such a political hot topic with the two major political parties in the US seeming to have opposing views on how to solve the problems or, instead, focus narrowly on police, courts, and prosecutors. And for Black parents like my mother, the negative perceptions and lack of progress in police reform for decades have forced them to have 'the talk' with their families.

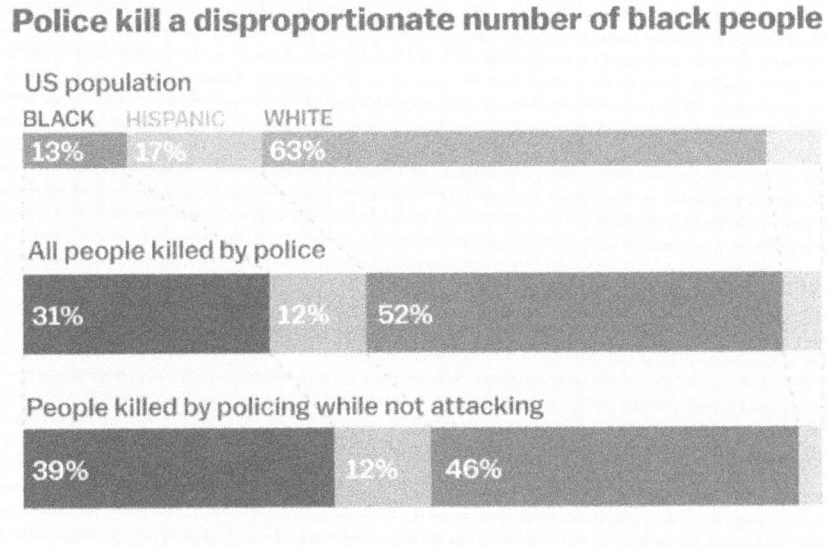

Police kill a disproportionate number of black people

US population

BLACK	HISPANIC	WHITE
13%	17%	63%

All people killed by police

| 31% | 12% | 52% |

People killed by policing while not attacking

| 39% | 12% | 46% |

Data from the FBI's 2012 Supplementary Homicide Report

The "talk" refers to what to do and not to do with interacting with the police has been passed down in many Black families for generations as a way to prepare their children for any unexpected interactions with the police, white police officers in particular. One of my daughter's favorite books *The Hate U Give*, was later made into a Hollywood movie dealing with Black culture and understanding. It had a scene where one of the main characters gets 'the talk' from her parents about sex and also about how to act when coming face-to-face with the police, an example of a film imitating life by placing a mirror in front of society. This distrust of police in the Black community is not just based on some unfounded fears that have been passed down from generation to generation, but they come from a history of police using methods that were not always used respectfully or honestly. Some of these tactics included undeniable lies about the evidence implicating Black men as the suspect, often referred to as "false evidence poly," where the police would tell the 'suspect' that they have video footage or an eyewitness from the scene of the crime, bluffing about the evidence that 'exists' against the suspect.

I had an encounter with a police officer in San Diego, California, in 2005 in the early morning hours before heading to work a day shift at the San Diego Air Traffic Control Tower. I had just completed a 5:00 a.m. gym workout at the local 24-Hour Fitness/Magic Johnson Sports health club. As I walked to my vehicle, exhausted from the early morning workout, I decided that once I got home, I would walk over to the nearby 7-Eleven store conveniently located less than fifty yards from the back gate of the condominium complex. After parking my vehicle, a black BMW-525 with shiny cast aluminum and steel wheels, in my assigned parking spot, I exited the back gate of the complex and hurriedly began walking toward the twenty-four-hour convenience store. Within minutes into my walk, I noticed a police vehicle parked outside the business next to the 7-Eleven, a self-service coin laundry facility. As I walked past the officer, he immediately began walking behind me. I could hear the sounds of his "cop" shoes as I continued to walk. Once inside the 7-Eleven, I walked directly over to the refrigerated beverage section of the store and grabbed a bottle of Tropicana pure premium orange juice.

I returned to the checkout counter where I picked up a USA Today newspaper and a yellow wristband inscribed with the words 'LIVE STRONG,' a charity set up by cyclist Lance Armstrong/

Lance Armstrong Foundation. Standing in line behind several other customers, I felt uneasy or anxious, as if someone were staring at me. I looked towards the front door and window of the store, and the officer was standing outside the glass window staring intently at me. Once I got to the front of the line to pay for my items, I couldn't help but take another look out the glass window. He was still standing there and staring directly at me. I thought, *What the hell, what did I do? I haven't done anything wrong, nothing at all.* After completing my purchase, I walked towards the exit, pushed the door open, and the officer stepped directly into my path. At this point, I became more irritated but continued walking without saying a word. I didn't have much time for small talk less than an hour before my scheduled shift to work at the control tower. In what seemed like a matter of seconds, as I stepped onto the sidewalk in front of the laundromat, I heard the loud, authoritative voice of the police officer, "Hey, Hey, Hey." It's 'that tone of voice' that is part of the 'progression of force,' with the first level being verbal commands, with each level escalating the situation from level 1 (verbal commands) to level 2 (physical direction) to level 3 (physical restraint). I continued walking, thinking, *I'm not stopping; I didn't do anything wrong.* So I just kept walking. Suddenly, seemingly out of nowhere, with sirens blaring and lights flashing, two police vehicles pulled into the parking lot of the laundromat on either side of me; I immediately stopped walking and leaned back against the larger glass window of the laundromat facility. I looked up in the direction of two vehicles, but their spotlights were so bright they temporarily blinded me. As I used my hands to shield my eyes, the police officer who was following behind me on foot, walked up a few feet away, and began questioning me, in that 'tone of voice,' "Hey, where are you coming from?" I was beyond frustrated at this point, and I'm certain he could detect this in my response, as I looked directly into his eyes and spoke with a stern voice, "You know where I'm coming from. You just saw me inside the 7-Eleven store, where you stared at me for several minutes." As he looked me up and down, he continued speaking. "Look, all I'm saying is a guy who looks just like you and was wearing the same color Nike sweatpants and top you are wearing just burglarized an apartment building around the corner." Before he could finish, I just started laughing. I responded to his description with a smirk and a "whatever, man."

The officer's radio chatter continued as he spoke to me. Still, I wasn't listening to his radio as much as watching his hands and wondering if he would pull his gun out of its holster. He never drew his weapon. But the fear of him pulling his gun was palpable, nevertheless. I remained calm and I continued to explain who I was: "Officer, I have a job as a controller, a certified air traffic controller, scheduled to work a day shift at San Diego (Brown Field) Airport within the hour." He responded by asking where I lived. "I live in that condominium complex right behind us." I slowly raised my arm and pointed towards the tall black gates surrounding the condominiums where I lived. I had just parked my vehicle minutes before my encounter with the officer. "I was about to go over and enter my security code on the access panel when you stopped me." Still staring at me as if he didn't believe a word coming out of my mouth, he asked, "Well, do you have any outstanding warrants?"

Shocked by his question, I begin shaking my head side-to-side to indicate 'no' before answering, "I've never been arrested." As the officer continued interrogating me, I noticed another large crowd from the 7-Eleven and surrounding stores gathering in the parking lot, attempting to see what was happening. I was mortified; strangers were standing around staring at me as if they were waiting for the 'perp walk' to happen. The 'perp walk' is a public showing of a suspected criminal being taken into custody by police. None of these people knew me, looking at me like, *Oh my God, look at this guy. Did he steal from the 7-Eleven store or rob someone in the store, or worse, did he murder someone?* I kept repeating the exact words to the police officer and, more importantly, to myself, "I didn't do anything." But regardless of that fact, I was being detained and publicly humiliated, a form of punishment in itself as I certainly felt dishonored and disgraced by the entire ordeal. I attempted to remain calm, but I was confused, anxious, and angry as two police cars were parked on either side of me, emergency lights flashing, while another officer stood in front of me shouting instructions and asking questions. I made sure to keep my hands in front of me and away from my body and avoided any sudden movements, all things my parents had told us to do if the police ever stopped us. I don't recall if the officers asked for ID or not; I also don't believe any of the officers had their guns drawn or their hands on their weapons; I just kept thinking to myself, *I didn't do anything.* I would later learn that California does not have a Stop and Identify law; therefore, it's non-criminal to refuse to identify yourself, the likely reason the officer did not ask for my identification. And yet there I was, standing in front of a closed laundromat business, surrounded by police officers, being made to look like a criminal. I could only imagine what my neighbors would think the next day when they saw me parking my vehicle or walking up to the security entrance gate; strangers who do not know me will be suspicious! It suddenly dawned on me that my college degree, a six-figure salary, high profile job, residing in an upper-middle-class neighborhood, or driving an expensive vehicle, none of those symbols of success mattered; I was just another criminal suspect! The encounter with the police officer was unnerving, and I left feeling more distrust of police officers than before. Although this happened in the early 2000s, it still surprised me that this still happens to everyday people who have done nothing wrong. After I was finally allowed to leave, I rushed home, grabbed my backpack, and hurriedly drove to work since I was running late for my shift.

When I arrived at the airport and entered the secured area for the air traffic control tower entrance, I sat in my vehicle for a few seconds, trying to regain my composure before walking into the tower. I could not shake off the negative experience. As I entered the building, I asked to speak to the shift supervisor downstairs in the training room; I explained to him what had happened and that I didn't think I could perform duties safely. Air traffic control is not necessarily dangerous, but it is about creating a safe environment for yourself and others. Sure, separating airplanes and ensuring crashes are avoided is serious work; it also requires the controller to be in a good mental space to make the best decisions possible. The incident had pushed me to a psychological brink, and I was still very upset about what the police had done to me!

The Education or Miseducation of Black Youth in America

Recent research studies published by the National Assessment of Educational Progress (NAEP) showed significant declines in American students' knowledge and skills and widening gaps between the highest and lowest-achieving students. The COVID-19 pandemic substantially affected the education system and student performance, with research showing a decline in math and reading scores by 15 and 10 percent between 2018 and 2022 (according to 2022 PISA results). But for Black children in America, other obstacles have created educational disadvantages, including:

- Access to opportunities

  Black students have less access to advanced classes, counselors, and certified teachers. They are also more likely to be below grade level for their age at age thirteen than white children.

- Learning gap

  The learning gap between Black children and their peers has widened, and their rate of progress has decreased. For example, in 2019, Black eighth graders scored lower on the NAEP reading test than in 2009 and 2017. According to the NAEP,

85 percent of Black students lack reading proficiency and 84 percent lack math proficiency.

- School discipline

  Black students are more likely to face disciplinary action than white students. For example, in North Carolina, law enforcement and school staff filed complaints against Black students for disorderly conduct at nearly four times the rate of white students between 2017 and 2023.

- Social challenges

  Black children may face social challenges when attending majority-white schools, such as white classmates correcting their English.

- Other factors that contribute to Black children's educational disadvantages include police presence in schools, excessive suspensions, and lack of personal responsibility from students and parents.

As a big proponent of the values of a progressive education system, not that it will resolve all our problems but that it could be an important step towards achieving equality, independence, and prosperity, I am greatly concerned about how our children are being educated, or not! Since the landmark Supreme Court decision, Brown v. Board of Education in 1954, a ruling that notably declared "separate is not equal" in response to the "separate but equal" legal doctrine in the United States that had allowed racial segregation as long as the laws applied equally to all people. The "separate but equal" doctrine was established by the 1896 US Supreme Court case Plessy v. Ferguson, which ruled that laws requiring racial segregation in public accommodations, such as schools and trains, were constitutional if the facilities for each race were equal. The doctrine was based on the idea that these laws did not violate the

Fourteenth Amendment's Equal Protection Clause, which states that states cannot deny equal protection under the law to anyone within their jurisdiction. In practice, however, "separate but equal" was a farce, as Black people often received inferior and inhumane treatment and facilities. Although Brown v. Board of Education declared the practice unconstitutional in 1954, many believe that not enough was done to make up for all of the damage that caused generations of racial discrimination and by the nearly sixty years of a "separate but equal" legal system. Another major gap that is impacting our education of Black children is a lack of diversity in teachers. Diversity is needed to sustain the education profession, but more importantly, it promotes achievement and cultural competency and provides role models. By no means am I saying that only Black teachers can educate Black students; in fact, some of my favorite teachers over the years were not Black, but evidence shows systematic biases in teachers' expectations for the educational attainment of Black students. Notably, non-Black teachers have significantly lower educational expectations for Black students than Black teachers do when evaluating the same students. In addition, Black students are also more likely to be placed in gifted education programs if they have a Black teacher and are less likely to receive suspensions, expulsions, or detentions (Center for Black Educator Development). Another external barrier that can negatively impact Black students is the presence of police officers on the school campus. There could be several factors that create this negative effect, including mental health, disproportionate assault, history of policing, and school climate. Whatever the cause, statistical data cannot be ignored; more than 80 percent of all students physically assaulted by police officers in schools have been black, according to data from the past thirty years. Latinx students have been assaulted at an 11 percent rate, and white students at a 3 percent rate, according to Advancement Project's analysis from Education Week (2023). To this point, I've only addressed external obstacles facing our Black students' educational journey, but let's be honest: we have also played a role in hindering our progress or success through our thoughts, behaviors, and attitudes.

In a study published in Education Week (1987), two anthropologists stated that "negative peer pressure" causes numerous Black students to perform below the level that standardized test scores indicate they should score. It's not completely clear how big of an impact the "acting white" ridicules or ostracizes students for making good grades and scoring high on tests. But what is clear is that the "acting white" criticism of high-achieving Black students results in those students being less popular with their peers and negatively impacts the attitudes of Black students' desire for schoolwork. As expected, the negative "acting white" peer pressure has emerged as a common explanation for the achievement gap between Black and white students, a gap that differences in demographic characteristics alone cannot explain away.

If the assumption is that students are deliberately underachieving to avoid social ostracism, then that action could explain the deterioration in the academic performance of middle adolescent African Americans (since the 1980s), according to the National Assessment of Educational Progress (NAEP). One more self-imposed barrier is the perceived or real issue of a lack of personal accountability in our communities. Parents abdicate their role in their children's development/education, instead placing the burden or obligation on teachers and the education system to educate their children. In researching this topic, I sat down for an in-depth interview with Mr. Thomas Cole, the co-founder (with his wife), educational consultant, and principal of Emma Jewel Charter Academy, a tuition-free public charter school located in Cocoa, Florida. The student population of Emma Jewel Charter Academy is 357, and the school serves K-8. At Emma Jewel Charter Academy, 29 percent of students scored at or above the proficient level for math, and 28 percent scored at or above that level for reading. The school's minority student enrollment is 95 percent. The student-teacher ratio is 18:1, which is worse than the district's. The student population comprises 43 percent female students and 57 percent male students. The school enrolls 85 percent economically poor and disadvantaged students. There are twenty equivalent full-time teachers on staff at the charter academy.

The following is an excerpt from a one-on-one interview conducted with Mr. Thomas Cole in the Spring of 2024. Thomas Cole has over sixteen years of experience in education. Over his educational career, he has served as a teacher, assistant principal, principal, and educational consultant. He holds an undergraduate degree from Florida A & M University and two graduate degrees in education from the University of Central Florida. He believes parents are the primary and most important educators in their children's lives. He currently serves as the Executive Director for Emma Jewel Charter Academy. Mr. Cole and I share the belief that educated people are more likely to have higher self-esteem, confidence, and a sense of purpose, which are essential for lifetime happiness. Believing in the importance of education means recognizing that it is a crucial tool for personal development, societal progress, and economic opportunity, allowing individuals to gain knowledge, skills, and critical thinking abilities to navigate life effectively and contribute positively to their communities. In the following interview excerpt, Mr. Cole shares his thoughts, ideas, and tips to parents about how to participate, be supportive, build relationships, and be culturally responsive and respectful in supporting their children and teachers in successfully educating our kids.

Excerpt from One-on-One Interview with Mr. Thomas Cole, Principal, EJCA

Dr. Robert Worthington: Recording has begun; good morning, Mr. Thomas Cole. How are you doing, sir?

Mr. Thomas Cole: Good morning, Dr. Worthington. Good morning, Brother Rob. Good to hear from you, man. It›s always good to connect with you, my brother.

Dr. Robert Worthington: Absolutely; I appreciate you taking the time to speak with me this morning. Before we get started, please briefly introduce yourself before we get into the Q&A of the interview.

Mr. Thomas Cole: All right, I am Thomas Cole. I co-founded Emma Jewel Charter Academy, located in Cocoa, Florida. We are a tuition-free public charter school. We serve scholars from DPK through eighth grade. We have about 98 percent African American students, 100 percent free reduced lunch, and 27 percent ESC population.

So, this is our tenth year of operation for Emma Jewell Charter Academy, and I've been in education since 1997.

Dr. Robert Worthington: Great, let's get started! You're a highly experienced and knowledgeable professional, ideally suited to address the topics we will discuss this morning. You're the perfect person for it.

We're going to begin this morning by talking about some issues and stuff in our communities, precisely the behavior and emotional development of African American boys growing up in a risky environment between the ages of nine and eighteen.

What's the most significant change, and what hinders that development?

Mr. Thomas Cole: Well, as with part one, you are a former basketball coach, let me take you on a very, very brief journey. In other words, if we were to go, let's say, three years ago at a middle school basketball game, specifically, I'm going to do a chartered academy. One disturbing thing for me is that there is no accountability when either (1) I have done something wrong, or (2) someone is just performing better than me.

I can sit in the stands and continually tell the adults and the parents at those basketball games to first watch their language because they're yelling and screaming at referees and constantly feeling as if the referees are cheating against them or they're trying to make them lose. The reality is that these referees do not have a dog in the fight. They are not professional referees where they would have some stake in seeing this team win over the others. Still, some of the parents have that lack of accountability to the point where they cannot (1) admit that sometimes the reality is that the other team may just be better than your team or is working harder than your team; (2) the fact that there's no conspiracy theory that everybody is against you; sometimes you just have to work harder and longer and be better than the next person as opposed to sitting there making excuses at the basketball games in terms of why your team is losing or lost the game.

But the reality is, Brother Worthington, that microcosm that I just broke down for you, that small microcosm, there is something bigger that you're seeing within the classrooms. And if we had that basketball game on a Tuesday night, Brother Worthington, the gym would be packed to capacity with our parents, okay?

But if we host an open house teacher-parent conference the next night on a Wednesday, we're going to be hearing crickets (silence) because we're not going to have that same level of folks showing up to be supportive of what's going on. Some of these parents that we have now, Brother Worthington, are not the same ones we had.

Dr. Robert Worthington: Yes, you are correct.

Mr. Thomas Cole: But this younger generation has been raised by a generation of parents who are not adequately ready to be parents. We have a lot; I think what you›re seeing now also too, Brother Worthington, is a lot of these teenage mothers that were never correctly ready to be parents to the point where they›re not, they›re loving their children so much to the point where they›re loving them and not holding them accountable when they›re wrong.

They're trying to be their friends. They're trying to be their homegirl. They call their kids, "That's my Jit." Or, for lack of a better term, "That's my little nigga." And those values that I'm talking about, Brother Worthington, start to seep into the educational system to the point where it deteriorates the amount of accountability.

This young parent, who's not ready to be a parent, loves her son so much that she doesn't want to see anything go wrong and nothing hurt them. But this same sixteen-year-old girl has had a rough time in school. So, she's taking whatever mindset she had when she was in school and not successful and trying to make sure it doesn't happen to her child to a point where she's not holding him accountable when he's wrong. He can come to that school daily and flip out of that classroom, laughing and talking to everybody how he wants to.

But the moment that boy comes home and says that the teacher said this to me or said that to me, she's (the boy's mother) ready to come up to the school with her hair bonnet on her head, wearing pajamas and flip-flops and 'curse out' everybody in the school based solely on the words of her son. Still, she's unwilling to sit down with the teacher or school administrators and listen to the totality of what happened and how the difficulty is in educating a young black boy. Both the young boy and his mother, who may have become a mother at a young age herself, may not be living in an environment of respect and boundaries; the child has probably witnessed adults smoking weed in front of him, unfiltered profanity, and confused and muddled topsy-turvy home life, where everything is 'upside down,' meaning their outlook on the world is the complete opposite of what it is. Now, the mother comes to the child's school with this mentality, which will probably not result in a positive outcome.

Dr. Robert Worthington: I agree with that, Mr. Cole. I want to change the topic because you reminded me of a conversation with a school resource officer. We had lengthy discussions about students using their cell phones to call their parents during school hours in the middle of an altercation with a teacher or administrator, and the parents immediately showed up at school, raising all types of hell with every schoolteacher or administrator in sight—still, no words to correct the behavior of their child.

Another example of how parents' behavior is different today versus 15-20 years ago. During the days we were attending school, if one of our parents received a call from the school officer or a teacher, we knew we were in serious trouble. When those '70s and '80s parents came out to the school, their child's behavior would change with just the sight of the parents because our parents would hold us accountable for our behavior. Does this still happen today? And if not, when and why did it change?

Mr. Thomas Cole: You›re correct. Let me say this. Whenever a teacher now calls a parent, they feel like they're the ones (behavior) that is being questioned. "What did you do to my child first?" Or what did you do first? "He wouldn't just do that, whatever the case."

That has changed because we no longer have the Mrs. Worthington-style values. We don't have the Mrs. Worthington-style values anymore because we don't have that; we don't have those same accountability levels for our young Black boys.

And our young Black boys are doing some very irresponsible stuff, getting a lot of these young girls pregnant early, and they're not ready. And they don't know how to be Brother Worthington; they don't know how to be young men. So, what's happening is they're getting these girls pregnant, brother Worthington, okay? Leaving these girls to fend for themselves and be able to raise these boys by themselves without a positive male role model.

That's part one of it, too. That's part one, okay? Now, I don't want to let the school system not be without fault as well, too, because there is also a lack of diversity in many of our schools, and this is not the only thing, Brother Worthington, but this also contributes to it, okay? This contributes to the fact that when you have a young Black boy who is going into an environment where he's going to be judged explicitly by white middle-class values all day long as far as how he acts and how he behaves. There are no positive males to put him in check. You have those white middle-class values that are enforced by primarily white female teachers who don't understand their values. What you're going to have there, Brother Worthington, you're going to have an over-representation of young Black boys being suspended. You're going to have an over-representation of young Black boys being referred to ESC programs for special ed. And third, you're going to have an over-representation of young Black boys being medicated because that makes it easier for those teachers to deal with.

So that's another part of it. So, one part of it is the fact that our young Black boys are not stepping up to raise our children, or should I say our young Black men. The second part is that we have an educational system that is not designed for success, and they lack diversity in the administration and teaching realm, okay?

Because what I think needs to be understood, what people need to understand, Brother Worthington, and stay with me on this, I'm going to come back to your question: is the fact that our young Black boys will be educated regardless, okay?

Brother Worthington, what are they being educated for? A lot of times within the school system, the only thing they're being educated for is to be a better hustler on the corner, a better con man, a better person doing conniving stuff.

Our role in the education system is to transform all those because this is the deal. I can have a child that comes into my school, and he is so independent, brother, because that young female I was talking about, she's probably working two or three jobs, and that young boy is at home taking care of himself, taking care of his brother. So, he's cooking for himself, cleaning for himself, and very, very independent.

Or that young Black female is addicted to whatever the substance abuse may be of the environment, and he is still taking care of himself. So, what›s more, when that young boy comes to school, now he›s so independent, Brother Rob, and now all of a sudden, Brother Rob, I'm telling him you will sit right here. I will let you know when you go to lunch, when you go to pee, and when you go to the bathroom.

He's like, "Wait a minute, who are you? You don't tell me what to do. I do what I want to do." And you know what, Brother Rob? He's authentic. He's telling the truth because he's so independent and cares for himself. He's taking care of his younger brother and younger sister. He is independent, but what I have to do as an educator and administrator is to be able to harness those leadership skills and turn them around. So, he's, he's the best leader on the corner in terms of selling drugs. He's the best person, being the leader of whatever local gang out there. He's the best person in the classroom to be the best lawyer one day. He can be the best doctor one day. So, he can lead and be the next CEO. We must refrain from turning our noses to some leadership skills that come across the client. We have to be able to find that middle ground, Brother Rob, so that we are harnessing those leadership skills in them and turning those into positive things as opposed to negative leadership skills because they're to be educated regardless of whether they're for the streets or educated for the boardroom, the medical profession, or the law profession. So those old school values that we lost came in because the fact we don't have Mrs. Worthington there anymore telling them as far as making yourself accountable.

Mr. Thomas Cole: If I were to give a message, honestly, it would be to our parents. As Black parents, we have a unique opportunity to empower our children academically by actively engaging with their education, celebrating their achievements, and advocating for their needs in school, ensuring they feel supported and confident in pursuing their full potential, regardless of systemic obstacles. Our parents need to be a part of the education process along with their children's teachers, in particular during the summer months, when many of our kids have two months of brain-dead time. Some important points for parents to remain engaged include:

- **Active engagement:**
  Regularly check homework, discuss schoolwork, and attend parent-teacher conferences to stay informed and provide support.
- **Positive reinforcement:**
  Celebrate your child's accomplishments, no matter how small, and emphasize their intelligence and learning ability.
- **Cultural awareness:**
  Discuss Black students' challenges in the education system and equip them with strategies to navigate these issues.

- **Empowerment:**
  Please encourage your child to be proud of their identity and use their voice to advocate for themselves.
- **Community building:**
  Connect with other Black parents and educators to share strategies and build a supportive network.

Mr. Thomas Cole: I would encourage all our parents to seek out reading clubs, reading camps, academic stuff, folks, anything that be academic as opposed to those two months of brain-dead time (during the summer months); by and large, African American children are on a grade level or more behind other students. There are several reading clubs and programs for K-12 students in the United States, including:

- **First Partner's Summer Book Club**: A California initiative that encourages children to read during the summer to reduce learning loss
- **Read Across America**: A National Education Association (NEA) program that encourages reading throughout the year and includes a Diverse Books Challenge.
- **Reading the World**: A virtual book club for K-12 educators that explores global challenges through literature
- **Scholastic Book Clubs**: A program that offers book clubs for children and families
- **Out school**: An online book club for kids and teens
- **Kumon**: A program that helps children build self-confidence through reading and math
- **Lexia**: A research-based literacy program that helps teachers personalize instruction for students

- Note: the list of reading clubs above is just a small sample of available reading resources for school age children.
- **Tips for starting a new book club**: Work with your public library to borrow books, eBooks, or audiobooks; Partner with your public library to get grant funding for books and book club programming; Seek out people who are already passionate readers
- **Dr. Robert Worthington:** I certainly appreciate your time, Mr. Cole. Thank you so much. You were very, very helpful. I'm looking forward to visiting Emma Jewel Charter Academy for a tour and an opportunity to speak with your faculty and students. Again, thank you very much. I truly appreciate your time.
- **Mr. Thomas Cole:** I look forward to your visit, Brother Worthington. You're welcome. All right, thank you.

These were the educational insights, opinions, and suggestions from this interview with Mr. Cole, an educator and administrator with more than twenty-five years of experience who has established partnerships with parents and worked collaboratively to ensure that all the students, past, present, and future who attend Emma Jewel Charter Academy receive a high-quality education. Although not included in the excerpt of my interview with Mr. Cole, we discussed another topic: the detrimental practice of book banning happening all around the country and its adverse effects on students' educational experiences. History teaches us that this practice can limit students to different perspectives, stifle critical thinking, and hinder students' understanding of important societal issues. Unfortunately, the momentum for banning books has not slowed down, with more than thirty states banning books by Black authors. According to the PEN American, the Black authors who have had their books banned include classics like *The Color Purple*; *The Autobiography of Malcolm X*, one of my favorite books, and *I Know Why the Caged Bird Sings*, to name a few. PEN researchers also noted that books about race, racism, or that feature characters of color make up 30 percent of the book titles that have been banned. The reason given for most of the banned books is part of efforts to stamp out "critical race theory" from being taught in K-12 public schools, which is a strange goal considering the second-year law school course isn't part of the curriculum in any K-12 public schools in the United States.

This was particularly challenging to write due to the susceptible topics, but sometimes hard truths must be told. Many of the sentiments expressed will not apply to every Black kid or family, but they apply to enough people in our communities who may make a difference between life and death.

white students

In 2016, there was a difference of five grade levels between white and Black students' math and reading scores.

Black students

Stacked books to represent the difference in grade reading levels between white and black students.   REBECCA RIRENBAUM

12

THE INVISIBLE VICTIMS: EXPLORING THE IMPACT OF INCARCERATION ON FAMILIES

M y brother is being charged with murder! Those were the words I repeated to myself over and over again as a shocked and confused eighteen-year-old first-year college student. I was looking forward to starting the 1984-85 college basketball season so that one of my lifelong dreams would finally be realized: I was the starting two-guard on a men's college basketball team. My older brother would see me play my first college basketball game. As my 'big brother' inspired my passion for basketball, I learned to play the game on the asphalt courts of Griffin Park projects, mostly playing one-on-one basketball games against him—games I never won! He played a significant role in my social and emotional development as my protector, guide, mentor, and friend. And, of course, he was my rival on the basketball court, which I guess is hard to call rivalry if you're always on the losing end of the score. But those one-on-one games at the park and later in our driveway built the foundation that developed an attitude of competitiveness that still helps navigate my life today. Tragically, my brother would never see me play my first college basketball game or any of the games I would play during my first year. In fact, he would never see me play another basketball game again! The shocking news that my brother had been arrested for deliberately killing someone was nearly incomprehensible to me. I watched the local news broadcast of my brother, a teenager, in police custody, being led into an Orlando police station in a manner that enabled the media to publicize the event: a perp walk! I read The Orlando Sentinel Newspaper article about the arrest, with the headline "Lawyer to the jury: Man slain with a machete was a case of self-defense." I was overwhelmed with emotions reading the news article and the details of the crime it provided; it just completely turned my world upside down. As I read the newspaper article again and again, my eyes returned to the first sentence of the first paragraph of the newspaper article, "Worthington is charged with first-degree murder." It elicited feelings of guilt, self-blame, and thoughts of *if only*. The last time I saw William was a Friday night just before the annual rivalry basketball game between local basketball powerhouses, the Evans High School Trojans versus Orlando Jones Tigers—a rivalry I had participated in for three years. He asked me to give him a ride to his friend Baby G's house. Since I hadn't seen much of him lately, I thought it would be a great idea if we attended the big game together. But after I repeatedly asked him to ride with me to Evans High School, he laughed and shook his head 'no.' Smiling while he spoke, he politely declined to attend the game with me, saying he needed to do something with Baby G. It has been hard to wrap my mind around everything that happened, *if only*.

After growing up with someone, sharing all your childhood secrets and hopes, you think you know who they are, but then something like this happens, and there is a mixture of shock, confusion, anger, and sadness. Grappling with the situation over the years has been a balance between supporting my brother, taking care of my mental health, and navigating the complex legal system. Sadly, I haven't visited William in person in several years, although I have had several video visitations with him. I still love him, obviously, but I can't help but feel like we no longer know one another. In just a few months, he will begin serving his fortieth year, four decades in prison, more than twice the number of years he's lived before being arrested at age nineteen. Throughout these years, William has been housed at some of the most challenging and most dangerous prisons in the state of Florida, including, Columbia Correctional Institution, Dade Correctional Institution, and Santa Rosa Correctional Institution, where he currently resides. It's a prison that ranks as one of Florida's worst prisons with over sixteen hundred prisoners and a high level of gang violence. Transferring prisoners to different prisons could be for many reasons, from security level change, sentencing plan, behavior, or planned transfers, and prisoners have little choice in the matter. In the nearly four decades (1985-2024) since my brother's arrest, conviction, and imprisonment for the crimes he committed, society has undergone some significant changes.

The most noted of these major changes is the widespread adoption of the internet and digital technologies. The internet was still in its early stages in the 1980s and was used mainly by research institutions and universities. Personal computers were just beginning to emerge, but the internet as we know it today did not yet exist. Over the past few decades, digital technologies like Apple iPhone or Samsung Android smartphones, social media, and streaming services have transformed how we communicate, access information, and entertain ourselves. In addition, over the past forty years, significant social and cultural attitudes have evolved significantly to include a growing acceptance of diverse lifestyles, increased focus on individual choice and personal values, greater emphasis on gender equality, broader acceptance of LGBTQ+ rights, rising concerns about climate change, increased reliance on technology, and a shift towards more progressive views on issues like racial equality and immigration, often accompanied by a growing polarization in political opinions. Another significant change in daily life is the dramatic rise in the popularity of electric vehicles (EVs), which were still nascent or non-existent in the 1980s. The most popular cars the year (1985) my brother was arrested were the Ford F-Series pickup truck and the Chevrolet Cavalier, available in five body styles: coupe, sedan, hatchback, wagon, and convertible. Four decades later, the best-selling vehicle in the United States remains the Ford F-Series. However, the electric car took off in the US in the 2000s, with millions being sold every year, including in 2023, when EV sales increased by 60 percent from the previous year. Tesla's Model Y and Chevrolet's Bolt EV, Blazer EV, and Silverado EV are all top-selling and award-winning vehicles regularly seen on our highways today but were only a thing of our imagination and Hollywood movies like *Back to the Future* (1985). However, grieving the death of loved ones while incarcerated is a uniquely difficult process. In prison, there is no space to grieve in private. Inmates are surrounded by people who reject and exploit signs of weakness and even fear dehumanizing prison regulations that may criminalize any showing of grief, like crying, wailing, or appearing unable to pull themselves together. And because inmates depend so much on family members during their incarceration, they are reluctant to burden loved ones with their feelings, so they often cope with isolation by compartmentalizing their emotions. "The prison environment is almost diabolically conceived to force the offender to experience the pangs of what many psychiatrists would describe as mental illness."

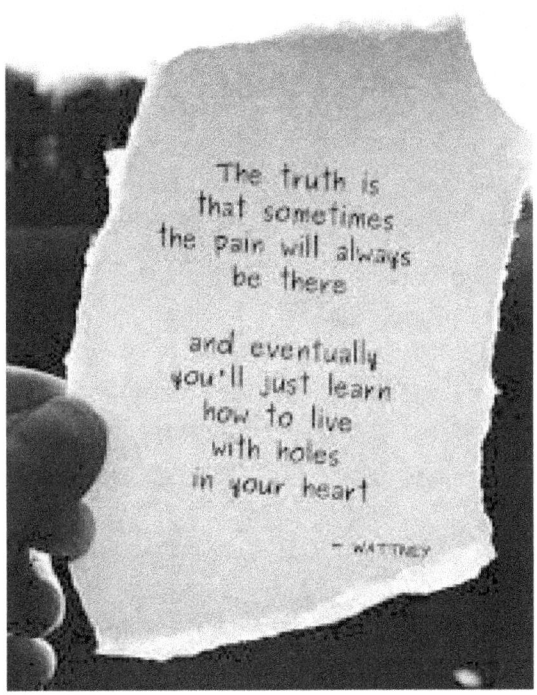

The truth is
that sometimes
the pain will always
be there

and eventually
you'll just learn
how to live
with holes
in your heart

— WHITNEY

Nevertheless, the burden William has had to bear hasn't been his alone; the impact on our mother's health has been devastating. She suffers from several chronic health conditions like hypertension, heart disease, obesity, and high blood pressure. She also has the added pressure of being the primary source for 'money on his books,' inmate accounts to access funds. She has been the consistent visitor for in-person visits at every single prison facility he has been in since his first year in prison; both significant factors are her elevated stress levels as a 78-year-old retiree on a fixed monthly income. No mother wants to go to bed at night knowing her child is in prison; it has been emotionally devasting for her.

William's arrest for murder wasn't just a shocking and unimaginable act but also left her and the entire family feeling humiliated and ashamed by the crime he had committed. We talked to investigators, lawyers, family members, friends, and the pastor from my mother's church. Still, none of us could understand how he got himself involved in something so far off and contrary to the values and beliefs our mother had instilled in us our entire life. My mother has often talked about how she devoted her life to her children in the hope that we would experience a better life journey than she had, but then to learn that your oldest son has been arrested unexpectedly and will be in prison forever, his life over— and everyday life will never happen! I can still hear the sadness in her voice when she spoke these words, "I am heartbroken, and my life will never be the same." William's life sentence and nearly forty years' incarceration, plus grief over the loss of family members and friends entered our lives during that period. We lost our maternal grandparents, my grandfather, Clarence Gaulden (1986), shortly after William was sentenced to prison; our grandmother, Claudia M. Gaulden (1997), and my sister's oldest son, my nephew, Sylvester "Junior" Walker (2007). Junior was murdered while walking with a friend, who, experiencing a mental health crisis, actually shot and killed Junior.

The death of a loved one is always tricky, but the constraints of prison life don't allow you to grieve in the same way as those who are not in prison. I spoke with my brother via phone and, with a heavy heart, told him the news of the death of our biological father, William E. Worthington Sr., who died on Thursday, November 16 (age 78), in Louisville, Kentucky. He is buried at the Kentucky Veterans Cemetery Central, Radcliff, Hardin County, Kentucky. William did not attend the funeral, something that would have been possible if the prison's warden approved a compassionate release or temporary leave, but it was not approved. However, the Office of Justice Programs, at the prison where William was imprisoned at the time, was authorized to provide him a grief pamphlet that included healing tools for dealing with the loss of a death, such as finding someone to talk to, allowing time in your cell for crying in private, asking family for a program of the service, and having a plan to have someone be with the inmate for support the day of the funeral. This grief pamphlet was designed for inmates held in prisons and jails to aid them in understanding grief and offer ideas and suggestions to cope with losses that have occurred in their lives. The healing process can be excessively challenging for long-term (more than twenty years) inmates as they seek to understand their emotions and feelings, such as regret, blame, hopelessness, and anger, while coping with their loss.

Prisons use different grief pamphlets. Still, much of the information and resources of support are similar and offered in a variety of printed booklets; for example, the Philadelphia, PA courts authorized a seventeen-page pamphlet, "The Multiple Layers of Grief," written by prison chaplain Phyllis B. Taylor and other mental health specialists, that presents detailed steps to understanding and coping with grief. See example below:

Cecilia Lee

THE MULTIPLE LAYERS OF GRIEF

Grief is the natural response to the loss of something important, such as a loved one, and is a process of learning to accept and live with that loss. There is no right or wrong way to feel during grief, and the time it takes to process a loss varies from person to person.

Some common symptoms of grief include:

- Emotional pain—Feeling numb, shocked, fearful, guilty, or angry.

- Physical pain—Tightness in the chest or throat, tiredness, or exhaustion.

- Behavioral changes—Crying easily, trouble sleeping, little interest in food, problems concentrating, and difficulty making decisions.

Stages of grief: The grief process is a complex reaction to loss that can involve a variety of emotions and behaviors:

- Denial

  A temporary response to overwhelming emotions, where you may feel numb or shocked and think the loss isn't real.

- Anger

  A natural response that can be directed at yourself, family, doctors, God, or the deceased.

- Bargaining

  You may imagine ways to reach an agreement or prevent the loss, or regret past actions.

- Depression

  You may experience sadness and emotional detachment as you understand the loss.

- Acceptance

  You eventually embrace the reality of the loss, even if the pain is still there.

Other reactions to grief can include:

- Shock
- Physical symptoms like headaches, body aches, or stomach distress
- Feelings of panic
- Guilt
- Inability to return to daily routine
- Return of feelings of hopefulness

There›s no correct length of time for grief, and it can last for several months or years. The length of time and depth of grief can be affected by many factors, including: your relationship with the person who died, how the loved one died, your own life experiences, what death means to you, and your cultural practices.

Some ways to cope with grief include:

- Talking with friends, family, or people you trust
- Seeking out online grief counseling groups
- Creating a routine to maintain a sense of order and purpose
- Honoring the loved one who passed
- Talking to a health care provider or counselor

The grief pamphlet example here is a duplication of similar booklets provided for real-life guidance for men and women at numerous prisons and jails throughout the United States to support those incarcerated individuals in coping with their feelings after learning of the death of a loved one. Grief pamphlets are available for free printing and reproduction for use in correctional institutions by contacting the authors of the booklets directly or through both local and national prison organizations, including Florida Department of Corrections, National Institutes of Health (NIH), The Lionheart Foundation, The Grace Project, National Hospice Association, American Correctional Chaplains Association, Office of Justice Programs, Prison Fellowship, and many others. The resources provided by these organizations are intended to aid inmates and their family members, often referred to as "hidden victims"— victims of the criminal justice system who are neither acknowledged nor given a platform to be heard. These hidden victims receive little personal support and do not benefit from the systemic societal mechanisms generally available to direct crime victims, despite their prevalence and their similarities to direct crime victims. Below is an example of a grief pamphlet designed for inmates held in prisons and jails to aid them in understanding grief and offer ideas and suggestions to cope with losses that have occurred in their lives.

Supports in My Life

When you lose a loved one, there is sometimes a temptation to stay away from people you've been close to or from organizations you belong to. Grief does tend to put you in an "antisocial state." However, reaching out to others is important to your health and healing. The grief journey will be more difficult if you try to go it alone.

List below the people and organizations that are supportive to you.

People Who Are Close to Me:
Immediate Family Members –

Other Relatives –

Neighbors –

Friends –

Others In the Community:
Pastor/Clergy –

Counselor –

Co-Worker –

Organizations:
Church –

Athletic/Recreational –

Clubs and Civic Groups –

Support Group(s) –

Now look over the names you listed. Does your support seem adequate at this time? If not, what more is needed? How could you help to make this happen?

Although I spent a great deal of time on the grief of family members and inmates as the result of long-term incarceration, it is not the only negative impact on family members, including:

- **Health**

  Children of incarcerated parents are more likely to have health problems, including developmental delays and poor mental health. Women with incarcerated family members are more likely to have obesity, stroke, and heart disease.

- **Behavior**

  Children of incarcerated parents are more likely to have behavioral problems, including aggressive behaviors and substance use.

- **Academic**

  Children of incarcerated parents are more likely to have academic difficulties and grade retention.

- **Financial**

  Families with an incarcerated member are more likely to have trouble meeting basic needs, such as food and housing.

- **Mental health**

  Incarceration can lead to depression and anxiety in both adults and children.

- **Housing**

  Incarceration can lead to unstable housing for the entire family.

- **Stigma**

  Many families need support but hesitate to ask for it due to stigma.

The fact that mass incarceration affects the overall quality of life for families isn't surprising. The fact that "almost half of the American population has an immediate family member who was formerly or is currently incarcerated" is staggering! Several studies have shown that the growth in incarceration of men with children contributes to higher rates of homelessness among Black children by dwindling family finances and placing additional strains on single-parent households. My brother was a teenage father when he was arrested, and his only child, my niece Che'na, was a preschooler and only four years old when her father was sent to prison; she's now forty-three years old, a mother, and a grandmother. She shared that her only memories of her father were visiting him in prison; there were no unique birthday gifts, no high school graduation hugs, no symbolic gesture of love, no support, and no possibility of her father walking her down the aisle for her wedding or a father to be present at the birth of her first child. Che'na has been wounded by lacking a significantly more robust bond with her father, leading to a more profound sense of connection and positive emotional support.

Unfortunately, after visiting her father in prison from the age of preschool to post-high school to early adulthood, and in later years visiting with her daughter, their relationship has fractured. Today, their relationship can be characterized by dysfunction, imbalance, and negativity. Che'na confessed to me during a phone conversation that she believes her father is emotionally immature, only concerned for his own needs and lacks empathy for others. She continued, "I don't talk to my dad; he's selfish." As I listened to her speak, I wasn't angry but more disappointed about the unhealthy relationship that had emerged after all these years. I told her that her father has been in prison for more than twice the number of years he lived as a free man, and incarceration hurts a young man's psychological maturity and mental health, including depression and anxiety. The human brain does not fully develop until age twenty-five; by this age, my brother had been in prison for five years…I think it's a safe assumption that his maturation process and parenting skills didn't improve over the next thirty-five years of imprisonment. The fundamental difference between childhood and old age is not physical or even mental. It's just the added weight of all the years accumulated behind you. Looking back on the ebb and flow of good and bad times, the journey that brought me from a military town with a small-town feel, Hinesville, Georgia, to a city with a mix of urban and suburban feel, and is known for its theme parks, entertainment, and diverse neighborhoods of Orlando, Florida.

I still remember the drive from Georgia to Florida as I relocated to Orlando with my mother and siblings. My big brother, William, eased my anxiety about the move, "Tan, man, I got you; I will be watching over your every move." He never got tired of the "He's copying me!" game that never seemed to end until we went to bed…at least until the next day. From that first car ride, I watched everything he did; I looked up to him—although I couldn't surpass his achievements in the classroom or the basketball court—I never gave up; I just kept watching, determined to work as hard as I needed to impress my 'big brother.'

The truth is—he was my hero, and being related to someone "as cool as Weo" is something every little brother wants. Being in a big brother's shadow can be good because it can help you develop essential skills and make you a better person. I realize the most profound lessons weren't taught in classrooms but in the heart of the challenges I faced on the asphalt basketball courts of the Griffin Park housing project. Playing basketball at the park became the most exciting thing about our day, not just for me but for nearly all of the kids in Griffin Park, playing pickup games with friends or watching NBA basketball games, mainly when the Philadelphia 76ers team played with the legendary Dr. J and Orlando's native son, Darryl Dawkins aka "Chocolate Thunder."

We could hear the sound of the basketball bouncing on the stiff surface of the asphalt court, emitting a loud characteristic "thump," followed by a high-pitched ringing. William and I would race down the stairs and out our apartment's backdoor, excited about the challenge that awaited us: a four-man team game or another one-on-one game that usually ended in William being victorious! But even as I lost another one-on-one game against my brother, the competition, the sound of nets as the ball went through the hoop, and the pounding sound of the ball would all be repeated in my dreams after I fell asleep. Suddenly, a loud pounding sound brought me to a different scene, the inside of four gray cinder-block walls, interrupted only by a small window, a steel toilet-sink combo, and a solid steel door. I awoke, still breathing hard, heart pounding; I sat up in the bed and rubbed my eyes with both hands—wishing this too was a dream and that I could wake up and walk across the hallway into my brother's room and see him sleeping in his bed…but then I awoke! Once searing, the scars of my past have transformed into guiding stars, illuminating a path where resilience and empathy are my compass. While the future remains unwritten, I carry the wisdom gleaned from my experiences, ready to embrace whatever comes next with an open heart and an unwavering determination to make a difference.

What's next is to take steps to seek a compassionate release from prison for William, a process that involves several steps: 1. Initial request: we need to file a request with the Bureau of Prisons (BOP). The BOP must respond within thirty days; 2. Exhaust administrative remedies; if denied, the inmate must appeal through the BOP's hierarchy; 3. Court petition, a motion can be filed directly with the court after a final decision or after thirty days without a response; 4. The sentencing court will convene a hearing to consider evidence, including the Bureau's recommendation and supporting documentation. The court's decision is final. Forty years is a very long time for someone to be conditioned to institutional living. It would undoubtedly be difficult, maybe even impossible, but it may be the only chance my brother has to ever see freedom again!

Some may wonder why securing my brother's release from prison after nearly forty years still matters to me. "Matter" is a term that refers to feeling valued and adding value to others and to us. It can also mean being appreciated, respected, and recognized. When I think of why it matters, it could be because my brother has always noticed me; he was always interested in what was going on with me because I 'mattered' to him. I felt important and motivated by his interest and fueled with a feeling of indebtedness, to make him proud. When I played basketball in our driveway alone, the imaginary opponent was always my brother. When I hit game-winning or buzzing beating shots in high school, college, and overseas, it was my brother's face with a look of approval I always saw. When I lost my way in college, resulting in losing my basketball scholarship, it was the thought of disappointing my brother that hurt the most. When I sat in an empty classroom or bedroom for hours studying for a college exam, the ASVAB (military entrance exam), or the Air Traffic Skills Assessment (ATSA), the entry-level exam that assesses candidates for Air Traffic Controller positions with the Federal Aviation Administration (FAA), it was my brother's voice I heard in my head telling me not to give up, and to study for just a few more hours.

Whenever I travel 'all over the world,' from Germany, England, Netherlands, Panama, France, Spain, China, Japan, or Guam, I always take a few minutes of private time with no one else around. I use the moment to reflect on my brother's journey, how he may never get an opportunity to walk these grounds or see the ocean, mountains, or famous world monuments. It is just my way of remaining connected to him. "Brother shares childhood memories and grown-up dreams." Playing basketball in the NBA and traveling the world were childhood fantasies my brother and I shared. Now, all these years later, we still share grown-up dreams, not one is as important as seeing him walk out of prison as a free man. We are both well aware that there are many things to consider when attempting to resume life after forty years in prison, including finding a place to live, finding a job, learning how to use the latest technology, and mental health support. Cognitive behavioral therapy (CBT) can help improve social skills, impulse control, and self-control, and accessing his eligibility for Social Security retirement, survivors, or disability are helpful benefits if you've worked or paid into Social Security enough years. You may also be eligible for Supplemental Security Income benefits if you are sixty-five or older, are blind, or have a disability, which is just the beginning. My brother would have to start his life all over again, building a new identity outside of prison, which may require him to examine "who am I now?" as part of his new life strategy. Whenever that day comes when he is finally released, I don't know if it will be one of the first things we do, but we can play pickup basketball, and it can be a great way to stay active, have fun, and enjoy some friendly competition. Unfortunately, the dream of playing one more time on the asphalt courts of the Griffin Park housing project ended when construction crews began demolishing Orlando's oldest public housing community, including the basketball courts. The housing units will all be demolished except for a six-unit residential building and the administration building. Griffin Park is on the National Register of Historic Places and has been a cornerstone of the Orlando community for more than eighty years.

Although William and I have used the term "playing ball" hundreds of thousands of times, the term means something different to a sixty-year-old than it did to an eighteen-year-old, twenty-year-old, thirty-year-old, or even forty-year-old. The challenge won't be winning on the court and running full-court games for hours at a time but walking several blocks to the court and shooting a basketball flat-footed for an hour on a smelly court after all of these years—playing ball means something different.

As does seeing your oldest brother walk out of prison a free man for the first time in forty years. The feeling will be incredibly overwhelming, joyous, and deeply emotional, like a flood of memories and a sense of time standing still, often accompanied by profound gratitude and renewed connection as if a significant piece of your life has finally been restored—because it has!

When Weo and I play a game of pickup basketball again, it will not be in our old community.

Orlando, Fla.—Crews have started demolishing Orlando's first and oldest public housing community, Griffin Park, with a mission to make it a better place. Source: Orlando Sentinel Newspaper September 5, 2024.

Understanding The Compassionate Release Program

Compassionate release is a process that allows incarcerated individuals to be released early from prison due to extraordinary circumstances. These circumstances may include illness, age, being too debilitated to commit more crimes, being too impaired to be aware of punishment, and being too compromised to benefit from rehabilitation. Compassionate release is also known as medical release, medical parole, medical furlough, and humanitarian parole. It can be mandated by the courts or internal corrections authorities. Some states have their compassionate release policies:

- Florida

  Florida's state prison system does not have a compassionate release program, but federal prisoners in Florida may be eligible for compassionate release through the federal prison system.

  To request compassionate release, a federal prisoner can:

  - Work with a federal defense attorney
  - Request early release in writing from the BOP
  - Wait at least thirty days for a response from the BOP
  - Exhaust all administrative remedies available through the BOP
  - File a motion directly with the court

A successful motion for release must demonstrate "extraordinary and compelling reasons" for early release. It must also show that early release is reasonable and does not put the community at risk. The motion should include proposed release plans that help inmates reintegrate after incarceration.

Some reasons for requesting compassionate release include advanced age, medical conditions, and family circumstances.

- New York

  Prisoners with a "significant debilitating illness" may be eligible for early release if their condition prevents them from posing a threat to society.

- Maryland

  All individuals are eligible to apply for medical parole, except those sentenced for sex offenses or those with sentences that are not parole eligible.

The United States Sentencing Commission has also changed the federal sentencing guidelines to expand access to compassionate release. These changes include removing procedural barriers and expanding the types of health and family needs that justify release.

The U.S. Sentencing Commission Policy Statement, §1B1.13
Grounds for a Reduction in Sentence

The following are "extraordinary and compelling" reasons that may qualify an individual to petition the sentencing court for a reduced sentence:

• Medical circumstances (b)(1)

- A terminal illness (a serious and advanced illness with an end-of-life trajectory).
- Applies to individuals who cannot adequately care for themselves (dressing, bathing, feeding) in a carceral environment because of a:
  - ✶ serious physical or medical condition, or
  - ✶ serious functional or cognitive impairment, or,
  - ✶ deteriorating physical or mental health because of aging

- Inadequate medical care*
  - ✳ This provision covers individuals who are suffering from a medical condition and require, but are not receiving, long-term or specialized care, putting them at risk of serious deterioration or death.
- Public health crisis*
  - ✳ There is an ongoing infectious disease outbreak that is likely to affect the individual who is at an increased risk of a severe complication if exposed to the infectious disease, and the risk of exposure cannot be diminished in an adequate amount of time.

• Age of the individual (b)(2)

- This applies to individuals who: (1) are at least sixty-five years old; (2) are experiencing physical or mental health issues because of the aging process; and (3) have served the lesser of ten years or 75 percent of their sentence.

• Family circumstances (b)(3) applies when:

- An individual has minor children (under eighteen years old) and the primary caregiver of those children has died or is unable to care for the children.
- An individual has a child who is eighteen years or older, who is incapable of self-care due to a physical or mental disability and the primary caregiver has died or is unable to care for them. *
- The incarcerated person's spouse becomes incapacitated and there is no one else who can care for the defendant's spouse.
- The incarcerated person's parent becomes incapacitated, and the incarcerated person is the only individual who can be a caregiver for the parent. *

• Victims of abuse (b)(4) *

- This provision covers individuals who are survivors of sexual abuse by prison personnel, as well as survivors of physical abuse by prison personnel. If the individual suffered physical abuse, that abuse must result in "serious bodily injury" as defined in the guidelines at §1B1.1. If the individual endured sexual abuse, the abuse must have involved a sexual act (penetrative, genital contact). In both cases, the misconduct must be established by a finding in a civil, criminal, or administrative proceeding, unless those proceedings are unduly delayed, or the individual is facing imminent danger.

• Other reasons (b)(5) *

- The Director of the Bureau of Prisons always has had broad discretion to identify reasons other than those described by the policy statement for a sentence reduction. The new provision provides a more limited authority. It gives the BOP Director and judges the discretion to identify unlisted extraordinary and compelling reasons. The other reason(s), however, must be similar in gravity to the ones expressly listed above in (b)(1)-(b)(4): terminal illness, serious medical condition, advanced age, extreme family circumstance, and sexual or physical abuse.

• Unusually long sentences (b)(6) *

- This provision gives judge's discretion, after full consideration of the prisoner's individualized circumstances, to determine whether a change in the law that would result in a lower sentence today could be a ground for sentence reduction. The person must have served at least ten years of an unusually long sentence, and there must be a gross disparity between the sentence being served and the one that would be imposed today. (Changes to the guidelines that are not made retroactive cannot be considered a change in the law for purposes of this ground.)

A few additional notes:

1. Rehabilitation of an individual certainly can be part of an argument for a reduced sentence. But rehabilitation alone cannot be the basis for a reduced sentence. To leverage an individual's rehabilitation as an argument for a reduced sentence, that argument must be made in combination with other circumstances.

2. Even though an extraordinary and compelling circumstance may have been anticipated or foreseen at the time of sentencing, it can still be considered by a court under a reduction in sentence motion. For example, if an individual had breast cancer at the time of sentencing, but files a reduction in sentence request three years into her term of imprisonment because it has advanced, the judge could still consider her motion.

   * An asterisk represents a ground for compassionate release that was added in the 2023 Policy Statement

FLORIDA COMPASSIONATE RELEASE

PRIMARY LEGAL SOURCES

CONDITIONAL MEDICAL RELEASE

Statute

Florida Statutes § 947.149 (2021), available through the Florida Legislature, https://www.leg.state.fl.us/statutes/index.cfm?App_mode=Display_Statute&Search_String=&URL=0900-0999/0947/Sections/0947.149.html

Regulations

Florida Administrative Code § 23-24.020(2021), available through the Florida Secretary of State, https://www.flrules.org/gateway/ruleNo.asp?id=23-24.020

Florida Administrative Code § 23-24.025 (2021), available through the Florida Secretary of State, https://www.flrules.org/gateway/ruleno.asp?id=23-24.025

Florida Administrative Code § 23-24.030, available through the Florida Secretary of State, https://www.flrules.org/gateway/ruleNo.asp?id=23-24.030.

Florida Administrative Code § 23.24.040 (2021), available through the Florida Secretary of State, https://www.flrules.org/gateway/ruleNo.asp?id=23-24.040.

Florida Administrative Code § 23.24.050 (2021), available through the Florida Secretary of State, https://www.flrules.org/gateway/ruleNo.asp?id=23-24.050.

A Letter from William

Hey Tan!   *February 20, 2022*

Man, I wanted to write and say how much I've missed you, bro…It's been a long time since I saw you, and you…it's kind of sad to be missing you so much, and not being able to hug you, bro… Tan, when you get this letter, do me a favor, and read it to Ketch too, okay? I want her to know how much I love you, Tan, and I never, never meant to leave ya'll alone, bro…I have to tell you, bro, that I cry at times…and I cover my head up at night, so no one can see my tears…Tan, I cry because I do realize that there was so much that I wanted to share with you, Tan, but I never had a chance to do so…Yes, we spent time with each other, man, but in my heart I held back a lot of things that I wanted to share with you…But, I just had so much other shit that stopped me from spending time with you, Tan, that I really needed! It hurts me to say this, but I was selfish, and only wanted to chase girls and do what I felt I wanted…

Tan, man, I love you more than you know, bro, and so I want to apologize for not being truly a big brother to you! You deserved everything of me, man, because you have always treated me with respect and love… I think about all the things we ever did together growing up as kids, and later as teenagers, and I know that our shared moments were never enough for the way I felt about you, Tan. Do you know that I've always had trouble expressing my personal feelings? To anyone? Man, you know how much I really did care for you all, bro…And when Mom had problems with Buddy, I was there, bro, for her mentally as well as physically… You know that? But, man, being able to say certain things, expressing my feelings was guarded, because all my life I NEVER wanted to seem weak to my brothers and sister!!!

Do you remember when you and I went to the Callahan Park to play ball, and Donnie Gandini "beat me up"? Tan, listen, the only thing that kept going on over and over in my mind, was I kept hearing you saying, "William, don't let him do you like that"…Bro, I felt weak and helpless in that moment and when I got up off the ground and drove to Winter Park in Mama's car, I closed my eyes twice on the freeway for about ten seconds each time, driving about 60 mph! Tan, I wanted to die that day…

Not because I lost the fight, but because you, Tan, saw me being treated like I was nothing, man…Just writing you this I am slowly shedding tears, cause the memory and possible thought that you were ashamed of me, Tan, broke my heart that day! If I wanted to be there to protect y'all, bro, I did not want you to see me not being able to protect myself!

Overtime

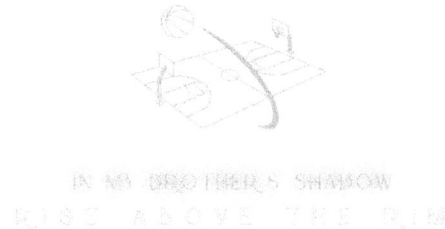

TERMS, PHRASES, AND SLANG USED IN BASKETBALL PICKUP GAMES, GYMS, AND THE NBA

(This list is by no means exhaustive, but it shows the kind of range that is used during most pickup games in the United States)

A

Active Around the Rim
When a player is constantly jumping and hustling for rebounds.

Air Ball
This phrase is used to describe a shot that misses the rim, the backboard, and the net entirely.

All Ball
Often said by the defensive player who appears to have blocked the shot but instead is called for a foul.

All Day
If a player can consistently make a shot, it's said that he can make it "all day."

Alley-Oop

An *alley-oop* is a type of assist in which one player throws the ball toward the basket, and another player jumps up to dunk the ball. It's a skillful way to bypass a tricky defense from the other team.

And One

This is when a player gets fouled while in the act of shooting but still scores the basket. He then gets the opportunity to make it a three-point play by getting one free throw attempt.

Automatic

Players who, when they shoot, anticipate that the ball is going in.

B

Baby Hook

A one-handed, high-arching shot that is difficult to block. It is primarily used by big men who are close to the basket.

Bail Him Out Defensively

When an offensive player jumps, he must shoot or pass. When a player is in the air and attempts an off-balance shot, and is fouled, the defensive player has "bailed him out" because he had no shot or pass to make.

Baller

A basketball player.

Battle for Position

When players bump and push one another to gain position close to the basket.

Beat the Defender

When an offensive player is able to drive past the defender guarding him.

Big Man

A tall player, often the center or power forward, who plays close to the basket.

Black Hole

If the ball is passed inside to the post and never passed back out to the perimeter player, the post player is a "black hole." Once the ball goes in, it never comes back out!

Box

Square area painted or taped above the rim on the backboard.

Break Ankles or Ankle Breaker

When a player makes a move that causes the defender to stumble or fall, the defender has had his "ankles broken."

Bringing the House Down

If a player is on a shooting streak, he is "bringing the house down."

Brick

A brick is related to an air ball in that the ball doesn't make it into the basket. But a brick shot bounces haphazardly off the rim or the backboard, prompting calls of "Brick!" from fans of the opposing team.

Bucket

The rim or a made basket. A player who is having trouble scoring "can't buy a bucket."

Buzzer Beater

A last second shot that is made as the final buzzer sounds. (In pickup games, since there are no shot or game clocks, these shots are game winners)

C

Call your own fouls
This phrase is used when players are not using an official ref. It means that players are expected to call their own fouls and be honest about it.

Cherry-picking
This phrase is used to describe a player who hangs back near their own basket instead of playing defense, waiting for an easy fast break opportunity.

Cut
To make a sharp turn or cut to free an offensive player so he can receive a pass.

Camping in the Key
Refers to a player guilty of a three-second violation in the key.

Charity Stripe
The foul line.

Check
A "checking" system is used to ensure that both teams are ready to begin play. This involves the offensive player saying "check" while throwing the ball to his defender. The defender then makes sure their team is ready and then throws the ball back to begin play.

Clean the Glass
When a rebounder swipes the ball off the glass backboard, he is a "Windex man" who is "cleaning the glass."

Clear Out
A halfcourt play designed to isolate an offensive player to go one-on-one against his defender.

Creating His Own Shot
This is when a player has to open up space for himself, thus giving him the opportunity to take a shot at the basket.

Crunch Time
The end of a game when the score is close. In Indiana, Reggie Miller has built a reputation for making the big shot at crunch time; Pacers fans call this "Miller Time."

Crossover
A crossover movement involves faking to one side and getting the defender to follow you before bouncing the ball back over to your other hand. This leaves the defender off balance and out of position, and leaves you open to take a shot, drive the lane, or pass. With enough practice, the crossover can be a deadly offensive weapon.

D

D Up
To play defense. This is also known as "checking your man."

Dagger
A basket late in the game that seals a victory.

Deep Threat
A player who has the ability to make long perimeter shots and three-pointers.

Defensive Assignment
The offensive player a defender is assigned to guard.

Defensive Help
When an offensive player drives to the basket, a teammate of the defender leaves his man to help cover the player with the ball.

Deliver in the Clutch
To make a big play at the end of a game, ensuring the win.

Denied
Describes a shot that is blocked.

Dish
To pass for a layup. A "3-D" man is a player that can drive (to the basket), draw (the defender to him) and dish (to a teammate for a layup). Toni Kukoc of the Milwaukee Bucks is known as "The Waiter" because he delivers "dishes" to his teammates.

Distribute the Basketball
To pass the ball.

Doing the Dirty Work
Hustling, rebounding, and getting back on defense on a fast break are all elements of "doing the dirty work."

Down to the Wire
A game that is decided on the final shot or possession.

Down
You have next game. If you have downs, you play the winner of the last pickup game and you can pick whoever isn't playing to be on your team.

Double Dribble
The ball must keep moving in basketball. A basketball player who catches the ball mid-dribble and continues to dribble—or who dribbles with both hands at the same time—is *double dribbling*.

Downtown
If a shot was made from an extra long-distance from the basket, you've made it from "downtown."

Draw a Foul
When an offensive player makes a move to the basket in an effort to initiate contact with the defender.

Draw the Defense
When the player with the ball attracts an additional defender, drawing the defender away from an offensive player. This player is now open for a shot.

Drive
To go to the basket.

Drive and Dish
This is to penetrate into the key and pass to an open teammate for a layup. "Drive and deal" or "drive and deliver" are often heard during NBA games and mean the same thing.

Drive and Kick
To drive to the basket and pass the ball to an open perimeter shooter.

Drop
To score. For example, "Shaq routinely drops thirty (points) on opposing players."

Dropping Dimes
Passing the ball to teammates for assists with a fancy pass.

E

Elbow
The intersection of the free-throw line and middle of the circle.

Empty the Bench
At the end of a game when the coach takes out his starters and puts in all bench players.

Enforcer

This is the toughest player on the team, usually a center or power forward, who tries to set the physical tone of the game with an aggressive rebound or hard foul. The Miami Heat's Shaquille O'Neal is an enforcer.

Established Position

When a defensive player has his feet planted outside the restricted area. An offensive player who runs into this defender will be called for charging.

F

Facial

To shoot or dunk directly in an opponent's face.

Fadeaway

A jump shot taken while the player's body is moving away from the basket. where one makes a jump shot while falling backward through the air.

Feed the Post

To pass to the low-post player on offense.

Fill the Lanes

Players who run on the "wings" close to the sidelines on the fast break are "filling the lanes." By spreading out widely, it is harder for the opposing team to defend.

Find the Open Man

To pass to an unguarded teammate.

Finesse Player

A player who excels in the skill elements of the game, such as passing, shooting, and ball-handling.

Finger Roll
A layup where the shooter rolls the ball off his fingertips into the basket. This is also known as a "lay-in."

Finish Around the Basket
To be able to score in the key. This can be on a turnaround jump shot, baby hook, drop step, offensive rebound, and/or layup.

Finisher
A player who is good at scoring on fast breaks, finishing the play.

Floater in the Key
A high arcing shot taken on a drive in the paint. This is also known as a "teardrop."

Flush
To dunk the basketball with authority.

Fouling Strategy
To purposely foul weak free-throw shooters in order to have them miss and the fouling team regain possession to score.

Four-Point Play
When a player scores a three-point basket and is fouled. He then has an opportunity to shoot one foul shot to complete the four-point play.

Franchise Player
The star player around whom a team franchise is built.

Full-Court Press
When the defensive team defends the offensive team in the backcourt. Full-court presses often have the defensive team double-teaming the ball to force a turnover.

G

Gamble on Defense
To try for steals, though this often leaves the player out of place defensively.

Garbage Man
A player that does the "dirty work." Bo Outlaw of the Memphis Grizzlies is one of the NBA's best "garbage men."

Get the Roll
This is when a player shoots the ball and it rolls around the rim, but eventually falls in for a score. This is also known as a "shooter's roll."

Get to the Line
To shoot foul shots.

Give and go
This is an offensive play in which a player passes the ball to a teammate and then cuts to the basket for a return pass and a layup or dunk.

Go Either Way
The ability of a player to handle the ball with both hands.

Go-To Guy
This is the team's best offensive player who is relied upon to score or create his own shot when his team needs a basket.

Go to the Bank/Bank Shot
A shot off the backboard.

Go to the Hole
To drive to the basket.

Good Look at the Basket
To get open for a shot that a player should be able to make.

Green Light
When a player is given the approval by his coach to shoot at any time regardless of the distance of the shot or time on the clock. A player given the "green light" to shoot has "no conscience," meaning he has no regrets about any shot taken at any time.

Gretzky Pass
In hockey, an assist is awarded to the last two offensive players to pass to the goal scorer. In basketball, often the most important pass is the one that leads to the pass for the assist. Canadian coaches have coined this "the Gretzky pass."

Gym Rat
A player who has spent a lot of time in the gym perfecting his basketball skills.

H

Hack
To foul a player. Also known as "hammer."

Handle
If a player has a good "handle," he is a good ball-handler.

Hanging Around
If a team is "hanging around," though they are losing, they are keeping the score close enough that they still have a chance to win.

He Got Game
A complete player who can shoot, pass, dribble, rebound and play defense.

"He's feeling it!"

When a player has made consecutive shots in a row. This player may be a streaky shooter capable of making many shots consecutively.

High Flyer

A player with the ability to leap high.

His Shot

A shot a player is comfortable taking and consistently makes. This is a high-percentage shot. Kareem Abdul-Jabbar of the Los Angeles Lakers was one of the few NBA players capable of consistently making his hook shot, known as the "sky hook."

Home-Court Advantage

The belief that a team playing with the support of its fans and in the familiar surroundings of its home court gives the team a competitive edge.

Hoop

Refers to a made basket or the rim.

Hooper

A basketball player.

Hops

The ability to leap high. A player who is excellent at jumping with the ball can make a name for himself with his *hops* (jumps). Ideally, a player with a lot of hops can make more baskets.

House

The key area. Dikembe Mutombo is famous for waving his index finger after blocking a shot and saying, "Don't come into the house of Mutombo!"

I

In the Zone

A player who is on a shooting streak, making a high percentage of his shots despite the level of difficulty, is "in the zone."

J

J

A word use in reference to a Jump shot. It is one of the most important shots in basketball. A basic shooting technique in which a player throws the ball towards the basket from a straight vertical jump.

Jordanesque

When a player performs a play that is reminiscent of Michael Jordan.

K

Keeping the Ball Alive

Tapping and rebounding the ball to oneself or a teammate in order to retain an offensive possession.

Keeping the Defense Honest

Defensive teams will often leave the perimeter player feeding the post in order to double-team the player closer to the basket. Perimeter players must be able to make outside shots in order for their defenders to have to guard them or "keep them honest."

Key

The key is the very large rectangle that extends from the free throw line to the base line. Also known as 'the lane' or 'the paint.'

Kicks

Sneakers or running shoes.

Kill the Clock

This is when an offense controls the ball for as much of the twenty-four-second clock or game clock as possible before releasing a shot.

Killer Crossover

This is when a ball-handler dribbles the ball across his body changing from right hand to left hand or left hand to right hand. If done quickly enough, it may leave the defender off-balance, allowing the ball-handler to pass, shoot, or drive. Tim Hardaway is famous for his Killer Crossover, also known in his college days at the University of Texas-El Paso as the UTEP Two-Step.

Knock it Down

To make a shot.

L

Leaner

A shot a player takes leaning into his defender as he shoots the ball.

Lock Him Up

To defend a player so that he cannot shoot, pass, or dribble.

Look Upcourt

To pass the ball to a player on the run closer to the basket.

Lose Your Man

When an offensive player uses a ball cut or screen to get open for a pass.

Low Block

The area near the basket outside of the key where low-post players create space to receive a pass.

M

Making the Cut
The coaches use a method to choose the best players during "try out." If you are cut from the team, you are not good enough. If you make the cut, then you are good enough to play on the team.

Man-to-Man
A type of defense where each defensive player is responsible for the offensive player he is guarding.

Mismatch
This is when an offensive player has an advantage in size and/ or speed versus his defender. In the NBA, teams try to exploit mismatches of size and speed.

Money Player
A player that makes clutch, game-saving plays at the end of a game.

Monster Jam
A powerful dunk.

Monster on the Boards
An aggressive rebounder.

My Bad
Often heard by a player to his teammates after a bad pass or turnover.

My ball or Your ball
This phrase is used to indicate which team has possession of the ball.

N

Nail-Biter
A close game.

Nailed to the Bench

Players who seldom play are said to be "nailed to the bench."

"Next" or "Next game"

This phrase is used to indicate that the current game is over and it's time to rotate the players and start a new game.

O

On a Roll

A player on a shooting streak.

On the Line

When a player is shooting foul shots, he is "on the line." When the game is "on the line," the outcome of the game is to be decided on the final play.

One-Dimensional

A player who is very good at one particular skill, often shooting. Teams will bring in a shooter for a last-second play for a chance at a three-point shot.

On Fire

In the metaphorical sense it means that you're "hot"… on a winning streak, doing something right for a long period of time. The phrase is commonly used in sports, such as basketball, where a player who has scored several consecutive baskets (three or more typically) is said to be "on fire."

Open Look

When a player has an unguarded shot that he should take and make.

OT

An abbreviation for "overtime." In basketball, games do not end in a tie; they keep going until one team has won. During the 2000-01 season, the Sacramento Kings and Toronto Raptors played in a triple-overtime game, with the Kings emerging triumphant behind thirty-nine points from Peja Stojakovic.

Over the Limit

When a team commits more than five team fouls per quarter they are over the limit and the fouled team shoots two free throws. When a player is over the limit, he has committed his sixth personal foul and cannot return to the game.

P

Packed

This means someone packed your shot, blocked shot.

Paint

This area in front of the basket is also known as the "key" or the "lane."

Perimeter Player

A player that sets up offensively on the perimeter, rather than in the low post. This is usually the team's guards or small forward. Perimeter players are usually strong ball-handlers and outside shooters.

Pick

A screen that's set, to free the offensive player from his defender.

To participate in the game two players (acting as captains) will pick (choose) their team out of the players available.

Pick Up Your Man

To begin defending an offensive player.

Pin

To block a shot by holding or "pinning" the shot against the backboard.

Pine Time
Time spent on the bench. This is also known as "riding the pine" or "getting splinters."

Pivot
The center who plays in the post uses pivot-foot moves to score. Because of this, the center position is often known as the "pivot."

Play Off Your Man
When a defender gives the player with the ball the room to shoot because he is cautious of the player's ability to drive. This is also known as "playing him for the drive."

Playmaker
A team's point guard who runs the offense and creates plays for his teammates to score. Also known as the "floor general."

Polished Offensive Player
A player who is strong in the offensive skills of passing, shooting, and ball-handling. A polished offensive player, like Antawn Jamison of the Dallas Mavericks, has the ability to make the open shot, post up, drive to the basket, or pass out of the double team.

Post Up
A player who positions himself near the free-throw lane for a pass with his back to the basket and a defender behind him.

Posterize
To dunk over another player. This word came about because photos for posters are made from these types of plays.

Pound the Ball Inside
To make a concerted effort to pass the ball to low-post players playing inside.

Pound the Boards
To fight for rebounds under the basket.

PT
This is short for "playing time." This is also known as "getting some run."

Pull-Up Jumper
To come to a two-foot stop to pop a jump shot. Also known as a "stop and pop."

Pure Shooter
A player who has the ability to consistently make long-range shots.

Put a Body on Him
To box out the player one is guarding when rebounding. Offensive rebounds lead to second-chance points.

Put-Back
To score under the basket off an offensive rebound.

Put the Ball on the Floor
A player who can "put the ball on the floor" is able to take the ball to the basket on a drive.

Putting Up Numbers
When a player's statistical production is impressive in a number of different categories, including points, rebounds, assists, steals, and blocked shots.

Putting on a Clinic
Some basketball games are so good that they feel more like a basketball lesson. Players in these games are *putting on a clinic*, which is a learning session for basketball beginners.

Q

Quick First Step
The ability of a player to beat his defender off the dribble. If a player has a quick first step, it is difficult for the defender to recover defensively once he has been beaten to the basket.

R

Range
The distance from which a player can consistently make shots. Dirk Nowitzki of the Dallas Mavericks has shown the ability to consistently make three-point shots; therefore, he has "three-point range."

Restricted Area
This is the dotted area close to the basket inside the key where a charging violation cannot be called on the offensive player. This is also known as the "no charge zone."

Ride Him While He's Hot
To continue to pass the ball to a player who is on a scoring streak.

Rock
The basketball. To "protect the rock" is to be careful when handling the basketball.

Run
An unanswered string of points scored.

Run the Floor
The ability of a player to run and handle the ball on the fast break.

Running the Point
To play the point guard position.

S

Schooled
A very talented basketball player may show off a bit when they're winning a game. The loser of that game can consider themselves *schooled* (also known as *taken to school*).

Second String
A team's non-starters or bench players.

Set the Table
When a point guard begins the halfcourt offense, he is "setting the table." From here, the point guard can "drive and dish" or "feed the post."

Shake Your Man
To "shake your man" is to fake out a defender for an open shot or layup.

Show and Go
A shot fake used before driving to the basket.

Sixth Man
The first substitute off the bench, replacing a starter in a game. Though the sixth man may not start, he often plays the fourth quarter and finishes a game.

Small on Big Screen
When a guard (who is usually smaller) sets a pick for a forward (who is usually bigger).

Soft on D
When a player is considered a weak defender, he is known to be "soft on D."

Square Up for the Jumper
To have your shoulders facing the basket when you shoot.

Squeeze the Ball
When rebounding, to "squeeze the ball" is to gain control of the basketball.

Starters
The first five players on each team to begin a game. The "starters" are usually comprised of two guards, two forwards, and a center.

Steal a Win
When a team that has played poorly plays well enough in the end to pull out a win.

Step Out and Face the Basket
For big men, the ability to shoot on the perimeter. Big men who can step out and face the basket, like Keith Van Horn of the New York Knicks, are tough for opposing players to guard because they are used to playing inside, close to the basket.

Stopper
A player known for his ability to "stop" players defensively. "Stoppers" are known for their ability to "shut down" their man.

Stretch the D with the Three
To make three-point shots, forcing the defense to come out (or "stretch") to defend the shooter. Teams that are not fearful of an offense's three-point shooters are known to "pack it in," meaning their defenders play close to the basket in the key.

Stroke
A player's shooting motion.

Sub

A sub or substitute player is one who replaces one of the players on the court. Substitute players that are not in the starting lineup (also known as bench players, backups, interchange, or reserves) reside on the bench and are available to substitute for a starter.

Suicides

A conditioning drill that involves sprinting different lengths of court (players start at the baseline, sprint to the nearest free throw line; half-court line; furthest throw line; opposite baseline, making sure to return to the starting baseline after each line touch).

Swat

To block a shot.

Swingman

A versatile mid-sized player who can play more than one position. Tracy McGrady of the Orlando Magic is a swingman.

Switch

When defensive players trade the players they are guarding on a pick-and-roll.

T

Taking Him to School

When a player is consistently beating his defender, he is "teaching him a lesson" or "taking him to school."

Test the Free Agent Waters

Players at the end of their contracts often discuss "testing the free agent waters." This means a player will consider contract offers from other teams when his current contract is complete.

Thread the Needle
When a pinpoint pass is thrown in traffic, like a needle being threaded.

Throw Down
To dunk.

Tickle the Twine
When a player "swishes" a shot, he is said to have "tickled the twine" or shot "nothing but net."

Top of the Key
The area around the free throw circle's farthest point from the basket is called the top of the key.

Traffic
When the lane is crowded with more than one defender. To "drive in traffic" is to penetrate the key with two or three defenders in the way.

Trailer
An offensive player bringing up the rear on a fast break who may get into position for a better shooting opportunity on a pass from the leader.

Transition
The fast break that results from a rebound, turnover or change in possession.

Traveling
This phrase is used to indicate that a player has taken more than the allowed number of steps without dribbling the ball.

Triangle
Also known as the "triple-post offense," used by Michael Jordan's championship Chicago Bulls teams under coach Phil Jackson. See the Basketball U tutorial on Halfcourt Offense.

Trifecta
A three-point shot. Terms for taking a three-point shot include "launching a trifecta" and "dialing long distance."

Tweener
This word is derived from the word "between," as in a player is between the height of a guard and a forward. "Tweeners" often have the skills of a big man, but the height of a guard. Though only six foot five, Charles Barkley was one of the NBA's greatest rebounding power forwards.

U

Up-and-Under Move
When an offensive player fakes going up with the basketball, waits for the defender to jump, then ducks under him before going up with another shot.

Upside
A draft term for a player with long-term potential. Players with "upside" are generally good athletes with great "tools," such as size, leaping ability, long arms, and quick feet. These players need some seasoning and experience before they can become effective NBA players. Jermaine O'Neal of the Indiana Pacers was drafted out of high school with raw athletic talent but needed five years in the league before becoming a solid NBA starter.

Use the Glass
To make a shot off the backboard.

V

Vertical
This is an abbreviated form of "vertical leap," indicating how high a player can jump vertically from a stationary position. Players

with large "verticals" are able to use their hops or jumping ability to "jump out of the gym." The Los Angeles Clippers have three young players with verticals over forty inches: Keyon Dooling, Corey Maggette, and Quentin Richardson.

W

Wet A shot that's automatic or on target. All net, that's wet.

Windmill
A dunk where the player brings the ball to his waist and raises it back up in a circular motion.

X

Y

Z

Zone
When players are assigned a certain area to play on the court instead of a certain player to defend.

Sources: NBA.com; The Basketball Dictionary; Streetball.com (Global Basketball Community)

OVERTIME
HOMAGE FROM KITH AND KIN,
COACHES AND PLAYERS

I don't know; he was different; even when he struggled with something, or maybe one of the other kids was teasing him, Tan would focus on what he was doing and not worry about how everyone else was doing. Tan was always mentally tougher than the other kids. Not in a way that he acted tough with other kids; he was resilient and had the courage and confidence to reach his full potential. Mental toughness is a personality trait that determines your ability to perform consistently under stress and pressure and is closely related to qualities such as character, resilience, grit, and perseverance. Maybe he developed this ability through being around team sports, as he would travel on the road with me to both my football and softball games. I am proud of him, man. I'm proud of Tan.

~ **Adolphus "Buddy" Jones**

Robert and I first met at Hurlburt Field AFB, Florida (1989); he had just arrived from Germany and was given a base tour by my supervisor. In the course of the tour, the two of them stopped by the squadron's orderly room, where I happened to be on a detail to the 'snack bar,' Robert asked if he could have some free snacks, but I said no and made him pay for the items he wanted. He looked at me with surprise, eyebrows raised, eyes wide open, and his jaw dropped open because I didn't make my supervisor pay for the bag of chips he grabbed and began to eat...needless to say, he doesn't recall that first encounter fondly.

We would have a second meeting several weeks later. I returned to work at my regular office in the munition's accountability department; Robert worked in an office across the hallway from me. After laughing about the initial meeting, we became fast friends and later began hanging out with the same group; from there, we just clicked! Our friendship grew into a personal and unique connection that has lasted to this day.

I attended many of his basketball games throughout the years; I never met anyone as passionate about anything as Robert was about basketball, and I truly enjoyed supporting him. He was incredible to watch, and his love for the game showed in every aspect of his on-court play...I was his biggest fan and loudest cheerleader!

Unfortunately, our relationship ended unceremoniously due to immaturity on his part, but sometimes, life happens unexpectedly. We shared a son and continued co-parenting him after our relationship ended. Robert and our son, William, have an extremely close father-and-son relationship, and they enjoy talking and joking with one another like best friends. Over the years, we ensured our interactions were positive and supported our son. Today, Robert and I remain best of friends.

~ Adrienne E. Grandjean

Tan and I have known one another since we were in junior high school (Robinswood Junior High School, Pine Hills, Florida), sitting across from each other in biology class. Tan and I have the kind of friendship, forty-plus years, that we will always be in each other's life no matter the circumstances. We haven't seen one another in years or lived thousands of miles apart at times. It doesn't matter if you talk every day, once a month, or a few times a year when you do talk, it's as if we just spoke a short time ago...the conversations are always so easy and exciting. And we know that we will be there for each other no matter what. Our friendship is truly one that has lasted a lifetime. It never matters how long it's been; we talk like there was never a break. I also have friends I've met in my adult life who are the same way. We have each other's backs and never feel like things have changed when we see each other. I've always treasured our relationship.

~ Andrea Distin

Families consistently display photographs that show a close bond between family members and project the image of an idyllic, harmonious family. But on this particular day, as I looked through the family photo album, there were unidentified family photographs of people I didn't know...so I took the picture from the photo album and ran to my grandma, whom we all called Mama. "Mama, who are these people?" I asked as I showed her the 5x7 family portrait. "Those are your Uncle Pete's children. Do you remember your Aunt Dorothy?" she asked. I responded, "Yes." "That's William Edwards's mother," she continued. "That's William Edward's brothers and sister, Robert, Derrick, and Sharon." That was the first time I had seen my cousin Robert; it would be over forty years before I met him. My first in-person meeting with Robert happened at the inaugural 2017 Worthington Family Reunion held in Louisville, Kentucky, and we hit it off. I found him to be intelligent, funny, and a man of sound principles, and like me, he was a basketball guy. Since that initial meeting, we have talked at least monthly. I have admired Robert's many accomplishments, drive, and perseverance. He's a master class in what focus and drive can produce.

My wife and I had the honor of attending his Doctoral Hooding Ceremony (Commencement) in San Antonio, Texas, this past January (2024), along with Robert's beautiful wife, daughters, and one of Robert's good friends. The ceremony is a unique recognition of the achievement of a candidate who has earned a doctorate. Each doctoral candidate is introduced individually during the ceremony. As they walk across the stage, they stop to have their hood placed on the stage in front of the facility, family, and friends. As I stood in among the crowd waiting to hear my cousin's name called, I reflected on how proud my grandmother and grandfather would've been, not to mention my Uncle Pete; I'm sure he'd shed a tear (he'd gotten a little soft in his old age).

Robert was about to become the first person in our family to earn a doctoral degree or "a first-generation doctoral student." I, too, felt very proud of my cousin and the discipline and persistence it took for him to complete this journey, as they called his name. He walked onto the stage to the announcement, "Robert Worthington, Doctor of Business Administration (DBA)." The feeling of pride and deep satisfaction with his accomplishment was nearly overwhelming. I'm sure we haven't heard the last from Dr. Robert Worthington. As they say in the Air Force, Onward and Upward!

~ Anthony "Bo" Chambers

I first met Dr. Robert Worthington while he was coaching a Wilde Lake Middle School team for the Howard County Youth Program, Inc. (HCYP). As the Director of Basketball Operations for HCYP, I quickly recognized Rob's exceptional leadership skills and unwavering drive. His qualities made him the ideal candidate to take over the middle school and travel basketball programs. Under Rob's guidance, the middle school leagues thrived, becoming one of the top middle school leagues in the country.

Rob's influence extended beyond just the middle school teams. He took charge of the boys' varsity, boys' JV, girls' varsity teams, and the travel league teams. His extensive knowledge of basketball and outstanding interpersonal skills revitalized the program and significantly contributed to its growth. Coaches and players alike benefited immensely from his expertise and mentorship.

Beyond his professional achievements, Dr. Worthington is a devoted family man and someone I am proud to call a friend. His impact on the HCYP and the community has been profound, and his legacy continues to inspire all those involved in the program.

~ BJ Borden

Through my many years of being involved with basketball, first as a fan, then as a player, and now as a current Professional Basketball Coach, I have never met a more passionate person about basketball than Coach Rob Worthington. I thought I was one of the few remaining dinosaurs who lived and breathed basketball all the time, but he may have me beat!! I first met Rob when I became Head Coach of the Brevard Blue Ducks USBL minor league basketball team in Florida in 2006. He had been the Assistant Coach the year before I got there under a Hall of Fame NBA player, Nate 'Tiny" Archibald, and having him there for me would be a big help since he had experience working with the team and organization. I was right. He made my transition smooth and easy, and I could focus on just the Xs and Os of basketball; as a Head Coach, it makes your job so much easier when you can deal with mostly on-the-court issues. He knew some returning players and their strengths and weaknesses; he ran our tryout camps and organized practices, among many other things. We talked basketball daily and worked as a tandem, not as

Head Coach and Assistant Coach, and we won 71 percent of our games that season. We have bonded since then as brothers out of respect and love for one another, and we still work together today with basketball camps, clinics, and training worldwide for players. You will not find a more knowledgeable and hard-working person than Coach Rob Worthington.

~ Brian Rowsom

Well, Robert "Tan" Worthingtn,

It was family as well as friends that made my life accomplishments achievable. When I first met you at Memorial Junior High School, I thought you and I were both newcomers to the area. It was at that time that I learned life lessons about family. You guys were the type of upper-class men who refused to quit, and that instilled in me a self-motivation that pushed me through high school and on to become a Florida A&M University Football Hall of Fame Member. It was never for me; it was always for the gentlemen who surrounded me that matter to me. Without them, there was no me. I always had great coaches who fathered me and figured me through points, but those teams whose bond was family-familiar won championships.

~ Bryan "B. K" Brewer

Two stories come to mind; in our first home game of the season, you kept slipping and falling to the floor as we tried to run our offense. The other team's players eventually stopped guarding you because you needed to stand up longer to be an offensive threat. However, later, during the same game, you hit some big shots down the stretch to help us win. Recalling our practices and how competitive some of them were, brings to mind the second story: one day before a big game, you got into an elbow-throwing contest with one of our "bigs" (power forward/center), and you hit him in the upper lip with your elbow, making him look like a fish. The next night, he had his best game ever…you had a strange way of getting our team ready for a big game.

~ **Coach Calvin Lingelbach**

Good morning, Brother Robert. Prophet Carl Murray. I'm not a writer, but I can speak things out. So, I'm going back to our high school days at Evans High School, playing basketball; boy, did we have some outstanding basketball players I can remember. During the time frame between 1982 and 1987, I graduated in 1985, and I believe you were a little before me (1984). I remember Tony Fluker, Cleve Williams, and especially you, Robert; back then, we called you Tan; a few others who stand out in my memory were Shannon James and Gary Napper, just to name a few. We used to have some battles on the court; everyone was so competitive, but all to improve each other.

I can remember the years ('82-'84) when you were playing, and man, your jump shot was just lethal; it made me a better player just by watching y'all compete on that basketball court. But we all liked playing together and cared about one another from a personal perspective; we were all just a bunch of good guys who enjoyed playing basketball and pushing each other to improve. I mean, those days were so awesome, man. But I still can see the image of you shooting that beautiful form jump shot and winning games; you were just a force and an example of what hard work looked like to all of us as younger players.

I also have fond memories of all of us going around to different neighborhoods in the city, visiting different playgrounds to play pickup basketball games. And we would play for hours, sweat dripping off our faces and clothes from our brutal battles on the basketball court. Those were some great times; I sometimes wish we could relive those days. But you spent those times competing on the court or just all of us sitting around and talking to each other, holding the others accountable to be better than you were the day before, on and off the court. Those times shaped and molded me into the man I am today. And I appreciate those times, and again, as I'm speaking, I visualize you shooting that jump shot, Tan. I remember talking to you one day about your shooting form; I was amazed that your form stayed the same whenever you shot the ball with your fingers spread apart, correct hand position, and elbow alignment perfect with the ball…. It was just a consistent shooting form stuck in my mind, just like the conversation we all used to have, honest from the heart with good intentions. Proverbs 27:17 proclaims: "As iron sharpens iron, so one person sharpens another."

~ **Carl "Tank" Murray**

Most young ladies meet the man of their dreams by reaching high school. That time came much sooner for me. I was ten years old when I knew Robert was my Prince Charming. I recall when his family moved into the Griffin Park housing development where my grandmother lived. My family had recently moved away, but we visited my grandmother daily. He was the conversion among the girls my age. He was tall and slender. His perfectly rounded Afro complimented his light-brown complexion. The young girls in the neighborhood went crazy over him, including me. I was "crushing" hard!

While my female peers tried to impress Robert, I displayed no interest. Robert and I played together regularly and attended the same elementary school, Grand Avenue. I don't recall when we officially shared our fondness for each other; it was just an understanding between us. Eventually, Robert's family moved away from the Griffin Park housing development, and I was devastated. I wouldn't get to see him when I visited my grandmother's house anymore; I was confused and unsure what to think: was our 'relationship' over?

We were finally reunited after the long summer months and the first day of junior high school at Memorial Junior High School

(MJHS). I was walking to my locker before my next class when I passed my uncle (Greg) in the hallway, and he asked me, "Have you seen Tan?" I thought my heart would jump from my chest! I wanted to rekindle our relationship, but I wasn't sure he felt the same. My high school years were spent at Jones High, and Robert attended Evans High. It wasn't long before I started hearing about "Tan" and his basketball skills. His ability to play basketball brought him a lot of recognition. I would listen to his name ring through the halls at Jones. The guys talked about his "jump shot" and love for the game. I remember thinking, *Why are they so excited? It's only Robert.* He was getting attention from the guys and the girls. Robert's greatest strength is his willingness to immerse himself in whatever he aspires to do for himself and others. As for his greatest weakness, in past conversations with Robert, he fails to understand that family, friends, or coworkers don't execute their personal or professional lives as he does.

~ Charlene Solomon

It's been several years since we played on the same basketball team, but I remember Rob being the most competitive player I had ever played with; he was consumed by competition. On the surface, for those who didn't know him, he was our team's alpha dog, go-to guy, and offensive scorer meant to lead with stellar play and adept leadership. But for those of us who knew him, we knew that he was deserving of those accolades only because he worked his ass off and earned the right to be placed in that role. I played more basketball while hanging with Rob, including 3-on-3 Hoop It Up Basketball tournaments and traveling with a military basketball team playing in different cities around the United States. Again, he was just a true competitor! I have one story in particular that stands out; just his work ethic and drive for the game rubbed off on other guys like me. When I see him today, he's still working, sharing his knowledge of the game, especially for young players.... imparting a higher basketball IQ to the next generation…that describes Rob to his core!

~ Christopher "Chris" Minters

Dr. Robert Worthington has been more than a good friend; he has been like a son, confidant, and colleague for over a decade and a half. *In My Brother's Shadow* is the book you would expect from Dr. Robert Worthington: Bold and exciting. Robert's book captures the idea that you can live any area of your life based on courage, love, and kindness instead of fear. Every day, I see people doing great things in the world. What do they have in common with Dr. Robert Worthington? They dare to go after their dreams and make a positive impact. Proverbs 27:17 — Iron Sharpens Iron: "As iron sharpens iron, so one person sharpens another." This verse highlights the mutual benefit of mentorship. We can help improve each other's character and wisdom through mentorship.

~ Clifford D. Garvey Jr, M.Ed.,
Prison Ministry Chaplain

I met Rob Worthington at Sembach Air Base, Kaiserslautern, Germany, located in southwest Germany, in 1986. We met at the gymnasium playing basketball. Rob was noticeable because that cat had a serious (excellent) jump shot with beautiful form. He was easy to notice because, on this particular day, he was hitting everything he shot…and shot every time he touched the ball (lol). Rob and I became fast friends over our shared passion for the game of basketball, which was of similar interest. Rob, unlike me, didn't drink any alcohol, and I drank a lot of Pilsner, the most popular beer in Germany, also known as 'Pils.' After many hours of playing pickup basketball, we eventually tried out for the basketball team at Sembach. We both made the team, with him at times a starter and me a reserve player during our first year in Germany. The relationship forged through the game of basketball blossomed into a trusted lifelong friendship of kindred spirits. Rob constantly invited me to his house for dinner and fascinating conversation. He always said, "C, I got to get you out of that dormitory before you go crazy." We had a certain rapport with one another, with no topic off limits to discussions and debates, although our upbringing happened on two different coasts, with him being from the South and me from up North. We shared a desire to want 'more out of life,' always seeking to go someplace new, do different things, and live on another level, like two peas in a pod. We were far from familiar surroundings, as Germany is nearly five thousand miles from the United States. Still, through a love for basketball and a strong competitive nature where we always thought we should be playing more (ha-ha) ...we built a strong friendship. He and I had many battles on the basketball court, with him usually complaining that I was fouling him...not true, of course! All in all, I have nothing but fond and cherished memories of the dude. I love him as a brother; he will always be my best friend.

~ Craig "Cee" Harrison

Recalling the '90s when we were members of the United States Air Force and basketball teammates...those days are pretty much a blur today; on and off the court, you were an individual I could trust and depend on, honest and direct. I remember you've always had a passion for hoops over all other sports. I can't recall one game or particular play from a past basketball game during our playing together, but you had quite a few tremendous scoring games, with great offensive performances, because you took all the shots...lol! I recall other players on the team thinking the coaches gave you too much leeway with the number of shots you got to take during games. One particular practice, we were all sitting on the bench having a post-practice team meeting, and the head coach was explaining to everyone what their role on the team was...after he didn't explain their role, one of the other players asked him, "Coach, what's Rob's role"? Coach, responded, "Rob has to score for us to have a chance to win...it's that simple." ...needless to say, the player didn't like the answer and responded (not loud enough for the coach to hear) ..." Well, he's doing all the scoring and we're still losing." Laughs, that was too funny! But, overall, those were good times; you were very passionate about the game, which motivated others to perform better. I'd have to classify you as an ardent lover of the game and a straightforward, honest guy. Although I'd have to admit, I don't know what type of guy you are today; you've been unsupervised for many years now...lol.

~ **Derrick Ligon**

I'm Derrick Worthington, the youngest brother of three brothers: William "Weo," Robert "Tan," and me, the youngest and tallest of us. We used to play basketball together at the outside courts in Griffin Park; Tan and I played on the same little league baseball team, George Stuart, at the Grand Avenue Baseball Fields, and we joined a lot of the neighborhood kids in Griffin Park sliding down the grass hills of Interstate-4 with our homemade cardboard box slides...we used to love the thrill of sliding down that hill! We also enjoyed riding our bicycles in other parks and communities throughout Orlando. I'm not surprised that Tan is writing a book; he always read comic books or baseball cards when we were kids. I mean, it's a great accomplishment! And I am very proud to know that my brother has written a book about some things we lived while growing up in Florida. We've laughed at times, experienced sadness and loss, dealt with fear and anger...but no matter what, there is no love like a brother's love. "We may fight with each other, but we'll always have each other's back."

~ **Derrick Worthington**

I have so many great memories of raising my children; they were the most joyous of times…they attended Sunday school together, and afterward, we all attended church service. We always ate Sunday dinner together; they were a joyful blessing. I worked hard for them and impressed upon them how important it was to get an education, which I felt particularly strongly about because I couldn't get the best education growing up. They enjoyed school and playing sports. William, my oldest son, and Tan both loved to play basketball. Derrick was my helper and protector, always helping me around the house. My only daughter, Sharon, has always been an independent thinker who makes decisions and cares for herself. Sharon was also an athlete.

I was always proud of my children and their accomplishments, such as getting an education, being hardworking, and making their way in the world. But when William got into trouble and was not in our life (in prison) anymore, it really broke my heart, broke me down, but with the grace of God, I've been able to get through it.

However, my middle son, Tan (Robert), recently completed his doctoral degree, which made me proud of him, and when he gifted me his doctor's diploma, I was overjoyed. His perseverance and determination inspire me; he has grown into a remarkable individual, and his success fills my heart with pride. "You make me so proud to be your mother, and I hope I make you proud to be my son, too. I love you!"

~ Dorothy Mae Worthington

I met Tan (Dr. Worthington) when I was thirteen in a small neighborhood in Orlando, Florida, called Carver Shores, and it was on the basketball court where our relationship grew. Tan (Dr. Worthington) noticed me as I played pickup basketball games on the neighborhood outdoor asphalt court. I believed he saw my potential as a basketball player (athlete) and thought he could help me improve with his experience and knowledge of the game. At this point in my life, I was playing on the Robinswood junior high school basketball team, and Tan (Dr. Worthington) was playing at a higher level as the star shooting guard and captain of the Maynard Evans high school basketball team, which ranked among the top teams in the State of Florida.

I was honored that someone outside my parents and coach was interested in my basketball abilities. I would be forever grateful for Tan's (Dr. Worthington) mentorship as I would eventually be a star basketball player on the Maynard Evans basketball team from 1984-1987. His guidance would contribute to my development into a four-sport star athlete at Maynard Evans High School. I earned a four-year college scholarship to the University of Minnesota to play football under Coach Lou Holtz as an All-American quarterback.

After my high school career, the next time Dr. Worthington and I would cross paths would be nearly twenty years. We both were pursuing our doctorate degrees at Walden University. I was at the end of my program, completing my Doctorate in Healthcare Administration in 2022. Dr. Worthington was in the last phase of his program; at this time, I shared my knowledge and experience to help my mentor, classmate, and friend navigate the most challenging part of the doctoral journey: the dissertation/thesis.

I was overjoyed when he completed his doctoral journey, also known as the quest narrative, and I was honored to be able to give back in the form of sharing my experience with my former mentor. Our shared quest narrative reinvigorates our friendship; today, our communication is stronger than ever. It's quite a blessing for both of us to have come from the same underprivileged neighborhood of Carver Shores, graduated from the same public school, Maynard Evans High School, and obtained Doctorate Degrees from Walden University, an accredited institution whose doctoral degrees are highly respected by society and peers.

~ Dr. Tony White

One of the things I will remember is your ability to connect with players. You have a lot of coaches that need to do that. They keep players at arm's length and don't care to know each of their players on not just a basketball level but a life level. I have three coaches that I would go into Hell with, and you are one of them. Your ability to connect with people has given you the longevity to impact younger athletes and older ones. It's a skill that only a few people have. I have been blessed to have great conversations with you twenty-plus years later about how the game has changed for the good and the bad. I cherish our conversations and talking to someone who knows the game and the ins and outs is good. I don't look at you as my coach for all these reasons. But a close friend. I appreciate all you have done for me to prepare me for life and its ups and downs. Love ya, Coach.

~ Emmanuel "Manny" Clifton

Tan (Robert Worthington) and I went to neighboring high schools (Jones and Evans) in southwest Orlando, Florida, a convenient area just a short drive from downtown central Florida and the rest of the endless attractions of Orlando. Although we had many mutual friends, I don't recall meeting Tan before our encounter during my first year at Valencia College West Campus... I remember him coming over to me and introducing himself while we were in the cafeteria or the breezeway of the college. Not sure what the conversation was about, but we walked and talked until I reached my next class. After asking if we could speak again, we exchanged phone numbers and agreed to call each other. We would see each other between classes during the week and often speak on the telephone; Tan was very easy to talk to. Eventually, our conversations turned into visits to my home and an introduction to my mom and two brothers. We became nearly inseparable away from the college campus; unless he was at basketball practice or a game, he would more than likely be at my house. We would spend hours in the family room watching television, talking, and laughing. The night would always end with a slow walk toward the front door, holding hands, a warm embrace, and a polite kiss. This was followed by each of us saying good night; you were the perfect gentleman. I don't know what feelings we were expressing, but our relationship was exceptional.

We never labeled what we were doing, but our attraction was not just about our physical attraction; it was more about the kindness, honesty, wisdom, and sense of humor we shared…our personalities seem to be so similar…but as suddenly as we had connected, our relationship ended abruptly after an uneasy conversation …. It would be more than thirty years before we would see each other again. After initially reconnecting via the social media platform Facebook, we began talking on the phone, and our conversations picked up as if they had never ended! We were at ease with one another, just as we had always been, our conversations moving seamlessly from one topic to the next without any thoughts of the hours passing. Reconnecting with Tan (Robert) and old friends from college reminded me of the people we used to be and helped get both of us in touch with parts of ourselves that might have become suppressed over the years. In addition, the reunion offered us a new perspective on how our lives today relate to the past…it was a heartwarming mix of nostalgia and excitement, catching up on lost years and comparing life's notes!

~ Eve Hall

I remember being the fastest when we played football on the field next to the basketball court. I also remember being the shortest [but fastest one] on the basketball court. I remember I always wanted to cover for you. However, you were doing crossovers and spins, making it difficult to guard yourself—sliding down the side of boxes on the highway. We also skateboarded underneath the road. I would never change those beautiful times growing up. We did not have much. But we were not just best friends. We were all Family. Oh, one more thing. Being the first ones starting the "Turkey Bowl."

~ **Frank "Pop" Allen**

I've known Rob for nearly twenty-three years. We met at Andersen Air Force Base in Yigo, Guam, in the summer of 2001. After meeting at the base gymnasium and playing a few hours of friendly but competitive basketball games...Rob and I forged a genuine connection on the basketball court.

Some of our earliest conversations revolved around basketball... past, present, and future. You could tell Rob was an astute student of the game. I want to think that, in some ways, my style of play reminded him of himself. Over twenty-three years, our connection has evolved into a true friendship predicated on mutual respect. I have had the honor and privilege of getting to know Rob as a colleague, mentor, family man, scholar, entrepreneur, and friend.

Over the years, he's been a constant voice of reason, perspective, and insight. He's been a sounding board with a wealth of knowledge through life experiences. As you can imagine, his journey, like many, from humble beginnings, personifies critically important mantras of identity, strength, resilience, positivity, determination, and focus.

In My Brother's Shadow is a journey of vulnerability and an expression of love, maneuvering the often-complex challenges and intricacies of family dynamics. His story will resonate with many, hopefully highlighting the importance of intelligent, thoughtful, and informed decision-making.

~ **Gene Uzoukwu**

Rob (Dr. Worthington) and I met at Sembach Air Base near Kaiserslautern, Germany 1987. We didn't run in the same circle of friends, didn't seem to have much in common, and were not particularly close friends, but we would cross paths at the base gym during evening pickup basketball games. During the winter months, we would compete against one another in an intramural basketball league. This competition did not help foster a closer relationship between us, in fact, quite the opposite. During the off-season, we would see each other around the base, maybe at a mutual friend's house or weekly Saturday morning pickup basketball games. We would later be reunited at another military base in the mainland United States, Hurlburt Field, and for some reason, maybe the mutual respect gained from all those previous battles or just the familiarity of the three prior years at the same base…we began hanging out and became great friends. This friendship has blossomed into a brotherhood today. Our relationship was so close that when he had a family tragedy—his uncle was murdered in the nation's capital, Washington, DC—Rob asked me if I would drive with him to attend the funeral services for his uncle, and without hesitation, I agreed to be there for my friend. The drive was 14.5 hours each way; the trip allowed us to talk about our lives, families, goals, and fears… our relationship changed during this trip; it was as if I had gained another brother.

~ James Eric William

Cuz (cousin), I'm so proud of you. Reading a short excerpt from your memoir, I realized that you're in the process of telling a great story; the word that comes to mind is phenomenal. The words you have chosen are vivid. I can visualize the story as you're telling it. Definitely, well written. The story is not only real but gripping and engaging. Powerful use of words and expression. Wow! It makes the reader want to know more. Unfortunately, I can see the shift you expressed in William and my son's behavior. You hate to see someone that you love have such a shift in their personality.

Especially when they're so talented. I can't wait to read more. As we reflect on our relationship, we see that we are cousins who are more like brothers. Aunt Dot (your mother) is my father's older sister, your Uncle Bobby. Aunt Dot was like the aunt everyone went to visit at her house. Therefore, we spent much time together in our formative years, as if we were brothers rather than cousins. I don't remember why we became so much closer than other family or cousins, but we seem to like one another, and our relationship has become considerably closer. Those feelings have endured even to this day, cousins who share a special bond and rely on each other for support throughout their lives.

~ **Jerado Gaulden Sr.**

I recall my first encounter with Rob (Dr. Worthington); he and I attended a social gathering at a mutual friend's home. We eventually would have a one-on-one conversation where we discussed many topics; his demeanor was strong and confident, and his opinions were sincere and straightforward. Our conversation drifted into personal relationships, in which he shared his thoughts and views, many of which I shared; I appreciated his honesty and ability to express himself with well-thought-out reasoning. We continued to talk throughout the evening, sparingly speaking with any of the other guests. Our conversation had an inexplicable sense of familiarity and understanding, like recognizing a piece of yourself in another person. Rob (Dr. Worthington) and I shared a kindred chemistry unlike anyone I have met.

There were several commonalities, such as we were both Floridians, athletes familiar with Florida athletics, both raised in economically challenged communities, and a surprising familiarity with young black men being disproportionately incarcerated throughout the USA. My comfort level was wholly calm and engaging. We shared countless stories of our past without feeling ashamed or uncomfortable.

We spoke for hours, thoroughly enjoying our time together. I knew that evening I had a friend in Dr. Worthington. We have continued speaking often (via cell phone) since 2017. Dr. Worthington and I respectfully confide in each other regarding life and family issues. I am honored to call Dr. Worthington a great friend and brother. I respect and admire his willingness to teach and serve youths throughout his community. He is a man of God and a great example to all.

~ **Jimmie C Gardner**

Robert Worthington, aka Coach Worthington, means the world to me as a coach but, more importantly, a man I could always look up to. I first met him in 1998, but I have grown to love him like a father or big brother. He helped me to become the best basketball player I could be by pushing me to work on my game. We spent countless hours together daily in the gym, helping me become a First Team Junior College All-American in 2000. I averaged thirty points that year and scored fifty-four points in one game with coach Worthington's help. He was relentless in our workouts, and we eventually became more than a coach-and-player relationship. It became a friendship that has grown now for twenty years. I became a big brother to his children, Robert and William. I can even remember one day going to William's baseball game; as I approached the field in the middle of the game, running from third base to home, he stopped and shouted, "Joey!" I waved and said hi to him and finally ran home. Coach Worthington has also been friends with my wife, Vianny; she has always loved and respected him as a coach and, most importantly, as a man. He has always taken marriage and family very seriously, which made an impression on both of us, which is why my wife and I are still married after being together for twenty years since high school. Coach Worthington is a godsend with the eye of a champion; everything he touches prospers, and there is no coincidence in his life's success. I wish only the best for a man I truly love and respect. I am honored to call him a friend.

~ **Joey Gordon**

I met Robert, or Tan as he was known then, in 1985. We were both students at Valencia Community College. Robert was a typical college ball player/jock. The guys wanted to be him; the girls wanted to be with him. Although our friendship began with a dare to obtain my phone number, thirty-plus years later, we remain the best of friends. Our relationship has survived thousands of miles and multiple marriages for both of us. We have gone for months or a year without communicating, but when we do, it is as if we just spoke yesterday. Though we've never been physically intimate, we share an intimate connection. We know each other's secrets, hopes, and dreams. So here we are more than thirty years later, having shared most of our life's journey with each other. It just occurred to me that we have spent more of our lives knowing each other than not. How awesome is that! Love you much.

~ Juanita Beason

Regarding basketball, especially basketball in the DMV, Robert Worthington is one of the GOATs for championing youth basketball. We were connected through the sport as Robert is the king of expanding his basketball network through thoughtful community partnerships. The youth basketball pipeline he has built throughout Columbia, MD and Howard County continues to showcase talented student-athletes in the classroom and on the court.

~ Kelsey Nicole Nelson

Serving on active duty in the US Air Force with Robert Worthington at Patrick Air Force Base in Melbourne, Florida was an enriching experience far beyond basketball. The characteristics that Rob emulated, both on and off the court, spoke directly to his attitude toward life in general. He was very conscientious and ambitious and had a strong vision of success while displaying a sense of humility and compassion.

The positive mindset Rob displayed to those around us provided a meaningful example, especially while many of us were navigating through trials. Remarkably, Rob was very instrumental during a specific experience that included the near death of a teammate. Somehow, we could always regain our focus and keep our heads together amidst it all.

Thankfully, my good friend and brother, Rob, encouraged me not to stay focused solely on the court but, as importantly, on my professional and personal life. Please continue to give us your best and thank you for being who you are.

~ **Kevin A. Rose**, USAF Ret.

I met Rob Worthington at my first duty assignment in the US Air Force, at Patrick Air Force Base, Cocoa Beach, Florida, when I was only nineteen years old. Being assigned to a military base whose mission included supporting rocket, missile, and space programs was my first experience being out in the world. When he first came, I was highly judgmental and thought, *ok, who is this guy, and why is he here?* I had decided that I wouldn't like him. But he wasn't paying me any attention. He seemed to be highly focused, even-tempered, and always under control. It was like a basketball game; he was a veteran point guard, and I was a rookie just out of high school. I had recently received my air traffic controller certification; I was on the honor guard and the best player on the inter-squad basketball team, so my ego was on ten. Rob, or 'RW,' wasn't impressed by that, but he seemed genuinely interested in me and looked after me like I was his little brother. It didn't take long for me to trust him, and he is one of the few I would call a friend; he is more than a friend. Rob is my big brother. He didn't ask for the job, but I made him my mentor because he seemed successful in everything he put his mind to. He would give me direction like a head coach and always stick to the play, even when it seemed that it wasn't working. I'm excited to read this book because I always wondered what drives him. Rob has the "it" factor and is the best basketball player I've ever seen. I used to watch him on the court in awe. I would watch if he missed, but nope, swish, then look up, and he has thirty points! He was grace on the court just as he was off the court. He was humble but confident, focused but flexible, and always there when I needed him. Rob was the first person there for my most significant life-changing experience. He had to make the hard phone call to my parents, and he was there to ease my pain, then my girlfriend's pain, and he has never asked for anything in return. Rob has a brilliant mind and is well-versed in any subject, and he will tirelessly research topics he needs to gain knowledge. People like him don't come around often, but they are a blessing when they do!

~ LaMont Robinson

Congratulations Dr. Worthington,

Following our very first conversation, a genuine friendship developed. Your pride, passion, and love for family, particularly for your brother, tremendously touched my heart from the very beginning. Listening to your memories throughout the years, I never doubted that this day would become a reality. You are a true inspiration, and I couldn't be happier for you. I can't wait for the screenplay!

~Dr. Marlene M. Jackson, Ed.D.
Founder/CEO, Biz Kidz Academy

We have known each other since the early 1970s, growing up in the Griffin Park housing project. I remember when you were so determined to become the best basketball player in the projects. I would (acting as your coach/trainer) have you run the line drill when you would make a mistake, unlike some of the other younger guys who were just quiet…you would always keep going at it and never been a quitter! Some of my best childhood memories occurred in the Griffin Park housing project, where everyone treated one another like family. There were days that all our friends would come outside on a Saturday morning after watching cartoons and play outside 'all day,' and we would go home when either our mother called out for us or 'the streetlights came on'…we all understood the street light rule, "have your butt in this house before the streetlights come on." We never worried about eating lunch because the neighborhood always had the 'flip lady' house, where you could buy popcorn, candy, cookies, and "flips" (freeze cups made of frozen Kool-Aid drink in a plastic cup, then flip over to eat from the smaller and sweeter end). At the park, we were very creative with the games we played to keep ourselves entertained, games like "Snatchie cat," where you would be walking and eating food when suddenly one of your friends would grab your food yelling, "Snatchie cat," your initial shock and maybe anger would turn into laughter. You laugh with the person who 'got you,' promising to return the favor when they least expected it.

We played every sport possible at "the park," basketball, baseball, and my favorite, sandlot tackle football…especially on Thanksgiving Day, we would watch the NFL football game on TV. When the game was over, we would all come outside to pick our teams for the annual "GP Turkey Bowl." Man, those were my life's most competitive, exciting, and enjoyable days. On the days we didn't have enough people to play a team sport, we got imaginative, taking old cardboard boxes and breaking them open to make homemade sleds and sliding down the grass hills of the two major highways surrounding the neighborhood. We even made a game of 'rock fighting,' never thinking about the possibility of injury any of us could have sustained if one of the thrown rocks hit one of us in the head or eye. We never felt as if we were poor or that living in the public housing project was considered a negative way of life...we were a family and took pride in living in Griffin Park...GP4LIFE!

~ Marvin "Man" Williams

I remember the first time I met Rob. I was a young twenty-two-year-old kid new to Patrick AFB in Florida. Now, at that time in my life, I thought I was the absolute truth in basketball. You couldn't tell me anything on the court. Well, with any base that I moved to, I always went first to the basketball courts. I wanted to find the best ballers on the base and politely introduce myself by giving them the business. Well, I remember walking into the gym, and there were a lot of young cats like me in there, but I saw this bald dude (Rob). He was old to me at that time...lol!! I would always sit and watch the players play and break down their strengths and weaknesses. I was a student of the game and always wanted to compete and beat the best of the best. So, I watched Rob play, and now he was the oldest dude on the court. However, he was giving it to these young cats. They could not stop that jumper of his to save their life. He was popping threes and mid-range jumpers like crazy. So, I was like, I've got to play against that old head and show him what a real baller looks like. So, the next game, I was up, and when I tell you we battled, BOY, it was like a Magic and Bird battle that day. From that day on, for the next two years, Rob and I always had mutual respect on the court. However, what I have always admired most about Rob was not his basketball game but his character as a man. Back then, I looked up to him (even though I never told him that). He was and still is a class act and continues to be a true inspiration to young people with aspirations of playing the game of basketball. It was a pleasure and a blessing meeting Rob when I was a young man. I passed on many things I learned from him to my daughters.

~ Mike Tyler

I am so proud of my cousin's accomplishments. This man is like a father, a friend, a cousin. He's had a significant impact on my life, and I'm so proud of him for being a man who has shown me how a man should be as a father, a husband, a friend, and a mentor. I'm truly honored and grateful for him being a part of my life. Words of wisdom: Isaiah 61:1 ~ The Spirit of the Lord God is upon me, because the Lord has anointed me to bring good news to the poor; he has sent me to bind up the brokenhearted, to proclaim liberty to the captives, and the opening of the prison to those who are bound.

~**Monica Gaulden**

I have many stories, but the author of this book, Robert "Tan" Worthington, is my best friend forever. My name is Moses Gordon. I am one of Tan's best friends. We met as first-year high school students at Evans High School basketball tryouts. I was unsure if I would try out for the team, but another friend, Tim Sherry, recognized my talents and urged me every day to try out. The next day, I was ready to show what I could do, and on the first day of basketball tryouts, I met my great friend Tan. It was our first meeting, but we connected as if we had known each other for years; he inspired and encouraged me as this was my first time trying out for a basketball team. On the second day of tryouts, I was proven to belong on the court with all of the other junior varsity players, and by the end of the day, I was practicing with the varsity team. In my first year of organized basketball, I became one of the team's best junior varsities (JV) players. Tan and I would lead the team in scoring and rebounds and to a country basketball championship. We would play together for the next three years and be like a big family; we had sleepovers and watched movies and would play a leading role in the team winning a Metro Conference and District championships by our senior year. Although we didn't win the state championship, a goal we set for ourselves in tenth grade, Tan and I earned all-star selections, being selected to the All-Metro Conference and All-Orange County basketball teams. We were not only two of the best players in Orlando; during our time playing together, but we also developed a lifelong friendship.

~ Moses Gordon Jr.

Tan (Robert Worthington) is my longtime childhood friend from my dad's friend's (Adolphus "Buddy" Jones) son. I met Tan when we played at the Southwest Boys Club and Carver Shores Poppy Park, where I grew up playing basketball and was the only female who played football. Deac (Buddy) is my father's friend. I always had a ball wherever I went. Tan is like a big brother; we shared a passion for basketball, and I enjoyed watching him play basketball and supporting him when he went overseas to play. It's an honor to know and grow up with him like a family member, a big brother. I attended Dr. Phillips High School in Orlando from 1988 to 1992. We won the Florida's Class AAAA state championship in 1992, where I was named finals MVP. In addition, I received several more honors, including being named to the Girls Dixie Dozen Team, a Parade Magazine All-American and Dr. Phillips HS Athletic Hall of Fame, 1992 Most Outstanding Athletes of the Year, Girls Season & Career Points Record Holder. In 1999, I graduated from Edward Waters College University... I played for the college from 1996 to 1998 and was a graduate student coach for the 1999 season after graduation. I live in Rochester, NY, where I live with my siblings, but I grew up in Carver Shores, Florida, with my momma.

~ Mosetta "Mo" Williams

I met Rob in 2012 while working as a Software Engineer at the Federal Aviation Administration in Oklahoma City. We quickly connected on our shared passion and love for basketball and sports.

Having just played amateur basketball on the streets in my home country of Senegal, I had limited experience and exposure to this sport as Rob, who has played at the collegiate and professional levels. Over the years, we developed a great friendship. My family had a chance to meet Rob's wonderful family, his wife Noena, and two lovely girls, Kaesha, and Sky, who left Oklahoma City as young girls and have grown so much now attending college. I was fortunate enough to work alongside Rob on his tremendous Hoop Drills for Skills program and on multiple camps where he would train young people with different skill levels in basketball and share his knowledge of the sport. It was an excellent experience for me to learn various techniques from him on mentoring and working with young kids that I still use today when I coach youth soccer. Thank you, Rob, for all these beautiful years of friendship and all the valuable life lessons you have taught me. I wish you continuous success in all your current and future endeavors.

~ Mouhamadou Bop

I met Coach Worthington about six years ago, in 2018, when I was looking for a private one-on-one basketball skills coach for my then-middle school son, Cameron, who played D1 AAU basketball. Hundreds of coaches worked in the field of player skill development. However, none of the other coaches had the depth of experience, national and international success, and range of players he had developed at all levels. My goal for Cameron was to develop his shooting form and technique to become a consistent shooter. From the first session, I was ecstatic with Coach Worthington's meticulous skill development and attention to minor details while holding Cameron accountable for his efforts with dignity and respect. He could identify flaws that no one else caught, and Cameron's perimeter shooting greatly improved, evidenced by sports articles that frequently talked about it.

Outside of practice, Coach Worthington devoted personal time to attending Cameron's AAU and high school games, recommended basketball training videos and reading material to reinforce skills, gave advice on displaying a positive character, or asked about how he was doing in school. Since our first interaction, Coach Worthington had dramatically impacted my son's basketball career both on and off the court, and our relationship had evolved from being Cameron's development coach to a genuine friendship. I have witnessed Coach Worthington's journey in developing players, his achievements, overcoming health challenges, completing his doctorate, writing a book, and loyalty and dedication to taking care of his family.

Thank you, Coach Worthington, for joining Cameron's circle in helping him achieve his dream to play in the NBA, for your passion for the game of basketball and unwavering support, for your family for being one of Cameron's biggest fans, and for your lifelong friendship.

~ Myron Whitmore

Coach Worthington, what have we yet to discuss since I was seventeen? You began as my Coach, then a fatherly voice, and finally, a friend. I learned so much from you as a Coach. You understood the game, you understood me, and you understood how to connect the two. Due to this knowledge, I loved bombarding you with questions. As I grew older, I still had questions, but they pertained to life, and yet you still entertained each of them with kindness and patience. With each answer, a story from your past was always included; this helped make your advice memorable and relevant. Lastly, you have served as a faithful friend because you have never allowed miles or years to get in the way. Your knowledge of basketball grabbed my attention, your understanding of people made me listen, and your loyalty made you a friend!

~ Dr. Nuria Butcher

I have had the privilege of knowing and working with Rob Worthington for nearly a decade. Over the years, our family-owned business, Bolt Athletics, has partnered closely with Rob, supplying his basketball camps and teams with uniforms, apparel, and equipment. Our collaboration extends beyond the court, as we have also supported his charitable initiatives in Africa, witnessing firsthand his unwavering dedication to making a difference locally and globally.

Rob's commitment to youth development and community engagement is genuinely inspiring. His efforts with Howard County Youth Program (HCYP) Basketball and the Hoop Drills for Skills Basketball Camp have transformed the lives of countless young athletes. My children, Serene and Marvelous, have thrived under his guidance, participating in HCYP Basketball, and developing as athletes and individuals.

Rob is more than a coach; he is a mentor and a friend—someone who has forged meaningful relationships within our community. His dedication and passion have been instrumental in establishing HCYP as a premier youth basketball program in Howard County, Maryland. It has been an honor to work alongside him and to support his vision of empowering the next generation of athletes.

~ **Paul Rihani**,
President, Bolt Athletics

I remember the first time I met Coach Worthington; he walked into the classroom with his shoulders straight back, always in a perfect posture, and spoke with a firm but gentle voice. I knew from that day I could learn a lot from this man. I moved from Pennsylvania to Florida when I was fourteen; I attended River's Edge, a small middle school right off US1 in Palm Bay, FL. When Mr. Worthington came to the school, I didn't know what to expect, a man with such a military-like attitude; I didn't think we would get along, and boy, was I wrong. Coach Worthington was the first to bring a basketball program to River's Edge; this man did everything from buying our uniforms to scheduling games in other cities; he got the school together. I would have never thought our school would accomplish and experience such great things, and with Coach's help, he turned some of our dreams into reality. It was an honor to be a part of the fantastic things he brought to our school. The basketball program in place helped many of us keep our grades where they should be and brought out the potential in each of us. Clearlake Middle School hosted our first game, my first official basketball game. I was so scared that I could not stop shaking. Coach understood what I was going through and did not hesitate to comfort me as he saw me slowly breaking down. He said, "It doesn't matter how many shots you miss as long as you keep shooting the ball." I will never forget those words because I may miss some shots in each game I play, but I never stop shooting. I grew up with only my mother as a father figure in my life, and she did a great job raising four kids by herself; with the help of Coach Worthington, I gained another father figure who I can give a lot of credit for molding me into the man I am today. Robert Worthington was not just a Coach but a friend, teacher, and role model. Thank you for everything, sir.

~ Rahim Brooks

Robert Worthington, writing a memoir sounds exciting! It's been so many years ago when we were both members of the Evans High School boys' basketball team. I remember your defense was great, but your long fingernails were lethal…I can't forget them! I also recall being envious of how well you could handle the basketball; I believe it was due to your larger-than-average hands. Whenever you're in town, you are always welcome at Chez Sloan!

~ Randel Sloan

In June 1986, I arrived at Sembach AB near Kaiserslautern, Germany. As on most Air Force bases, the first place you go if you play basketball is to head to the base gym. That is where you find all the gym rats and aspiring (wannabe) ball players. As I got in the gym, a couple of the players caught my attention; one was a guy named Martin, and the other was a very active talker named Rob. Later, I came to know him as Robert Worthington. Trash-talking is an art form; in no other sport is it displayed more openly than basketball. It can be used as a psychological tool to shake up an opponent or to deflate some overblown egos of wannabe ballers (basketball players). I noticed that Rob had a nicely formed jump shot, which reminded me of Dennis Scott (at that time, an NBA sharpshooter with the Orlando Magic). In other words, he (Robert Worthington) could shoot the lights out. The team had its tryouts as the season (around September) approached. I can't remember the head coach's name, but he assembled the team. In every practice, you would always get 100 percent from Rob. Rob showed great energy, and of course, he could talk. The best trash talkers can back up their hubris, which makes their words so devastating. Rob played with a lot of passion for the game. A player like Robert Worthington is a coach's dream, and we all say we wish we had ten players like him. So, it's a blessing to see him decades later still passionate about the game.

~ Coach Ray Elliot Lee

Tan was a great friend to hang around growing up; he was like a brother. I always respected his basketball skills. We both played basketball when I got to high school, Maynard Evans High School. I was on the junior varsity team, and he was on the varsity team. Although basketball wasn't my best sport, I am more of a wrestler. But Tan would come by my house every morning, and we would walk to the bus stop together, usually laughing always there. We became good friends, and I am incredibly proud of my 'big brother' for overcoming our bringing up in some of the most dangerous and poverty-stricken neighborhoods in Orlando, Florida, including Parramore, Washington Shores, Mercy Drive, Richmond Heights, and Carver Shores by becoming economically prosperous enough to ("make it out of the hood") live outside of it.

~ Robert "Hershey" Alston

Dr. Worthington, fondly known as "Coach," spearheaded the creation of the first-ever basketball team at my son's middle school (Wilde Lake). His dedication went beyond the court, as he nurtured the boys' skills, organized tournaments, and even introduced them to professional basketball (with a two-hour practice/training session on the home court of the NBA's Washington Wizards, Capital One Arena). Not only did he emphasize athletic success, but he also prioritized academic achievement, requiring a minimum GPA, and providing tutoring resources when needed. Dr. Worthington's influence extended far beyond basketball, as he became a positive role model and mentor, fostering a sense of camaraderie among the team. With him at the helm, what began as a team evolved into a close-knit family.

~ Rosa Richmond

When I became the Coach at Evans, it was a challenging transition for the team. From the first day of practice, Robert was supportive and understood my coaching views and what it would take to win. It was a successful season, with twenty wins and a loss in the regional finals. I tribute this to Robert. He was an outstanding leader, on and off the court. It was my pleasure to have been his coach and part of his life.

~ Coach Rudy Tapia

Robert, where do I begin? I have always looked up to you; even as a child, you always seem to have the most level head in the family. You always knew what direction you wanted to go. It has indeed been an honor to call you brother. I have lived my life through your success and experiences. Your accomplishments are all the things I wanted to do, like skydiving and scuba diving. Traveling the world and being successful at anything you touch. You are a massive inspiration to me. And I often tell my boys that if there is anyone they want to admire and look up to, then their Uncle Robert is a perfect example of what a real man looks like. I love you, brother. Keep moving forward, and I look forward to all your accomplishments.

~ **Sharon D. Washington**

I've known Coach Worthington for over twenty years. Although I don't recall exactly when we met, I believe HOW we met was at Patrick AFB gym. I was in high school and was constantly at the base gym playing ball against grown men, some of whom were twice my age and size. They probably looked at me as the annoying girl who just got in the way, but it didn't matter to me because, at that time of my life, the ball was life, and I knew that if I wanted to get better, I needed to play against bigger and better. I remember seeing Coach play pickup games, but you could tell he wasn't just a "pickup" player. He knew how to manage the floor. And no matter who he played with; he made them perform better. I've always gravitated to players who are more than just physically talented but also organized on the court. I believe that translates to the type of person you are off the court.

Coming out of high school, I didn't have a lot of offers to play, but I was fortunate enough to play for our local Junior College, Brevard Community College, as it was called at that time. I was ecstatic when I found out I would be playing for Coach Worthington. I'd known him for a while, and I couldn't think of anyone else I would have wanted to play for. Unfortunately, the results of our season didn't reflect our coach's abilities or our team's talents. We didn't win a single game that season. You can imagine how difficult this was for someone like me who was coming from a middle school team that never lost a game and a high school team that was #1 in our district and state contenders every year. And I know Coach was used to being a winner most of his career, so I'm sure it was just as gut-wrenching for him. But he never let us put our heads down, be negative, or feel sorry for ourselves. As hard as it was, that season taught me so much, and I attribute that season to being my first big "life lesson." It taught me how to persevere, stay positive through adversity, and, no matter what, don't give up! As life happened, Coach and I would drift apart periodically, but we always made our way back. I don't have a lot of twenty-plus year friendships. I've known quite a few people for twenty-plus years, but that's very different. Our friendship was founded on basketball and our love and respect for the game. Still, it developed into career advice, counseling regarding family matters, intense conversations about politics, mentorship regarding life-changing situations, and, yes, still to this day, BASKETBALL. That was our core foundation, and it is incredible that this "game" could bond two people for a lifetime. Side note: I am incapable of calling him by his first name to this day. He's a Coach and will always and forever be a COACH!

~ Shawnta Price

I first met Tan, Robert Worthington, when my sister Cynthia was dating his older brother, Weo, William Worthington. I started hanging out with my sister more and, leading to us becoming better acquainted. It was great hanging out with Robert because he was calm and protective, something I was used to growing up in my grandmother's care. In other words, he wasn't a thug or someone who liked to argue; he was quiet and laid back. More my speed of the type of guy I was interested in meeting. We didn't spend much time together; when our siblings' relationship ended, we also faded apart. But I never stopped thinking about how wonderful a person he was as the years passed, and we both continued life's journey. We continued to communicate for years from afar, but we finally saw one another in person again after many years. Unfortunately, it was not under happy circumstances, but an end-of-life ceremony for my older brother, June (Gilbert Lake). They had shared a great friendship for many years and seeing him at the funeral was comforting. I hope to see him again in happier times!

~ Stephanie Lake Knowles

Here are a few stories I remember about being your teammate/friend...The first regular season game we won, you had a good game; the next day, the Orlando Sentinel did a game re-cap that read something like this... *KUHL LEADS EVANS TO VICTORY*! Evans star Jimmy Kuhl scored eight points and grabbed six rebounds, leading the Trojans to a decisive victory. The junior had four points and a rebound in the decisive second quarter. Senior Robert Worthington chipped in twenty-two points in support of Kuhl's effort. I asked you if you had seen the story, and we joked that you needed to contribute less to get the headlines! 😊

In the second story, we had beaten the Colonial High School basketball team the night before by about fifty points, and you scored something like twenty-five points while I hit two FTs in the last minute of the blowout. The next day, I told a girl that you and I combined to score twenty-seven points. You said, "Yep, he hit the clutch free-throws." I also remember you giving Jimmie Kuhl a "duck lip" with an elbow to the mouth one day in practice; you had complained to me earlier that if "he elbows me again, I'm going to beat his ass," and he elbowed you again!

~ Tim Sherry

When reminiscing about meeting Robert (Dr. Worthington) or the coach, my first thought was admiration. He exuded joy, strength, and compassion while working with many people, including youth groups. He expressed himself as a lover of people and nature that furnished the world he admires. Robert always had a passion for helping others and loved the idea of being considered a dependable person. He welcomed and enjoyed when others came to him to talk about the hardship they were experiencing and being able to provide them with feedback or helpful advice.

The following quote reminds me of Robert: "Help others without reason and give without expecting anything in return. Service to others is the rent you pay for your room here. We know too well that what we are doing is nothing more than a drop in the ocean." His incredible achievement, completing his doctoral journey, filled me with a substantial sense of accomplishment from caring for Robert and enjoying the friendship that has stood the test of time and is more precious to me than time itself.

~ Tracie Dancingstar Johnson

I am sharing some thoughts about my son, Robert; he's laid back, curious, and not much trouble; his personality is more compliant than a rebellious one. As a child the most vivid memory I have of him is as a five-year-old; he had a little basketball he always played with, like being outside, and few arguments with his siblings, but standard stuff. I have not been in his life very much, so I'm not too familiar with his friends, neighborhood, or schools he attended.

As for our father/son relationship, we didn't have one early on. I separated from their mother many years ago, but after rekindling the relationship, it is much better now. We communicate pretty frequently and enjoy the conversation. William has always been outspoken; he's a self-confident leader who is pretty well reassured of his positions. His self-assurance is his greatest strength… Innovative like his daddy. Great mind!

What is the area where improvement needs to be made? Some people take his robust approach the wrong way, even referring to him as an "educated butthole," so he would benefit from toning it down sometimes and not being so opinionated. But all in all, he's a well-rounded young family man—he's all about family, loves family, and has an incredibly close relationship with his family—I am proud of him for that.

He wanted to go into space at one time, and he shared with me that he would one day work at the International Space Station. My best advice to him would be…Life can start one way, so be open to what life hands you. Start planning, some five-year plan, and see if you can achieve that goal. I retired from the military (United States Army) at age thirty-nine, then had a career as a carpenter and law enforcement for another fifteen years. I told Robert to have planned financially. I'm seventy-eight years old. If you smile and are happy, you'll live long.

~ **William "Pete" Worthington Sr.**

IN MY BROTHER'S SHADOW
MUSIC PLAYLIST

YouTube Link:
https://youtu.be/4V40BQtAGIQ?si=pHmu1b-FjGaObhV9

First Quarter: s 1-3
Uptown Saturday Night **Soundtrack – "How I Got Over" (1974)**

~Performed by Gospel Choir

"Cornbread" Cornbread Earl and Me **Soundtrack (1975)**

~Performed by The Blackbyrds

"Le Freak" (1978)

~Performed by Chic

"This Is It" (1979)

~Performed by Kenny Loggins

Second 'Quarter: s 4-6
"Try Again" (1981)

Performed by Champaign

"Marvin Gaye sings American National Anthem" (1983)

~Performed at the NBA All-Star Game

"Basketball" (1984)

~Performed by Kurtis Blow

"Believe In the Beat" (1984)

~Performed by Carol Lynn Townes

Third Quarter: s 7-9

"Vision Of Love" (1990)

~Performed by Mariah Carey

"Mind Playing Tricks on Me" (1991)

~Performed by Geto (Ghetto) Boys

"Fortunate" (1999)

~Performed by Maxwell

Fourth Quarter: s 10-12

Music from the *Love & Basketball* Movie Soundtrack (2000)

~Performed by various artists

"Fabulous" (2002)

~Performed by Jaheim

"Mesmerize" (2002)

~Performed by JaRule feature Ashanti

"Signed Sealed Delivered" (Barack Obama 2008 Campaign Theme Song)

~Performed by Stevie Wonder

"Lost Without U" (2009)

~Performed by Robin Thicke

"This Is America" (2018)

~Performed by Childish Gambino (Donald Glover)

"Lift Me Up" (from Black Panther: Wakanda Forever, 2022)

~Performed by Rihanna

"All My Life" (2023)

~Performed by Lil Durk feature J. Cole

"Philip Glass: Metamorphosis 1-5" (2020 – 2023)

~Performed by Philip Glass

Bonus Track:
"Faded Rose" (originally released in 1977)

~Performed by Shirley Caesar

Connect with Dr. Robert Worthington

To book Dr. Worthington to speak at your company, upcoming conference, retreat, meeting, or as a guest on your podcast:

Email: rworth2533@gmail.com

Let's connect on social media:

Facebook: https://www.facebook.com/robert.worthington.359
https://www.facebook.com/HoopDrillsForSkillsBasketballCamps
Instagram: https://www.instagram.com/dr.robworth/:://www.
instagram.com/hdfsbballcamps
X: https://x.com/hoopdrillscamps
TikTok: https://www.tiktok.com/@rworth2533
LinkedIn: https://www.linkedin.com/in/dr-robert-worthington

If you are a fan of this book, please tell others...

- Write about *In My Brother's Shadow* on your blog and social media channels.

- Feature Dr. Worthington on your podcast or radio/TV broadcast.

- Suggest this book to your friends, family, neighbors, coworkers, and company leadership team.

- Write an authentic, positive review on Amazon.com.

- Take a selfie of you holding the book, then post and tag Dr. Robert Worthington on your social media channels.

- Purchase bulk copies for your sports teams, families with incarcerated loved ones, and classrooms with young adults in need of guidance.

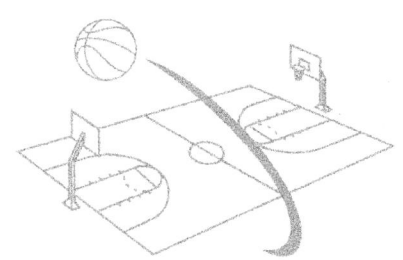

IN MY BROTHER'S SHADOW

RISE ABOVE THE RIM

www.ingramcontent.com/pod-product-compliance
Lightning Source LLC
Chambersburg PA
CBHW041624140626
46547CB00030B/746